W9-BGT-099

Advance Praise

"No city shines and shimmers like Jerusalem, and no city pierces and burns like her. Sarah Tuttle-Singer, in her lyric and soulful prose, captures both the light and the shadows, the holiness and the heaviness, of one of the world's most magnificent, maddening places. In a bold and deeply personal journey, she searches bustling alleyways and ancient stones, intimate rooms and holy texts, to unlock the secrets to Jerusalem's beauty, energy, and pain, which are found, most of all, in the souls of its inhabitants."
—Daniel B. Shapiro, Former U.S. Ambassador to Israel

"Sarah Tuttle-Singer has taken her experiences of the city of Jerusalem and crafted a masterpiece of her heart. Sarah's distinctive voice will give you the chills on every single page as she celebrates the beauty of Jerusalem while detailing the complexity of loving a city so embattled, so diverse, and so difficult. This book is simultaneously a love letter and a declaration of frustration; a poem and a song; a masterpiece of confusion and undying affection."
—Mayim Bialik

"Raw, dark, funny, this book brings you closer to the truth of the Old City today than any other I've read. Sarah Tuttle-Singer captures the sensuality, anger, and promise of the Holy City in a narrative that moves from one incredible true story to another. Her pilgrimage is intimate, irreverent, unashamed—and written with haunting beauty."
—Rob Eshman, former editor in chief of the *Jewish Journal*

"Sarah Tuttle-Singer, who loves Jerusalem passionately, offers us an unvarnished, intimate, and sometimes shocking look at life within the walls of the Old City. Her stories of modern existence in ancient Jerusalem come to life through in-depth portraits of this historic city's residents. In spite of the fact that perspectives are deeply polarized, and fear and interpersonal conflict are a constant reality, Sarah Tuttle-Singer gives us the 'real dirt' that shows us that co-existence is not only possible but happening each and every day. This is a hard-hitting book about hope that offers us glimmers of humanity that can help us imagine a time of peace and acceptance that, today, seems so far away."
—Peter Yarrow (Peter, Paul & Mary)

"Sarah Tuttle-Singer's book is a real love story, maybe even a love song, for the city of Jerusalem. In this brilliant and fascinating book, Tuttle-Singer brings us Jerusalem in all its ugliness and beauty, darkness and light, bad and good. With the honest, funny, and sad stories of her life and of the city, one can not stop reading until the end."
—Avi Issacharoff, journalist and co-creator of the hit TV series "Fauda"

"Sarah Tuttle Singer has written a brave, honest, and fiercely personal love letter to Jerusalem. Whether you've lived there your whole life or have never been, she is the tour guide you want to the world's most beautiful and broken city."
—Daniel Sokatch, CEO of the New Israel Fund

"Part searing personal memoir, part psychic and political exploration, this is Jerusalem's Song of Songs, an exquisitely written love poem to a city at the centre of many universes. It also marks the debut of a major new talent. Sarah Tuttle-Singer is a force to be reckoned with."
—David Rose, contributing editor with *Vanity Fair* and special investigations writer for *The Mail on Sunday*

"Beautiful, intense, mad, exhilarating: Sarah Tuttle-Singer hasn't just written a terrific book about Jerusalem, she's written a book that is now a part of Jerusalem. Taking us through the back alleys of the Old City, she introduces us to its world-class characters, their dreams and fears and most of all daily lives. In Sarah Tuttle-Singer, earthy Jerusalem has found its lover."
—Yossi Klein Halevi, author, *Letters to My Palestinian Neighbor*

"An intimate, bracingly honest, beautifully written memoir of life in the most captivating city in the world."

—Peter Beinart, author, *The Crisis of Zionism*

"If you love Jerusalem, you will love this book. Sarah Tuttle-Singer in her life love affair with the city, new and old, people from across the political and religious divide brings it all together like only Sarah could. *Jerusalem Drawn and Quartered* is a rollercoaster of culture, senses, emotions, and experiences. It reads like a diary, a very personal diary with dark secrets, but reflects the holy city that is so much for so many and has so many secrets of its own."

—Lieutenant Colonel Peter Lerner, retired IDF spokesperson

"*Jerusalem Drawn and Quartered* is a vivid evocation of the city in all its contradictions, showing its Jews and Arabs with their mutual fears and hatreds and contempt that do not altogether preclude moments of shared humanity. The story of the city is also the story of Sarah Tuttle-Singer, which is told affectingly, with unblinking honesty."

—Robert Alter, author of *The Art of Biblical Narrative*

"Sarah Tuttle-Singer brings Jerusalem's Old City to life like no writer before her, penning a ferocious love letter that will infuriate zealots and enthrall most everybody else. *Jerusalem Drawn and Quartered* is at once a biography of the tiny walled world in which a mosaic of anguished peoples struggle to coexist, and Tuttle-Singer's own story—rollicking, wrenching, coarse, and wise.

Making several homes in the different quarters of the torn, treasured enclave over the course of a year, Tuttle-Singer creates friendships from the most unpromising encounters with people of all faiths, dreams, and prejudices. But her readiness to think well of all those she meets unless proven otherwise costs her dearly too. All of which she describes with sometimes shocking candor.

Her love for the city and its residents spills from the pages. So, too, her delight in each new discovery she makes, each new character she wins over, each new world she insists on entering.

Tuttle-Singer's book sparkles with zest and originality: Who, hitherto, has dismissed the idea of rebuilding the Temple because they mistrust Israeli building contractors and wouldn't want to see a revival in the sacrifice of all those "adorable" goats?

Written with too much real-world knowledge to be easily dismissed by more conventional experts, Tuttle-Singer's book is ultimately a plea for Jerusalem, as she puts it, not to be 'ripped to ragged pieces by those who say they love her the best.' If there were more Jerusalemites like her, that simple, elusive aspiration might even be realized."

—David Horovitz, Editor, *The Times of Israel*

"Dangerous. Seductive. Laugh out loud funny. Sarah Tuttle-Singer has created a savvy and sexy *Innocents Abroad* for the internet age. Tuttle-Singer's stories are at once wildly original yet vaguely familiar, weaving nostalgia for her former life as a free-spirited moppet on Venice Beach with indefatigable optimism for peace in Jerusalem, her adopted ancestral home. *Jerusalem Drawn and Quartered* is a revelation and the best of the new voices covering the world's most maddening conflict: the millennial struggle for the Holy Land."

—James Oppenheim, co-founder and lover-in-chief of Crave Gourmet Street Food

"*Jerusalem Drawn and Quartered* is stunning, devastating and brimming with wisdom. Tuttle-Singer's curiosity and courage drive her to open worlds otherwise impermeable; her tireless quest for human connection and understanding tear at your heart and make you question everything you've assumed to be true. Her voice is not only raw, provocative, and always honest, it is also fiercely sensitive and desperately needed in these confounding and conflicting times."

—Rabbi Sharon Brous, IKAR

"The story leaves the stones and all who walk them in Jerusalem bare, raw and lovable."

—Gail Doering, pastor of Danville Congregational Church

JERUSALEM DRAWN AND QUARTERED

One Woman's Year in the Heart of the Christian, Muslim, Armenian, and Jewish Quarters of Old Jerusalem

Sarah Tuttle-Singer

Skyhorse Publishing

This is for my mother and my father, and my son and my daughter, and my great grandmother and the stranger she kissed on that roof at midnight, and for the love of my life.

Author's Note: I have tried to recreate events, locales, and conversations from my memories of them. In order to maintain individuals' anonymity and the rhythm of the narrative, in some instances I have changed the names of people and some identifying characteristics and details, as well as the order of certain events.

Skyhorse Publishing books may be purchased in bulk at special discounts for sales promotion, corporate gifts, fund-raising, or educational purposes. Special editions can also be created to specifications. For details, contact the Special Sales Department, Skyhorse Publishing, 307 West 36th Street, 11th Floor, New York, NY 10018 or info@skyhorsepublishing.com.

Skyhorse® and Skyhorse Publishing® are registered trademarks of Skyhorse Publishing, Inc.®, a Delaware corporation.

Visit our website at www.skyhorsepublishing.com.

10 9 8 7 6 5 4 3 2 1

Library of Congress Cataloging-in-Publication Data

Names: Tuttle-Singer, Sarah, 1981-author.
Title: Jerusalem drawn and quartered: one woman's year in the heart of the Christian, Muslim, Armenian, and Jewish quarters of old Jerusalem / Sarah Tuttle-Singer.
Description: New York, NY: Skyhorse Publishing, [2018]
Identifiers: LCCN 2018005301 (print) | LCCN 2018005999 (ebook) | ISBN 9781510724907 | ISBN 9781510724891 (hardcover)
Subjects: LCSH: Jerusalem—Biography. | Yerushalayim ha-ʻatiḳah (Jerusalem) | Tuttle-Singer, Sarah, 1981—Travel.
Classification: LCC DS109.86 (ebook) | LCC DS109.86 .T88 2018 (print) | DDC 956.94/42055092 [B]—dc23
LC record available at https://lccn.loc.gov/2018005301

Cover design by Mona Lin
Cover image courtesy of iStock.com

Print ISBN: 978-1-5107-2489-1
Ebook ISBN: 978-1-5107-2490-7

Printed in the United States of America

Contents

Introduction

THERE'S A STREET in Jerusalem that has two names: Al-Wad in Arabic and Ha-Gai in Hebrew. And it's my favorite.

It runs from the north end of the Old City to the south and back again.

It's the street that leads you from Damascus Gate to the Western Wall, the holiest site where Jews are allowed to pray.

It's also the street where a quick turn and a step or two takes you down a little road to one of the Aqsa gates—one of Islam's holy sites, and a spiritual and political flashpoint between Jews and Muslims. The Cardo ran underneath back in the day.

The street smells like coffee and ripe strawberries and saffron. You can buy bags of pink and blue almonds, and Christmas lights during Ramadan, to illuminate the night. There's a guy who runs a money changing station—his voice box was removed a few years ago, but he'll press on his windpipe and sing something by Fairuz.

There's also a Yeshiva, heavily guarded by guys in pants and black shirts with black yarmulkes on their heads and black guns on their hips. The kids are escorted to and from the Western Wall by at least one armed guard—sometimes more, depending on how many kids and what's happening in the news cycle. The mothers push pink strollers quickly from the front; they don't stop, even if their baby is crying. They keep walking fast, their eyes moving left and right until they reach the Jewish Quarter. And then they stop and breathe. And buy a coffee for six shekels at Cofix.

Late at night, you can hear the guys in the Yeshiva singing.

During the day, you can hear Palestinian hip-hop or Oum Kalthoum.

Five times a day you can hear the call to prayer.

On Friday afternoons, there's the Shabbat siren.

There are these old women from the villages outside Jerusalem who bring figs during late summer, artichokes in winter, and they sit on the street on woven rugs and sell their reapings. They look old but they probably aren't.

Then there are the dudes who sit around and play backgammon, their bodies smushed into metal chairs. They are the masters of their own fate, the kings of the street. Until their wives call them home.

There are a lot of kids—Jewish, Arab—they're the same ages, and they play the same games, but I've never seen them play together.

And then there are the Border Police who are stationed at the major intersections—they mostly point their guns down, until they don't. I've seen them buy coffee from the old guy who sells juice and popsicles and other drinks one day, and then interrogate and frisk his son the next.

This is the street where there's an indentation in one of the walls that some believe was left by Jesus Himself when he stumbled and almost fell on his way to being crucified. Although maybe the indentation is there merely because so many thousands—maybe millions—believe that *that* was the spot, and so day by day, year by year, we've helped make that indentation by placing our own faithful hands against stone.

I've done it. The stone feels warm.

But the part that makes me reel, the part that is hardest to understand and bends knees in humble supplication, is the intersection between Al-Wad/Ha-Gai and Via Dolorosa. Especially on Friday afternoons, and especially when the sun softens the stones and makes the street shine like seashells or fair skin.

It's where you see it all—the Christian pilgrims carrying the cross up from Lions Gate, wafting past the shops, stopping at each station, singing, praying, sorrow by sorrow on their way to the Church of the Holy Sepulchre. The Muslim guys heading toward Aqsa with their prayer rugs, the young women in hijab, and moms pushing babies, buying candies, or going to pray. The Yeshiva boys heading to the Western Wall for Shabbat, and whole families—beautiful families, with six or seven kids, all dressed in their finest, their faces scrubbed and their hair shining—going to pray, too, or maybe going for a meal, or just walking together during the holiest time in the holiest place.

But it's also around the corner from where my friend got the shit beaten out of him by Border Police when he was nineteen because his papers had expired the week before. Where a soldier the exact same age kicked him in the head. Over and over, until his face was a strawberry pulp. But when my friend looked up, that soldier was the one crying.

And this place is also around the corner from the spot where two Jewish fathers were stabbed to death by a terrorist, where they bled out on the stone street, where their injured and screaming and terrified wives were kicked and spat on by the shopkeepers.

And it's just down the street from where I stood one night when I was eighteen, covered in my own blood.

But it's also the street where I carried this grey kitten with the moth's wing fur, like my two cats that disappeared, only this one was rescued by Palestinians in the Muslim Quarter, and I took him to a woman in the Jewish Quarter who is caring for it to this day. And it's the street where the Border Police, and the Yeshiva kids, and the Palestinian merchants, and even a random priest have asked me separately and on different days, "How's the kitten?"

It's the street that flows from two directions where we drink coffee, where we kiss, where I looked for my mother years after her death, where I imagine my great grandmother walking with her hair blown back like seawalls, and her head held high.

It's my favorite street because it is an injured artery from Jerusalem's holy heart to the rest of us, and terrible things have happened, but lovely things have happened, too.

And it's the street that I walk the most, because if you expect to find a miracle in Jerusalem, you have to start looking in a place like this where all roads—beautiful and terrible—meet.

How It Happened

THIS IS A love story.

I didn't expect it to be this way, but it is.

And like all love stories, it's many other things, too—but mostly it's a love story. It started the summer I was sixteen, when my parents sent me to Israel for the first time.

I wasn't expecting to fall in love—in fact, I was pissed off when my mom told me they were sending me for the summer.

"No way," I said. "I don't want to spend my whole entire summer there."

"Why?" she asked.

Why? Because I was fifteen, and I wanted to spend the space between ninth and tenth grade strolling the 3rd Street Promenade with Aimee and Emily. I wanted to sit by the phone and wait for Matt Johnston to (*OMG please!*) realize he still wanted me and *call.* I wanted to make out in the Century City AMC theater, and buy clothes at Forever 21, and paint my nails black, and sneak out to Mar Vista swimming pool with a bottle of Sun-In and a bathing suit my parents would never allow carefully hidden under a Nirvana t-shirt I'd wear as I left the house.

In other words, I wanted to be, like, sixteen and super original.

My mom had other plans.

She had been to Israel before she met my dad.

"It was right after we won the Six-Day War," she had told me when I was even younger. "Jerusalem was ours again—all of it—the Old City . . . our very heart." And I thought it was funny at the time that she said "we," as if we'd been there, invading the Egyptian Sinai, seizing East Jerusalem and the West Bank.

"But we aren't Israeli, Mom," I said.

"We aren't, but we're Jewish . . . and Israel is our homeland."

Jerusalem was her favorite place in the whole wide world, she told me, and my bedtime stories were about how she rode camels in the desert, and picked oranges and sweet clementines in the orchards on a kibbutz way up north, and swam in the Mediterranean amongst the ancient Roman ruins of Achziv, and sang songs around a campfire in the middle of nowhere. But mostly she told me about Jerusalem. About the nun who painted icons on old pieces of wood, and the man who fried sweet dough into little balls dusted with sugar, and the family who lived in a wooden shack on the roof of the Church of the Holy Sepulchre, and how each morning she'd leave a little note with a secret wish and a whispered prayer tucked into the cracks of the Western Wall.

She had only been there that one summer after the war, and she said the streets were filled with a fantastic energy, and everyone was singing "Jerusalem of Gold," celebrating the fact that they could return to the Western Wall and explore the ancient alleyways of our forefathers and mothers . . . the places that the poets and the sages wept and dreamed over, the very place where our exile began 2000 years ago.

Of course, I know now that's much more complicated, but at the time, this is what I knew. And as a kid, I was intrigued, and I would look at her old photos and coin collection from her weeks there, and ask her questions and listen to her stories.

Jerusalem was in her blood in other ways, and in mine too, she told me. Her grandmother, Sarah, whose name I had been given, came to live in Jerusalem nearly one hundred years before as an au pair to a rich Polish Jewish family from the town near her shtetl.

"She fell in love," my mother said. "I don't know much about it except that this was during the Ottoman times, and he worked for the sultan, and they would meet at midnight to kiss on a roof overlooking the Temple Mount."

"What happened?"

"Well, the family she was working for found out and shipped her back to Poland where her parents sent her to Chicago—as far away from Jerusalem as they could send her—where she met my grandfather, your great grandfather."

I liked that story, and I would fall asleep some nights picturing my tall, strong great grandmother with the raven hair she refused to cover tumbling down her back while a handsome man cupped her face with the same strong jaw as mine between his hands and kissed her on that roof, while a million stars shone in the sky.

But now I was fifteen, and there was the mall, and my friends, and boys, and making out behind the air vents. Israel and Jerusalem and all those old stories were ancient history to me.

But not to my mom. I remember she was sitting at the big library table in her office, wearing her stupid blue-and-white bandana that she always wore, in a cloud of blue smoke from her GPC 100 Ultra Lights.

"Oh, you're going to Israel," she told me while she smoked. "Besides," she added, "you'll meet some nice guys."

I didn't want to meet nice guys.

I was still heartbroken over my first guy—Matt—with the maroon Billabong shirts and the skateboard, with the shiny brown hair and shinier smile, who made hash pipes out of tinfoil with little Green Day, Soundgarden, and Nirvana stickers on the bowl.

I didn't smoke, not then at least. But I would watch Matt's fingers separate the blossoms from the leaves, with more dexterity than he ever showed while unhooking my bra; he would roll and fold, pack, and light, and I would watch his eyes deepen to opacity.

Then we'd kiss and kiss and kiss, and rub each other blue and pink.

But young love lasts about as long as a twelve-track CD—remember those?—and he broke up with me, and I was crushed.

My parents were *those* parents—curfew was 9:00 p.m., and my dad would copy down the license plate numbers of anyone I went out with. "Seatbelts!" he would bellow after us as we'd pull out of the driveway. But for some reason, my parents trusted Israel—didn't matter that I would be gone for nearly two months, which was a whole lot of nights without curfews or parents to write down license plate numbers. But as visions of all of us singing "Hava Nagila" around a campfire floated through my mother's head, the meta-message wasn't lost on me: Israel was safe. Why? Because it was a country full of Jewish people who would take care of one another.

❖

It all started on a road off the main highway you take from the airport, heat-stricken, parched, and yellow, while the bus with the LA ULPAN sign in the window kicked up dust, as it chugged up the hill and through the gates of the kibbutz where we would be living.

That bus held 120 of us with our heavy Jansport backpacks and heavier jet lag. I was the only one on that bus who didn't have a seat, and probably the only person on that bus who didn't want to be there. I sat on the top step by the driver, my legs tucked up, my arms around them, and my eyes wide open.

But it wasn't long after that bus ride that it happened.

I fell in a mad rush with Israel—in a tumble, like my first kiss behind the air vents at Century City Mall when our braces got stuck together. This was like that, sudden and shocking and out of control. It happened in Jerusalem on a rooftop overlooking everything—that mosaic stretched out before me, a mosaic of peoplehood, of faith. The mosques, the churches and the synagogues . . . each part integral, and yet just part of the whole.

It was during Havdalah services, when we welcome the new week, after one of the counselors lit the braided candle that symbolizes the wholeness of the new week, and all of us were gathered in a giant circle, singing and swaying side to side. With my two roommates on either side of me, all of us reeking like the perfume section at Walgreens, I felt engulfed in a sense of belonging that I had never known before.

This was the first time I didn't have to explain why I didn't eat pepperoni pizza or shrimp tempura, or why my family stayed home on Friday nights and I couldn't go ice skating like everyone else, or why we faced east when we prayed. Everyone here already knew, because I was home.

I was always Jewish, but for the first time, my Judaism was awake and singing, and I felt hungry and full at the same time. My eyes sparkled, and my heart pounded, and I was more awake than I had ever been in my whole entire life.

And Jerusalem was the center of that—especially the Old City. Although I'll tell you the truth, when they took us the first time to the Western Wall—when they had us close our eyes before we saw it from one of the overlooks, and told us to take a deep breath before we touch it, and when I finally put my hands against it—can I just tell you? I felt . . . absolutely nothing.

And oh man I wanted to feel something.

Because everyone said I would. From our rabbi back home with the LA Dodgers yarmulke, to my Sunday school teachers who played guitar and sang songs about Jerusalem in English, to my friends who had been to Israel, and especially my mother who had touched the wall all those many years ago.

"It's unlike anything else in the world," they all said.

And I felt like there was something wrong with me for feeling nothing when I touched it.

So I nodded along with everyone else when they went on about how spiritual and meaningful it felt. But honestly? I can tell you this now: I just felt a wall.

But the Old City itself thrummed with holy energy all around me—the different people passing one another between the stones, the priests and the imams and the rabbis, the women in hijab and the nuns in blue habits and the women with flowing scarves wrapped around their heads . . . *that* felt special, and I was in love. And the smells all around me, from the spice shops to baking bread to the crisp falafel balls to the plumes of rose-scented smoke billowing from the water pipes. . . . And the different languages, and the upturned eyes of the faithful. It was my spiritual epicenter, right there, all of it.

And I reeled with it.

I ate falafel by Jaffa Gate. I drank coffee in the big plaza in the Jewish Quarter next to a tree growing out of the stone. I saw the Armenian seminary students march toward Zion Gate in their black slacks and jackets, each step clipped and measured, their hair neatly combed to the side.

I explored the alleyways and thoroughfares that our counselors told us we could explore—the ones that were "safe enough." Because while I was feeling this deep and powerful connection through that first summer, I didn't yet know that there were others who cared just as deeply but in different ways.

We weren't to meet them, though.

That was also the summer I wore cut-off shorts and scarred my knees rappelling down a mountain. That was the summer right after my braces came off. That was the summer I kissed a man who had stubble, who wasn't worried about his AP History test, who tasted like Goldstar and Noblese cigarettes, and who would go to Gaza the morning after I slept curled up like a cat beside him in the middle of the desert.

I went back to LA and missed Israel so much it hurt, and I would dream about being back the way you dream about a lover who is out of reach. Especially Jerusalem. Jerusalem of stone and iron and Roman glass. Jerusalem of spices and smoke from the hookah pipes. Jerusalem of shofars and Sabbath candles. I would troll Ventura Boulevard where all the Israelis hung out, meeting guys with shaved heads and a lot of jewelry who smelled like sun and sex. There was Itsik who always knew stuff, and Arik who always got stuff done, and Eli who had seen too much.

And then there was Moti, but we don't talk about him because he's in jail.

I spent my Saturdays writing letters to the Israeli friends I had made—Elad with the purple hair in Tel Aviv, Daniel who lived on the kibbutz where we had stayed, Yuval who was in a special forces unit in the middle of the desert, Elinor who kissed her Bon Jovi poster every night before going to sleep.

I guess she was my best friend in Israel because I met her on a week-long exchange, and I stayed in her apartment with her parents and brother, and I slept next to her in her bunk bed, and we put on the same purple eyeliner and black tank tops, and we would hang out with the other kids our age and smoke cigarettes and drink coffee, and I felt all grown up.

She lived in Migdal HaEmek, a dingy little city in the worn seam of farmland country. A land of wheat and corn and maybe strawberries, where the air smells like manure and diesel and rotting fruit. Too far from the sea on either end, not close enough to the mountains or any river worth mentioning, Migdal HaEmek just sits there with a few pizza places and a bunch of kiosks one after the other, and an old park with rusted swings and a slide that smells like tetanus. But that's where I stayed with Elinor, where there were no camp counselors or curfews, where I watched the sun rise with a bunch of Israelis my own age who were two years shy of the army. We didn't know it then, but one of them would come home one weekend on leave and shoot himself in the face.

I loved Migdal HaEmek almost as much as I loved Jerusalem because it felt like a real part of Israel where no one really spoke English, and these were just ordinary folks who were building cities brick by brick and planting things seed by seed.

My parents were right—Israel was good for me. My skin was clearer in Israel. My muscles stronger. My allergies disappeared.

But during the school year, back in California, I lived a half life, sleeping through each day, dreaming. I yearned for the smell of fish heads and parsley in the shuk, the way the light hit the Jerusalem Stone or the waves of the Mediterranean. I craved salt and earth and all the things that I had felt when I was in Israel, barefoot in the fields, or sleeping in the desert. I missed my friends, especially Elinor, and I missed staying out all night at the scrap metal park in the middle of that gritty little city.

I didn't have many friends in high school. I was the girl with the frizzy hair and the bad skin, the girl who sat with the cafeteria manager because no one else wanted to sit with her, the girl who never got invited to the parties, and was pretty much invisible on a good day, or harassed, shoved, and tripped in the halls on a bad day.

I didn't fit.

But in Israel—especially Jerusalem—I wasn't the fish flopping on the shore, or the cat thrown into the deep end. I made sense.

I went back to Israel again the next summer and the next. The summer before my senior year—the summer my mom started getting stomach aches and going to the doctor, before they knew that a tumor the size of a grapefruit had wrapped itself around her left ovary and fallopian tube, the summer before I took my SATs and applied to universities, that last summer when I knew what each Monday would look like—every feeling, every hope, every thought squeezed down into a tiny little ball of desperate wanting, and I found it in Jerusalem.

And that was the summer that I ran away to Jerusalem from Migdal HaEmek because it was the only place I could go after what happened, happened.

Because Jerusalem was the only place that felt safe, that felt grounding. The name literally means City of Wholeness—*Eer Shalem*—and after what happened, I needed to feel whole again.

It happened because it was night and I had just gotten off the phone with my mom who tried to hide the pain in her voice when I asked how her stomach was feeling, but I heard it and I knew that something was wrong, and when I got off the phone, this guy who wore the same cologne as my ex-boyfriend started talking to me. We met the summer before, and the summer before that, he said, and didn't I remember?

Kind of.

"You're Sarah from Los Angeles," he said. "Everyone knows who you are."

And I felt like I was home.

He had a little silver stud in his eyebrow, and he was tall and thin, and on leave from the army, and when he told me he had some pictures from the time we all hung out at the pizza place near the park, I said *Yalla*, I'd love to see them.

"I live just around the corner," he said, so I went with him.

("Maybe you'll meet someone wonderful," my mother had said.)

I'm pretty sure I would have kissed him, except when we got to his house, I hit my head on a low beam, and the world went white and silent. I woke up on a rumpled bed, the long peasant skirt I borrowed from my mom hiked up around my waist and my thighs wet and sticky.

I got up slowly. My head hurt and everything I saw was in little pixels like stars coming into focus.

He was dressed and sitting at the tiny kitchen table when I found him drinking tea, a steaming cup across from him at the empty seat.

He looked older than he did when I followed him home, and his skin was pockmarked, and his nails dirty.

"What happened?"

"Nothing," he snapped. "You hit your head. I helped you lie down."

But he wouldn't look me in the eye. I drank my tea and he drove me back to Elinor's house a few blocks away.

He didn't even show me the pictures he said he had.

"What happened?" I asked again when we he stopped the car outside of Elinor's place, the light from the streetlamp yellow and jaundiced on him.

"I told you, nothing happened. You're fine."

I wasn't fine, but I didn't know what happened so I went up the stairs, my head pounding and my skin rancid.

I wasn't fine, but I didn't know what happened, so I took a shower until my whole entire body turned red and pink like hamburger meat.

I wasn't fine, but I didn't know what happened, and suddenly I was very tired.

"What happened?" Elinor asked me, and I couldn't answer.

"*Stupid, stupid, stupid,*" I said to myself, because I just knew that whatever happened, it must have been my fault. I shouldn't have gone with him. I shouldn't have been there.

The next day at dawn when the sky was the color of a bruised peach, I took my suitcase and snuck out of Elinor's family's apartment without saying goodbye, and I rode to Jerusalem, because it was my favorite place, and my mom's favorite place, and going there seemed like the only thing I could do to make sense of everything I knew, and everything I couldn't remember.

The bus lurched to the Central Bus Station in the middle of a hot and heavy Friday afternoon a few hours before Shabbat.

You have to understand something about Jerusalem: There is only one city in the world where you really feel Shabbat. And that's right here. Signs are posted everywhere with Shabbat times. Everyone knows when Shabbat comes in because a citywide siren announces it. And everyone knows when it goes out because the shops open and public transportation starts up. There's a rhythm to Shabbat in Jerusalem like nowhere else on earth.

But before it happens, there's this crazy kinetic energy in the air, and everyone is running around like kosher chickens with their heads cut off trying to get the last-minute ingredients for their meals before the stores close, and everyone is yelling about prices and parking spaces, and pushing each other out of the way, but also shouting, "*Shabbat shalom!*" which makes it all okay. The whole entire world outside the Central Bus Station on that hot August afternoon smelled like challah and zatar and candle wax.

And everyone had somewhere to go . . . everyone except me. I stood there in that filthy peasant skirt and my black tank top, carrying a suitcase without wheels, there in the hot August sun, baking against the Jerusalem Stone, and I wanted to cry.

I had 150 shekels in my wallet, which was less than fifty bucks back then. I had a plane ticket home for the following night, too, but nowhere to go right then. I felt light years away from my parents, and AP History class, and homework, and my curfew. The only thing that existed in that moment was my suitcase, the clothes on my back, and this little corner of the universe that was closing in on me.

So I did the only reasonable thing I could think of. I started walking east, the sun over my shoulder, toward the Old City, because that's where I had fallen in love with this place the first time, and I needed to remember.

It seemed like a good idea at the time, but remember the suitcase had no wheels, and I was tripping over that stupid soiled peasant skirt, and my whole body was aching in the hot sun, and every step measured with fatigue and anguish. But each step took me further from the rottenness of the night before, and closer to Jerusalem.

I saw Gideon by Jaffa Gate, leaning under a palm tree, only I didn't know his name yet. He had a joint in his mouth, and he was picking out "Jerusalem of Gold" on this old beat-up guitar that was nowhere near in tune. The case by his feet was open, and there were a few shekels in it, and a book titled *Jerusalem's Guide to Hostels,* or something like that.

He was wearing a shirt made out of hemp cloth, and torn jeans, and those leather Jesus sandals, and had a Phish yarmulke on his head. He smelled like weed and patchouli.

He reminded me of Jewish summer camp, and that first summer in Jerusalem. He reminded me of the sixties, like my mom's summer in Jerusalem all those years ago.

I sat down with him, and said, "Hi, I think I'm supposed to follow you."

"Groovy," he said. "My name is Gideon."

"I'm Sarah."

"Like Sarah Imenu, Sarah our Mother," he said in American Hebrew, referring to the biblical Sarah.

"You're making me sound old," I said.

"No, Holy Sister! Sarah Imenu is where it's *at.* She is the ultimate Woman of Valor who went forth from the land of her birth with her husband Abraham on a journey of danger, and of faith, to this very land on which we are sitting."

He patted the pockmarked grass next to him, the color of old pee—the same grass where a crumpled bag of potato chips lay baking under the hot August sun a few feet away. "This is holy land, dude," he said. "People should fucking treat it that way." He picked up the trash, tucked it in his pocket, put the guitar in the case, closed it, stubbed his joint out on the side of the palm tree, and reached his hand out to me.

I took it, and we walked through Jaffa Gate, and into the Old City.

It was nearly sunset by then, and the afternoon had turned to honey, and there were actual shadows to walk through, and for the first time all day, I didn't want to tear my skin off.

"There's this place up here," he said, pointing to a quick turn down an alley, and then another one, and another where there was an old staircase past a surly guy selling scarves that fluttered in a rainbow. "It's only five shekels to sleep on the roof. You down?"

Sure. Why not? One hundred and fifty shekels minus five for one night, and also, I thought about my great grandmother and the man who kissed her on a roof. Maybe it could be the same roof. ("You might meet someone wonderful," my mother had said.)

And something about sleeping under the Jerusalem moon and a million stars felt wild and free, and also safe—like, the complete opposite of that stale room with the rumpled sheets, the dingy room in that cramped little town. Jerusalem was the wellspring, and I would be reborn underneath the sky.

Because that summer I was eighteen, half woman, half child, a little broken in places, and seeking wholeness. I felt saturated and electrified by every experience, and I wanted to live it all as fully as possible. Both the awful and the beautiful.

So I did.

I wasn't expecting to walk up a narrow staircase and walk into another world, but I did that, too.

The room was sky blue, and the entire eastern wall was a glass window overlooking the rooftops of the Old City, just like the view I had seen that summer two years ago when I stood on the roof with all those other Jewish-American kids and lit the Havdalah candle.

The main room was strewn with Bedouin rugs, and there were hookah pipes, and a whole bunch of people just sitting und smoking and talking, popping sunflower seeds, drinking coffee.

And there was music—Bob Dylan's "Like a Rolling Stone." And it felt exactly like that.

The rooftop was perfect and I sat there for seconds—or maybe hours, doesn't matter—while the sky deepened, and the stars came out over the Old City. I heard the Shabbat siren, announcing that the Jewish Day of Rest was beginning. I heard church bells peeling from one of the steeples. I heard the Muslim call to prayer echo across each stone and each rooftop. I breathed deeply for the first time since I had woken up on those rumpled sheets, and I was free.

The guy behind the front desk was named Jono—he had tattoos snaking up and down his arms, and there were track marks along the veins. He had a sunken face, except for his chin that jutted out and just dared you to punch it. I am sure no one ever did because he also had these eyes that were two hot coals, and there was no way to tell the difference between his pupils and his irises.

His girlfriend, Rachel ("Rachel Imenu!" Gideon had said when he met her, "Rachel our Mother!"), was older than him, with tired blue eyes, and a smile that made her look a lot younger.

"Let's get a drink," he said. And since you could drink legally at eighteen, I choked down Arak at a dusty little hotel bar just inside Jaffa Gate.

Jono was divorced.

"We used to live on a kibbutz," he said. "I moved here from Brooklyn, and met my wife, the fucking bitch. She ran off. She took the kids."

"Wow, that sucks," I said.

"Yeah, if I ever see her again, I'll kill that bitch myself."

"You don't really mean that, do you?" I said.

He laughed, and his eyes were dead.

(Now that I'm a mother all these many years later, I know he meant it.)

Rachel squeezed his hand.

Gideon kept Shabbat, so he had gone to the Western Wall for candle lighting and prayers, and I had decided to explore the Old City with Jono and Rachel.

It was a good time to be in Israel.

Even though the Land is often marked by violence—almost everyone you'll meet, Jewish or Arab, knows someone who was either killed or maimed in a terror attack, a war, a demonstration, or reprisals—1999, unlike the terrible years before and the terrible years that would follow, was a little easier on everyone.

People in the region were still optimistic that peace between Israelis and Palestinians was just around the corner. Any minute we would get our act together and reach an agreement. Israel was still reeling in the aftershock of Rabin's assassination, and yet still hopeful that the handshake between Rabin and Arafat on the White House lawn really meant something.

So yes, it was a good time to be in Israel. It felt so good that I didn't think twice about strolling through Jaffa Gate that Friday night with Jono and Rachel, hooking a right around the ancient walls of the Old City, and toward Damascus Gate.

"It's called Damascus Gate because back in the day when you'd walk out of it from the Old City with your camels or donkeys and head straight, you would reach Damascus," Rachel explained as we walked along the walls. "It's really cool. Have you been in the Muslim Quarter?"

"No, not yet." I said. "They didn't let us go there on my trip."

"Well, girl, you're on a different trip now," she laughed. "Explore!"

They kissed me goodnight—each on each cheek—and headed up toward the bars on Jaffa Street.

I continued to follow the walls of the Old City.

Rachel was right.

Damascus Gate was like something out of a fairy tale where knights slay dragons while princesses watch from high turrets. The moon was rising and the gate gleamed pearly white, and I could smell Nutella crepes and hot corn.

I squinted my eyes and pictured how it must have looked nearly a century before when my great grandmother was there—with camels and donkeys, instead of kids on skateboards, and soldiers standing guard, their guns pointed at the ground.

I walked down the path toward the gate and then . . .

And then . . .

I don't remember. Really, I don't remember, because my body lurched forward, and I was nearly splayed across the stones. My left shoulder throbbed, and then searing pain spread down my neck from the back of my head.

I smelled blood. I reached back to touch my head, and it was wet and sticky and smelled like the bottom of a river.

And I was back in that house in Migdal HaEmek, the world turned white, my head exploding, just frozen and lying there, unmoving, and being torn apart from the inside.

I got hit again, twice? Ten times more?

What did it matter, I was back on that bed, not remembering, but reliving it in my skin and my bones, each breath measured only to breathe and get through it.

I don't remember, except there were so many people—mostly men. They seemed grownup to me, but I'm remembering this through the eyes of an eighteen-year-old who was terrified. Maybe if it happened now, I'd see they were just young boys, same age as I was. Maybe even younger.

I do remember that instead of running away from the gate, I ran toward it, and into the Muslim Quarter. The gates aren't straight shots—you go through and you basically hit a wall, and you either turn left or right. I turned left. There was Arabic scrawled all over the walls, and it looked spidery and dangerous and to this day I have no idea what it said except it was written in crimson, like the blood on my fingers from the wound in the back of my head. Music throbbed from different shops, and people were shouting and laughing, and everyone was pushing and shoving through that narrow little passage, and I smelled smoke, and I had no idea where the fire was, or if I was just imagining it, and I couldn't remember what had happened, and my thoughts were stuttering in loop between waking up on that filthy bed, and standing at Damascus Gate covered in blood, and that's all I was . . . broken.

There were so many people all around me, and I pushed through them without seeing, my legs tangled in that stupid peasant skirt, until I found two soldiers and said in English, "Help me." And they walked me out of the gate, and up toward Jaffa Street where I sat for a long, long time and cried for even longer.

"Stupid stupid stupid," I said to myself just as I had the night before. Because this, too, must be my fault.

That was my last summer in Israel for a very long time.

The night in Migdal HaEmek that I *still* can't remember even now—except in that never-ending spool that something terrible happened, something terrible happened, something terrible happened—and then the night right after where I was pelted with rocks and bled in the shadow of the Old City, had shaken me.

I came home quieter than usual and went back to AP History class and sitting alone at lunch.

That was also the year I hated my mother. And I had good reason to. She was leaving me.

An hour after I had finished taking the SATs on the first Saturday of November, my parents sat me down for a family meeting.

My mom sat to my right in a blue cloud of smoke. She was wearing her "Howard Berman for Congress" shirt. She had that blue-and-white scarf tied around her head, like always. Even before I was born, she always wore that blue scarf.

("Saraleh, when I was in high school, I had such long black hair, and I ruined it with Aquanet. . . . Don't make the same mistake, dear one.")

Her scarf was part of my vocabulary early on. I remember once, in the throes of preschool, when my mother told me it was time to go, I broke a red crayon and hissed, "I hate you and I hate your scarf."

I didn't really mean it then—I didn't hate her, and I didn't hate her scarf. But I sure would mean it during that long last year I lived at home.

And on that first Saturday in November, my parents looked at each other—and in that moment, when their eyes met, I realized that they were more nervous than I was. "Sarah, we have some news."

"Dr. Bernstein called yesterday, and I have cancer."

Type 3. Ovarian, if you're keeping score.

She'd have surgery in a week, the Thursday after my essay on *Heart of Darkness* was due.

She'd start chemo the week after, just before Christmas vacation.

They'd stick a portacath in her stomach—I'd never see it, but I would feel it when she'd hug me.

She bought clip-on bangs to tuck under her scarf—espresso black. The first time she wore it was on Hanukkah at her parents' house because she didn't want them to see the signs of what they already knew was happening to their firstborn baby.

She bought a wig and hated it. ("I look like Ronald Reagan.") She only wore it once—to my high school graduation.

("Well, at least no one will notice when my hair falls out, since I always wear a scarf anyway.")

And I hated her.

We were already locked in a power struggle, my mother and I, well before that first Saturday in November. We were already caught in the tug of war between being her daughter and breaking away. And this, oh this, this motherfucking cancer, was like a dark music score in a movie—cellos moaning, a harbinger of doom.

With every pound she lost, I hated her. With every apologetic smile, I hated her. With every treatment, every scan, every doctor's visit, I hated her. Because in her frail body, in her pleading eyes that lost their lashes, I saw only the years stretching by one after the other, endlessly, without her.

This was my mother, but she was leaving me.

How dare she leave me! I should leave *her*!

And I would cry at night like a small child locked in a tiny space with no light and no sense of the coming dawn.

And I hated her for her modesty, for trying to hide the disease from me, for covering her head every time as though her hair grew as always beneath the blue bandana, for hiding the scars on her stomach, for covering her bones with three layers of clothes in the middle of July.

And if she had showed me the signs that she was leaving? I would have hated her, still.

The last day in that house, in that house where my mother and I would lie head to toe on the green couch in an LA winter watching flames dance in the fireplace and listening to recordings of old broadcasts from the forties, in that house where my mother and I had planted purple roses outside my window because they were my favorite, in that house where we baked meringue cookies, and watched "Mystery Theatre," and played "Heart and Soul" on the piano, I broke my mother.

We were packing the last of the boxes and we had a tug-of-war over Howard Zinn's *A People's History.* And here's the fucked up thing: I don't remember why we were fighting over it. Maybe she wanted me to take it and I didn't want it, or maybe she didn't want me to have it, but I wanted it with me. But in that struggle over paper and words, I could smell underneath the cigarettes and the patchouli oil, underneath the Bounty fabric softener and Irish Spring soap, I could smell my mother—so like me, only leaving. And I hated her more than I hated her all year.

And with a scream I would only recognize years and years later when I heard my daughter for the first time, I reached down over my mother and ripped her scarf off.

And she stood there in the soft light of dusk, her eyes shocked and shining, like a baby sparrow she stood there, her skull covered in soft tufts of grey feathers, the light shining through like spun silver.

My stomach clenched.

The scarf floated to the ground.

She lunged as though to pick it up, and instead, with a roar that came from somewhere infinite and endless inside her, she sprang on me, and bit me on my left arm.

Her teeth sank into my skin. I yelped.

She pulled back. There was blood on her lips, and her eyes were fierce.

She stood there, a single exquisite spark of kinetic energy trembling in the fading light. "You're leaving me," she growled. "You're leaving me. You're breaking away from me. You're moving away. You have to, but I hate it. And this is what a mother lion has to do when her cub leaves the pride. And you will forgive me for this, dear one . . . for all of this. And you will forgive yourself, too."

I forgave her, but I haven't forgiven myself.

I guess I have to tell you that after I moved away to university, six days after my mom bit me, I met someone.

I met him on a golden day in August, days before freshman year. I remember the exact spot where I saw him—in a sunny strip just outside a cafe on the north side of campus. He was sitting between the door and the shadow from the building across the street. He glowed.

He started talking to me because of my chai necklace. I had bought it in Israel. Chai means "life," and I wore it every single day.

"Are you Israeli?" he asked, pointing to the chai.

"No, but I love it there, and I want to live there someday."

"Cool. I'm from there."

Maybe you'll meet someone nice.

That night, when we kissed, he tasted like that first summer in Israel.

So, how could I not fall in love with him?

Nearly four years later, I was working four jobs and taking four classes, and I lived an hour away from campus in an apartment next to the train station.

I taught Hebrew School. I was a teacher's aide at a local high school. I cataloged Hebrew books in one library. And I worked in the main stacks/circulation at another.

I volunteered at the Student Advocate's Office and I studied folklore and anthropology and Middle East history and peace and conflict studies.

I lived on caffeine pills and a bottle of Adderall I scored from one of the frats.

My mom had gotten sicker, and it took every bit of strength she had to go out to the garden and pull the yellow leaves off the plants that grew outside her window.

I also lived on heart-pounding, sweat-prickling, stomach-wrenching fear.

Because he had changed. It happened suddenly, overnight, but by the time my mom was in a last-ditch clinical trial in an effort to save her life, he would knock me down on the floor and pin my arms to my sides and snarl that he would "fucking kill you, you stupid bitch," because I brought home a B- on a paper.

He threatened to leave me if I spoke to my friends from back home.

We had these two cats, Sigmund and Crumbum, both grey and brown and in between like moths, and they were sweet and they'd curl up against me at night when we'd go to sleep, and they'd purr, and if I was scared, they somehow knew and crawled into my lap, just to sit there. One night he filled the bathtub with water and held them under and made them "disappear."

I didn't tell my parents, or anyone, and I would get home every night at 10:55 p.m.—still with two hours of reading left, maybe an essay to write—to a man who would hiss in my ear, "You better bring in this month's rent and make straight As, or else."

And every morning I had to be at the library at 8:00 a.m., which meant waking up at 6:00 a.m. (or else) to take the train.

Once, on the way back from Trader Joe's, we were listening to Counting Crows's "Mr. Jones," and I was singing the words, and he asked innocuously, "How do you know all the words?"

"I googled them."

"YOU STUPID BITCH, IF YOU HAVE TIME TO GOOGLE THEN YOU HAVE TIME TO GET A'S ON ALL YOUR PAPERS."

That night he hit me. I didn't scream. I never screamed. I was too afraid the police would come and take him away if I did. But he yelled. He yelled so loud the neighbors banged on the walls.

And he kept yelling, until they called the police.

Then sirens. Then loud footfalls against the thin carpeting in the hall. Then a heavy knock.

That night, he looked at me and said, "You better tell them you're fine."

That night, I opened the door.

"Ma'am, are you okay?" they asked.

I was only twenty. But I looked old—face fish-belly white from crying, swollen lids, red eyes. And underneath my long-sleeved shirt, I could feel bruises blooming like blue bonnets along the insides of my arms.

Where did I go? This silent "ma'am" who had taken over the girl who danced and sang in front of bonfires, who shouted into canyons, who climbed roofs, talked to strangers, who laughed with friends. Where did I go?

Please don't let them find out please don't let them find out please don't let them find out. They'll take him away they'll take him away they'll take him away.

I couldn't live without him then.

"Ma'am, are you okay?" they asked.

"I'm fine. Just a little argument," I whispered.

"Are you sure?" they looked at me.

"Yes. Really. I'm fine. We're fine. Thanks for checking."

My voice stuck in my throat. Where did I go, the girl who made up bawdy song lyrics with her best friend, the girl who struck up conversations with people over books they were reading, the girl who slept on roofs, the girl who called her parents and told them things.

Please don't let them find out please don't let them find out please don't let them find out. They'll take him away they'll take him away they'll take him away.

So that's why I was tired. Every night before getting on the 9:55 p.m. train to go home, I would stand on the platform, my toes over the edge. I would watch the digital clock on the consul—I *lived* by that clock. Ten minutes until I had to go back home. Then five. Then four. Then three. And at two minutes, from so far away, I would hear the roar of the train barreling south, a yawn that grew into a roar as it got closer, and with one minute to go, I would see the lights down the long tunnel, that faint glow, almost like the light they say you see before you die.

How often I thought about jumping in front of that train, mouth open, silent scream.

Because I knew I was headed back home with only a few hours to sleep next to a man who terrified me, next to a man that I was equally terrified of losing.

And let me tell you, being pinned between these two fears is the absolute worst—because your life ekes out into his, and you can't live without him, even though living with him means slowly, slowly you are dying.

So, *God damn,* I was tired. And every morning I would bring this little alarm clock with me in my bag—this was before I had a cell phone—and I would set it for 7:35, five minutes before my train was due to pull into the station.

That hour ride, through the flatlands and over the hills, was the only time I could really sleep.

I would tuck my legs up against the seat in from to me, and I would put my jacket against the window, my bag clutched in my lap, and I would finally sleep.

The whoosh whoosh of the train engine felt so safe, I was vaguely aware of people moving around me, but they became gentle dream sounds . . . lilts and lulls and then a laugh. . . . Life moving on around me, safe. And as I would drift off, I would pretend I was on one of those old-timey trains that would bring me to a station in the middle of Small Town Anywhere-But-Here, where people milled about and sold flowers and apple pie, and went fishing, and no one beat their girlfriends or drowned her cats.

God *damn,* I was tired.

And I would sleep sweet and deep until my alarm went off, and then I would get off the train and go to work.

Each day, the same.

Each day, silently checking books, or cataloging, teaching Hebrew in a whisper, in my own classes quietly taking notes, writing essays, reading, but no longer Googling song lyrics.

Then at night, standing on the platform again, my toes over the edge.

Would I jump this time?

And then one morning, I was curled up again as usual, head against the window, my legs tucked up, my bag in my lap, when I realized half-asleep that there was a hand between my legs. And it wasn't mine.

And I woke up. And the man sitting next to me was touching me—his hand pressed between my thighs—and he stared at me, like ,"What are you going to do about it?"

So I'll tell you what I did about it: I did what I didn't do when I woke up on that fetid bed in that terrible room in Migal HaEmek. I did what I didn't do all those nights that the man I loved hurt me. That morning I screamed.

I stood up in the middle of that train—a quiet train full of men and women in suits with briefcases, students in coats and scarves, old men with walking sticks, a woman in a wheelchair—and I fucking *screamed.*

"How dare you! *How fucking dare you!*"

My voice was mine, but it wasn't mine. It was bottomless and infinite, the roar of a thousand generations of strong women who had had enough.

My voice was mine, but it wasn't mine, and yet it sounded like it could be mine, and it tore through my throat and filled the train, and everyone turned to stare at me, a warrior goddess born of fury, standing there, my jacket on the ground, my bag splayed open.

My voice was mine—yes, my voice was *mine*, because no one else on the train said a goddamn word, no one would stand up for me except me. So I did it with a roar.

"*Don't you ever lay a goddamn hand on me ever again you son of a bitch!*"

And I stalked out of that train at the next stop before my stop, and I was late to work, and I lost my voice, and I didn't give a shit because I felt great.

Because I wasn't just screaming at him on the train. I was finally screaming at the other him, the him still sleeping an hour away.

And by the time I got my voice back three weeks later, I had left him.

And I never took that stupid morning train again.

I never told my mom about what happened with the man I loved. My dad knows now, but my mom never knew. She was dying in LA during the months after I left him, and I was up at school doing my best to ignore it. I worked in a bar at the edge of the world that reminded me so much of that hostel with the hookah pipes and Bedouin rugs just in Jaffa Gate.

The bar was next to this little park, a patch of hopelessness that looked like Ground Zero for the Zombie Apocalypse if the Zombie Apocalypse had happened in 1968. The folks there reminded me of those pilgrims staring out that big old window at the hostel looking toward the Temple Mount just a few months before the year 2000 when some folks kinda hoped that the world would end.

They all had zealot's eyes, the lot of them: too bright one minute, too cloudy the next. Whether in the dregs of this small town, or the rooftops of Jerusalem, too much faith unhinges the mind.

I worked in this little bar called Dream Cuisine—a shack, really, but covered in colored Christmas lights, with more beers than I could count in the rickety fridge and on tap.

That was the summer I learned to love beer. Especially the sour ones like Red Seal.

I wore halter tops back then, and I had a little belly button ring that sparkled.

I was also working at the library, and as a Bat Mitzvah tutor, and thinking about my senior thesis, and smoking a shit ton of weed, and saying a long goodbye to my mom back and forth to LA.

And Dream Cuisine was my *spot*. The place was wild, just like that hostel in the Old City with its cast of characters where I slept on the roof my last night in Jerusalem when I came back covered in blood. There was this guy named Phil who was in Nam. He was old with broken teeth, and the best smile in the world, and he would belly up to the bar and say to me, "Hey, Angel Face. Get me a beer. I don't care if your name isn't Angel Face. Get me a fuckin' Road Dog."

Sometimes he brought his boyfriend with him, and that guy would always bring a jar of pigs feet.

Then there was Shroom. (Guess what he was on?)

And Psycho Mike who had anger issues, and then this guy we called Super Psycho Jay who got his name because he beat up Psycho Mike—like literally threw that motherfucker through a plate glass window across the street like nobody's business.

Through it all, the owner would make Massaman curry, and chicken masala, and some Brazilian dish, and nachos and beer in the kitchen that was about as big as my kitchen table.

Meanwhile, out in the front, we would dance on the bar—usually to Natasha Atlas, or the Cure. I did a mean sexy routine to "Tainted Love," and then I'd belly dance to the *Monsoon Wedding* soundtrack, and sometimes one of the mix tapes that Itsik or Arik or Eli gave me back when I was in high school and trolling Ventura Boulevard for Israelis. Moti never sent a mix tape because he was in jail.

There was weed smoking inside and outside, and the frat boys would all show up around midnight and buy their one-dollar pitchers, and the street kids would come in and dump their paper cup full of quarters out on the counter and say, "Just give us everything you've got."

It was a scene.

That was the summer I learned to use a butterfly knife—I think it was Turtle who lent me his, or maybe Maurice, or Shroom.

We were a mixed crowd of every religion (or non-religion), every color, a ton of languages. Guys would make out with guys, girls would make out with girls, and it was all good.

It became our Jerusalem—our spiritual epicenter, as insane as that might sound.

And so it went that summer with our Massaman curry and our beer and our weed and our music and our colored Christmas lights in that little shack. We were cool. We were family.

Shit got real sometimes, but we took care of one another.

Why am I telling you about this?

Because that's where I met the man I would marry.

I hadn't been back in Israel since that summer of 1999, and I missed it, but it was a dull ache, like a bruise that wouldn't quite go away, but that I could ignore unless I pressed it.

And then this guy came in, smelling sweet and clean, and he ordered a Sierra Nevada—an aromatic, almost flowery beer, which earned him some serious points in my book, and when I carded him and saw the ridiculously Israeli name, I flirted with him.

"Where are you from in Israel?" I asked in Hebrew.

"Wait, what?"

He was not expecting the blonde-haired, blue-eyed girl with the chubby cheeks that the bar folks called "Angel Face" to know he was from Israel, or to speak Hebrew.

We went on our first date the next night, and were living together within a week.

And my mom got sicker, and just a few months later, on a warm morning after the longest night I had ever known lying beside her in bed and counting her breath, she died.

Before it happened, time stretched and bent and stretched again, and so did the spaces between each breath she drew. 86 seconds. 87. 88. 83. 78. 90.

She was holding on so tight.

The rabbi had called us around midnight: "You have to let her go," he told my dad. "She's won't leave until you tell her it's okay to let go."

My dad had spent the last few weeks urging her to rally. "You can do this! You'll be up and dancing again in no time!"

She couldn't do it, but she couldn't let him think she didn't want to.

So she lingered in that space between here and not here, and it's the worst because it's forever, and it's nothing.

We lay in bed with her, my dad and I on either side.

92 seconds between each breath. Then 94.

A week before, when she was still able to sit at her desk and drink coffee and smoke her cigarettes, she would quote that line from *Peter Pan*: "To die will be an awfully big adventure."

Her vein thumped between her left ear and her hairline. Her eyelids fluttered.

"You can go now," my dad whispered to her as the sun streamed in on a day too beautiful for her to die. "You can go now."

I wouldn't have believed it unless I had been there, holding her hand, now slack in mine while her face softened as that last breath blew through her and into the morning light.

For days, she had been stuck in limbo between our world and that next "big adventure." For days, she had lain there in a space in between.

But this, she heard. I saw her let go, and every moment of her life, every joy and every anguish, had been sucked down into that one last breath, and it was gone.

A scream ripped through the room, too horrible to hear, a keening wail without words, the noise a trapped animal makes while it tries to gnaw its own leg off.

I wanted to shout, "shut up shut up shut up shut up shut up," until I realized that I was the one screaming, my whole body rigid and shaking while people poured in: my aunt, my uncle, the neighbors. But the room was really empty because she wasn't there anymore.

"Bring her back, bring her back," I screamed. "Bring her back, bring her back," I shivered and shook as the light shifted in the room and the shadows fell across the bed, across the shell of the woman who held my world together.

This woman, the granddaughter of the woman who kissed a man on that roof in Jerusalem, this woman who wandered the same streets that her grandmother did, and that her daughter would, this woman was gone.

And when she died, the world became less safe, so I measured my life in what ifs and reruns. The girl who climbed roofs had faded into grey over the years, and I craved routine the way I used to crave the stars.

❖

The following year, my boyfriend and I flew to Israel to visit the kibbutz where he had grown up. The smell of grass and cigarettes outside the kibbutz pub made me heady and reminded me of that first summer and the next and the next. Drunk on a lot of cheap wine and possibility, I told my boyfriend that (and I quote) "I'd *totally* love to live in Israel someday."

We got engaged, and three years and two babies later, he called me out on that promise.

I was a mess then. I had two babies back to back, both of them still breastfeeding, and my life revolved around old episodes of *Friends* and *Sex and the City*, and driving to Coffee Bean just around the corner on Sepulveda and Palms.

My mom was still dead, and I was afraid.

But I had made a promise to live in Israel, and we went because somewhere buried deep inside me was that kernel of a golden memory of that first night in Jerusalem on that rooftop overlooking the Old City when I was sixteen and felt that real sense of home and wholeness.

So we flew to Israel.

And again, it's worth repeating: I was a mess. I was in a new country with a nine-month-old who spent more time with my boobs than my high school boyfriend did back in ninth grade, and a two-and-a-half-year-old who had mastered the word "no" (in Hebrew and in English), and I had no friends. I barely spoke the language, my whole entire family was in another time zone, and my marriage was falling apart for the above reasons.

Hell, it isn't like I was even a virgin when I got married, but I still wore white.

Because for all my experience playing grownup in that little house on that pretty street where we lived and loved, when it came down to it, I was seeing the world through a filmy veil of good intentions.

In many ways, I was very, very young when we got married and started a family.

Those were easy times spent eating four-dollar sushi and sipping Sierra Nevadas on Friday afternoons on the south side of the city where the houses were handmade and the flowers bloomed all the time. Easy times spent sharing a big red umbrella when it rained and a tiny kitchen space where we'd cook pasta with butter and garlic, getting stoned then watching *Spaceballs*.

Easy times spent thinking it would always be like this. Sure, the kids would come, but nothing would really change unless we let it, which we wouldn't.

Just a few steps from where we lived, there was a twist in the road that I loved with all my heart. It was just behind the main drag with all the restaurants and cafes, three steps away from the doughnut shop where I would get a rainbow sprinkled doughnut on the way to the book store that smelled like patchouli and hydroponic pot and was run by a man who swore he was two hundred years old and the wizard Merlin's long lost cousin.

I loved that little bend of road because in early spring the cherry blossom trees that lined it would turn to blushing brides in gauzy white veils.

And I was a bride-to-be, floating in dappled sunlight even when it rained, and I'd walk beneath that big red umbrella we would share when we'd head down College Avenue to the place with the cheap sushi.

And during those early days after I told the man I loved that I would, like, totally move to Israel some day and raise our kids there, for sure, when the ring on my finger sparkled extra bright, and while I'd dream about all the Very Important Things a marriage needed—like a really good kosher caterer and a DJ who would play "Hava Nagila," Flock of Seagulls, Eminem, *and* Billie Holiday—I would walk past the elegant trees swathed in white and think about the most important thing of all: my wedding dress.

The most important thing of all: my wedding dress.

Really?

Seriously?

My wedding dress?

But at the time, a marriage meant a ritual and a costume change. What would really change between us? We were in love.

I saw myself each night just before slipping into sleep—the awkward, off-kilter girl with the bad skin and hopeful eyes standing beautiful on her wedding day like those exquisite trees that would bloom those few short weeks each year.

Blink and you will miss it.

And I found my dream dress online on the first click, like it was *bashert:* fated.

So I spent $150 of my father's money on that creamy white satin gown with its lace overlay and the pearl seeds that gently caught the light.

This was a dress that would erase the past that I had spent living on my knees with my head pressed to the ground pleading for redemption from every mistake, every misstep.

This was a dress that would make me beautiful.

(This dress, now rotted to grey, and laced with mold. This dress that my daughter will never wear even when playing dress-up. This dress that I can only remember from the pictures in the Facebook album that I've set to "private.")

"Behold, by this ring you are consecrated to me according to the laws of Moses and Israel," we said to each other while our rabbi looked on and smiled as we read from the wedding contract that we had written ourselves, that I had sketched with colored pencils, and outlined in gold pen.

I was barely twenty-six when I stuck my index finger out beneath the huppah my preschool students had painted for us with watercolor paints and droplets of gold glitter, when the man I loved slipped the gold band halfway down. When with a deep breath and the sound of breaking glass, it was sealed.

I wore white on my wedding because that's what brides spoon-fed fairy-tale dreams do—despite the years of living that came before, that bruised the bloom off this rose. The fights that I should have paid more attention to. The churlish silences that stuffed the spaces of our studio apartment. My (over)reactions born of seething neuroses. The memory of another man from long, long ago who knocked me down and crammed his foot against my throat. The memory of my mother dying next to me.

That desperate need to be seen always for who I wanted to be but *soooo* wasn't.

So, I painted my fingernails a pale pink, not because I liked the color but because the name on the bottle read "Blushing Bride," and that's how I wanted to be seen.

But two weeks in, I was puking my guts out while a teeny tiny life made her presence known deep inside me, and our lives sped up to Ludicrous Speed. (Because Light Speed is for amateurs.)

Two years: two kids.

Two years more: two separate homes.

And two years of living in two, we stood clear-eyed the two of us, one before the other, my hands outstretched as if beseeching, waiting for that folded sheet of paper that would end what we thought would never change but did, while surly old men in long white beards told the man I once loved what words to say.

"Banished, banished, banished."

Just a simple costume change. I stood there silently, in a long black dress I bought for this occasion that skimmed the hips that had borne our two children. The tan line from the ring I once wore had disappeared. My nails were painted in my favorite color: red. Red like cherries. Red like blood. Red like the first traces of dawn.

A few days after that was when I found Jerusalem again.

Back to Jerusalem

I HAD ONLY been in Jerusalem twice since that summer of broken memory, but when I did, it was only to visit the Western Wall with my dad, and my kids.

And when we went, we went the route I knew from that first summer on the Jewish program—the safe way—down through Jaffa Gate, into the shuk, past the glittering necklaces and mosaic signs, past the mirrors and IDF t-shirts, past the olive wood crosses and the menorahs and the guy selling pomegranate juice, to the little turn toward the Western Wall.

I remembered that path from nearly fifteen years ago when our counselors led us down the steps and through the alley, and I knew it from my dreams, too, and I knew that it was safe.

"Have you been to the Muslim Quarter?" someone asked.

"No," I answered.

"Why not?"

I thought about the stones hitting my skull, and about the writing on the wall in bloodred paint.

"Because it's dangerous."

It was fifteen years since that night by Damascus Gate, and negotiations between the Israelis and the Palestinians stalled and failed, felled by a Jewish assassin's bullet and an onslaught of terror attacks against Israeli civilians on busses and cafes and even a discotheque. A lot of innocent people died, including my friend's brother who got on the wrong bus a few months after his wedding. All they could identify of him was his blue yarmulke and his gold wedding band.

Israel built a wall high and mighty, cutting into large swathes of Palestinian land, and expanded the settlements.

Artists and activists came and painted on the wall.

And it's true, after thousands died during the Second Intifada, the Wall stopped a lot of the carnage.

But a new generation of Israelis and Palestinians grew up on different sides, never seeing the other, not learning the other's language, not knowing that there, just on the other side of that big, tall, ugly wall, there are other kids, just like them.

It was the winter two years after my divorce, the winter of the snow fall and the ice storm that swept through the land, turning it a blinding white, and I was already working at *Times of Israel* as their new media editor, and I became friends with one of Israel's leading journalists.

This journalist is like those guys I knew back in LA all rolled into one—Itsik who knows stuff, Arik who gets stuff done, and Eli who has seen too much. He's many things, but mostly he's charming, really smart, and radiates warmth and a little mystery.

He's the guy who walks into the bar, and people turn around and notice. It's not because he's particularly tall or broad-shouldered—he is neither, and like most Israeli guys in their late thirties and forties, his head is shaved down to the skin. But he's got it. Charisma.

He also smells fantastic.

And a combination of his intelligence, his warmth, and his street smarts honed from living in Jerusalem have helped make him a damn good journalist who knows everyone, and has access to everywhere (and did I mention that he smells good, and that's kind of my thing). I liked him, and one day he called and asked, "Want to come with me to meet the Sheikh of the Waqf?"

He said it so casually, like it ain't no thang to be a Jewish Israeli journalist and go sit with the man who oversaw Al-Aqsa, the place that seethes with contention. Many argue it was ground zero for the Second Intifada, when Ariel Sharon ascended the Temple Mount in the middle of a very tense period between Jews and Palestinians.

Today, it is the epicenter of the tensions that reverberate throughout the region, and already there were rumblings and riots between Jews and Palestinians over the holy site.

I didn't realize that saying yes would mean we would walk through Damascus Gate, but it did.

He didn't notice while I trembled, clutching my pearly scarf around my shoulders, my eyes darting left and right, my body tense and ready to run.

"*Yalla*, let's go eat kenafe," he said as he led me to this little place that sells fried cheese and semolina. He walked in and spoke Arabic and Hebrew to the guys behind the counter, and we sat down and ate the sweet cheese.

I waited for someone to hiss at me. I waited for a rock to graze my temple. Instead, I had dessert.

We continued through the shuk and toward the perfume market. "This is the best place to get spices," he said. "Smell!"

It smelled amazing.

"They make the best *siniyeh*," he said, pointing to a small place tucked behind crates and boxes, where three men bent over large bowls of steaming stew.

It smelled amazing, too.

I started breathing more slowly, my breath in soft little clouds hanging in the chilly air, just like the breath of everyone around me, and my eyes stopped darting, and instead of looking for danger, I started looking at people.

I watched a woman in hijab soothe a crying child just as I would soothe my own crying babies.

I watched these two grizzled men play backgammon outside a shop just like the old-timers on the kibbutz where I had lived that summer in 1999.

I watched old women lean on canes, their bodies bundled and cozy beneath their long robes, and then a boy run past carrying a bird cage. I saw pilgrims dressed in white float by singing in Latin. I saw girls in glossy hijabs and designer sunglasses point to a young guy and giggle. Really, I just saw people being people. People just like the people in my little town in the center of Israel. People just like my friends. People just like my kids. People just like me.

Ordinary folks.

After I went with the journalist that day, I decided to go back. First I went with other journalists—this tall Dutch correspondent who had green eyes and smelled like Christmas. We went together and I felt safe with him. But as the cold, hard winter passed, I started getting bored just following the same roads that others had forged.

So I decided to go alone.

And I went through Damascus Gate by myself one day, past the guy selling crepes, and the Border Police with their guns drawn, past the huge crate of strawberries, and this little girl with a Hello Kitty balloon.

I walked by myself through that same gate where it all had happened, where I smelled my own blood, brackish and sticky, from the back of my head, the same head I had hit the night before that knocked out everything I still can't remember.

I walked by myself through that same gate where it all had happened, where I turned left and saw red scrawled all over the wall. Those spidery letters were still there, still crimson, and I still had no idea what they said.

I walked by myself through that same gate where it all had happened, where I needed soldiers to walk out with me, where I was shivering, and struck, and broken.

("Do you know what they do with broken objects in Japan?" my mom had asked me after my first heartbreak, when I lay in bed staring at the ceiling, my heart shattered into several jagged pieces. "They don't throw them away, sweet girl. They repair them. They melt gold and mend the everyday clay objects with the precious molten material."

"That's kind of stupid. Why don't they just get new objects?"

"Because they understand that the broken thing is far more beautiful for having been broken in the first place.")

Jerusalem of gold, and I am the earthenware bowl.

I went through Damascus Gate a lot that spring and into the summer.

I didn't go into any of the stores, or talk to anyone, because I didn't know how to.

But then one day, one of the guys at the kenafe place called to me in Hebrew, "Hi, I've seen you pass this way a lot. Come have kenafe."

So I did.

We didn't talk about politics. But we talked about his kids.

We didn't talk about God. But we talked about the rosemary his wife had planted in their little rooftop garden.

"How do you say, 'thank you' in Arabic?" I asked.

"*Shukran*."

"Okay, *Shukran*!" I said.

"*Bevakasha*—you're welcome!" he answered in Hebrew.

And I've kept going back—not just there, but to other places all up and down that street, and on others too.

And that's where I met Musa.

Deep in the Old City of Jerusalem, tucked into a dark little corner, there's this jewelry gallery that's always shining. I like bright, shiny objects, especially on dark days, when the shadows nip close at my heels, which they do even in the early spring here in Jerusalem. And when I saw the lights of the shop winking off the tables of gold and silver and crystal for the first time, I went inside.

The man who owns the shop is my age and he's got eyes the same color as the Roman glass he sells behind the glass case near the register. The first time I saw him, he was sitting behind the counter holding Muslim prayer beads, hand-carved, one two three, four five. . . . There was a calendar next to the cash register that read "Bank of Palestine."

And in this shop, deep in the still-beating heart of the Old City, he sells menorahs, and Sabbath candlesticks, kiddush cups, and Jewish star necklaces alongside murals carved on marble of Al-Aqsa, wrapped around by the Shahada, the Muslim declaration of faith.

We speak in Hebrew, because my Arabic hasn't grown beyond the simple.

"Kif halik habibti?" How are you?

"Mabsuta. Kif Halak?" I'm great, how are you?

"Al hamdullah." Thank God.

Sometimes, we switch to English for a sentence or two. And sometimes, we have to use Google Translate, because words are hard.

It was spring, but raining still—soaking through each layer from jacket to sweater to tank top, all the way to my very skin—and I had walked through the gleaming streets, to this shop where it's always warm.

"Tea, *habibti*? You know you aren't leaving without drinking a cup, especially in this rain."

So we sat over spiced tea in the corner, next to the table with his prayer beads and the Bank of Palestine calendar.

"Did you hear about the soccer match?" he asked, referring to a game where Arab fans of Sakhnin waved Palestinian flags and shouted "*Allahu Akbar*—God is Great" after Jewish fans of Beitar Yerushalayim screamed "*Mavet l'aravim*—Death to the Arabs."

I shuddered.

"My sons play soccer," he said quietly.

"So does mine. Not very well. Show me pictures of your kids!"

He clicked over to Facebook and we scrolled through his albums. Oh such cute kids, smiling in each picture, in their soccer uniforms. The younger one wore glasses and a lopsided grin. "He loves learning, that one." The older one's face was nearly split in two with his smile. "He takes care of his younger brother. He's really a sensitive boy. I try to teach them to love everyone, but they hear things from their friends that make it hard."

I wonder what my kids will hear from their friends some day about "The Arabs," the faceless, nameless, Other.

They've been through a war, my kids.

For the whole entire summer before, we slept with our shoes on, with one eye open. When the sirens would wail, we would run for our lives, over dry earth, to our public bomb shelter.

We had ninety seconds to get there, but try doing that with two little kids who are blank-eyed and screaming.

I'll never forget the second time we had to run. I had my daughter in my arms because she was sick that day, and my son was running as fast as his sweet little legs could carry him, but he fell, screaming, crying on the dry earth when, suddenly, out of nowhere, someone I had never seen before—surely a neighbor—doubled back, swooped my son up, and we all of us ran the rest of the way.

We made it on time. And the rocket landed in a field close enough to smell the smoke and scorched earth.

There were pieces of shrapnel scattered across the field we had run through earlier—the field where my son fell and I couldn't carry two children at the same time.

We still have nightmares. A low frequency hum, and it feels like wild birds are beating their wings in my chest.

My kids don't sleep with their shoes on anymore, but they line their shoes up by the door.

"*Yalla*, let me show you my babies," I said to Musa, pulling out my phone.

He scrolled over the album, flicking through each photo.

"Oh my God, that smile!" he said when he looked at my son mugging for the camera and doing jazz hands. "And your daughter—wow, she has your expression. You can see her soul shining through her eyes." He paused for a minute as his finger hovered over a photo of my sweet girl standing next to the fields by our house.

"I want to give her something," he said as he stood up and walked over to the display case near the window. "Don't say no, it will break my heart if you do," he added as he returned with his palm held out to me.

I looked down at his right hand, and there in the middle, halfway up his lifeline, was a tiny Star of David charm sparkling with blue and white crystals, these shining colors, the colors of the desert and the sea, the same ones on our Israeli flag, shining like the tears he must have seen in my eyes.

My daughter is still young and she knows only what she's directly experienced. She still lines her shoes up by the front door just in case we have to run to a bomb shelter, but she doesn't know about terrorist attacks. She doesn't know about checkpoints or reprisals, either. She doesn't know about the fathers at the synagogue who were butchered in the middle of prayer. Or about the night that a man drove his car into a crowd of people and sent a baby girl flying high, higher, higher still into the air before she landed limp and lifeless. She doesn't know about the busses that have blown up, about my friend's newly married brother, or the family in Itamar that was butchered in their beds. She doesn't know about the beatings, or the riots, or about the stabbing that happened just inside Jaffa Gate in the Old City a few hours after I had walked past that very spot on my way home to her, with her Star of David shining around my neck.

My daughter doesn't know abut what happened to me that night at Damascus Gate, and that many of us feel that we have reasons to be afraid of the people with whom we share this land. Nor does she know that many of the people we fear feel that they have reason to be afraid of us, too.

But she will know that an Arab Muslim man gave her her first Star of David.

"Who is Benny Sharon?" my father asked me while he sifted through the ziplock bag of photos I had purloined from my mother's desk after she had died, the bag I carried with me all the way to Israel in a purple carry-on.

He was sitting in my favorite armchair by the window, looking through each picture.

A treasure trove, this bag—photos of family past, the photos my parents took at a carnival booth, the photos my grandparents took next to a sepia sea long before my mother was even a dream, the photos of faces that look like ours, and faces from far, far away.

"Who?"

"Who. Is. Benny. Sharon?" he asked again as he held up a picture of my mother. She was glowing even in black and white. Her cheekbones rounded in a smile, her teeth bright against dark skin . . . and her left arm around a man with a smile as wide as hers.

"It says Benny Sharon on the back. In your mother's handwriting," he said, "and I want to know who he is."

I knew he was joking—never once did he doubt my mother's love.

My parents met three days before the spring of 1968, her arms still toned and tanned from her year in Israel picking oranges.

He proposed on their first date over Irish coffee. She laughed at him with all her teeth showing, but she took him seriously enough to go out with him again and again and again until finally, on a late night ride back from the valley, while they passed the Wilshire Boulevard exit on the 405 freeway, she turned to him and said, "Yes."

He knew my mom adored him. That was never the question.

You could see it in the way her eyes would glow and her cheeks would flush when he would call her his "beautiful bride," every day, throughout the years, when she would wash the dirt off her hands after gardening, when she would bend over the typewriter, her fingers flying, when she would tie the bandanna around her head after her hair had fallen out three weeks after she began chemo.

He knew she adored him. That was never the question.

You could see it in the way they'd laugh, in the way they'd fight, in the way they'd make up again, in her simple kindnesses, the brush of her hand, his favorite meal on the table, her "oh, let your father sleep another hour, he had a hard week," on Saturday mornings.

But "Sarah, who is Benny Sharon?" *was* the question.

And I wondered too, while I looked at her smile and the way she's leaning toward this man, the way her arm wraps around his waist, and the way his arm drapes over hers—I wonder, too, if maybe I wasn't the only one to fall in love with Israel through the eyes and arms of an Israeli . . .

Who was Benny Sharon?

And more importantly, *who was my mother?*

Who was she before she nursed me night after night and took me to the pediatrician and wiped my nose and sang "You Are My Sunshine" and "Feeling Groovy" when my stomach hurt and drew faces on the hardboiled eggs she put in my lunches and waited at home for me to come back and asked me questions about my day and drove me to Hebrew School and helped me write my history papers . . .

. . . and who was my mother that year in Israel when she walked the alleyways of the Old City, when she swam in the turquoise waters of the Mediterranean Sea, when she hiked through the rippling desert, and rappelled down steep mountains, when she danced in front of bonfires, and held hands with a man who made her smile.

And I wished I could ask, and hear about her life before mine, and about this man, this man who may have helped her fall in love with this country, enough to send me here so that I may fall in love with it, too.

So, I took the picture and put it in my wallet, so I would remember to find out.

I won't lie to you.

When a new wave of terror began in October 2015, I didn't want to be in Jerusalem.

I was angry.

Especially when I thought about those two women watching the lives eke out of their husbands while they lay there mewling on the stones and the merchants stood around cursing them and spitting on them.

I was angry when a mother died defending her children, her face and arms and body slashed to ribbons.

I was angry when a family was ambushed on their way back from a holy site late at night, the kids watching their parents bleed out right before their eyes.

I was afraid, too.

I remember one afternoon when I was walking from the Western Wall toward Damascus Gate on my favorite street with two names, and there was this group of guys behind me. They were young, their hair cut like that soccer player everyone was copying—short on the sides, gelled at the top. They were just laughing and hanging out, but they were the exact same ages of all the other guys on the news—the guys with knives and scissors and screwdrivers—just like the nineteen-year-old law student who murdered two fathers, Nehemia Lavi and Aharon Bennett, just a hundred meters away from where I was walking.

I turned my body to the side so my back was parallel to the wall. I took my headphones out so I could hear them behind me in case they got closer. I walked faster.

My heart hammered my chest, my little ribs a fragile cage to protect my beating heart, just like the buildings and walls we build that can't really protect us, either. Bones and stone can be broken, and underneath we are vulnerable. We are afraid sometimes, and we are angry, and yet full of hope.

But I thought about that night at Damascus Gate—the night that changed me and started everything—and I remembered that the only way through fear is literally through it, step by step.

And I thought about that day when the journalist took me back through Damascus Gate and through the shuk and past all those ordinary folks.

So I stopped, my back still to the wall, and as they passed in a wave of cologne and cigarettes, I said "*Salaam Aleikum*," peace be upon you.

"*Aleikum Salaam*," each answered. "And upon you, peace."

I was never a brave person. But I didn't have to be.

Because when you're a kid, growing up in a sweet life with three meals a day (plus snacks), and you build sandcastles at the beach in your pink-and-white Strawberry Shortcake bathing suit, and you sleep in a soft bed with stuffed Baby Bear and Special Blanket, and you have a garden, and a best friend, and good books, and a purple flashlight under your pillow, and nothing ever happens except for finding pretty shells by the sea, or the once-in-a-while lightning storm in the middle of the night, or your cat goes missing for a day before he turns up with singed whiskers and a bruised ego, you think you'll live forever.

And this is even truer when you have the kind of mother who is strong and capable, with hands worn from gardening, who can fix a broken shelf, and play the piano, who writes books, and brews strong tea. The kind of mother who pretends not to see that you're reading an R. L. Stine book (with your purple flashlight) way past your bedtime, who doesn't bat an eye when you bring home a hermit crab you found at the beach.

The kind of mother who goes outside and dances in the middle of the once-in-a-while lightning storm, and who always finds the cat.

But then a week before my twelfth birthday, she crashed our Toyota Corolla on Olympic Boulevard—barreled into a Mercedes who slammed into a Jag, who bumped a Maserati, because #LABaby. We were on the way to see my gramma in the hospital. (She had sinus surgery, and we were coming back from Thrifty's Drugs. I could still taste mint chocolate chip ice cream on my lips. I held a coloring book.)

She was smoking and Bach was on the radio and maybe she was worried about *her* mother in the hospital, and I was in the backseat staring at the fine gold dusting on my legs that had somehow deepened from the color of corn silk the year before to the color of wheat, even though it was summer and usually my hair would get lighter in the sun.

This was the beginning of being the growing-up me. My thighs were softer this year, and covered in that wheat-gold dust, but the little star freckle just over my right knee was still the same as it always was.

(And it still is.)

And then, in a flash, there was nothing except white. Blank, open, endless, white that finally deepened into shape and texture; but as the color emerged, so did the pain as the world came into focus.

I think I cried—I *must* have cried—but I don't remember that sound, just the blare of the horn while my mother lay slumped over the steering wheel. I couldn't see her face. I hoped her eyes were closed because then she'd just be sleeping.

Two police cars and a fire truck. Then an ambulance. When I was a little kid, I had always wanted to ride in one, to feel like something Very Important was happening, but when they lifted me out of the car, my arm dangling like cooked spaghetti, I just wanted to be in the normal flow of traffic somewhere, where my arms could move and brush the hairs on my leg, or pick up a pen and color in my coloring book.

And then the paramedics cut my shirt off—my favorite shirt, the purple one with Ariel the Little Mermaid on it—and it was the first time I cared that someone besides my mommy and daddy were seeing me like this. It was the first time I realized that my breasts had changed from mosquito bites to soft pieces of gum.

I tried to cover them, but my arm was shattered.

Then I cried.

First pain, then euphoria. That's the thing about breaking bones, or busting skulls, or tearing skin. It hurts—*oh God* it hurts, but then the body does this thing, and you're flooded with sweet light and it feels great. Even though everything slows down, even the beep of the heart monitor. Even your own pulse.

It would be another seven years before I sucked weed deep into my lungs for the first time (at a Counting Crows concert behind the Greek Theatre). I remember that, too. But this was better. This was a pure, sweet, clear subliminal rush of coming home where you know yourself better than anywhere else, the same warm glow like all of us around the table on Shabbat.

And then I was just floating in soft light. My hair like sea reeds, but I was still tethered to that girl on the stretcher besides my mom. I could see I was still breathing.

I think my mom was, too.

But she was so, so still, and the paramedics started the IV drip into her arm, and even though I was floating, I moved my lips through subliminal waters, and I said, "Don't give her iodine. She's allergic. It will kill her."

They took out the IV.

And then a cough—her annoying smoker's cough, and it was the best thing I'd ever heard.

And this was the beginning of wisdom for me, when I learned my mom could die, which meant that I could die; and it was as though the angel who makes the cleft above our lips when we're born and tells us, "shhhhhh . . . forget everything you know so you may learn it all again . . ." bent down and began to whisper all the secrets of the universe in my seashell ear all over again.

And my collarbone never healed completely. Look, you can see the wobble in it. And I like it that way because I remember that we aren't here forever, so what we do now really, really matters, even if we get a little broken in the process.

I was feeling especially broken that winter, and afraid sometimes, too.

The thing about the wave of terror in that fall and winter was its epicenter in Jerusalem, and unlike the war the previous summer, there were no sirens to warn you before something terrible happened.

Stabbings can happen anywhere at any time. Stabbings can happen in a park on a quiet bench. They can happen in the market with police and soldiers standing just a few steps away. They can happen in front of a school or in a synagogue.

And everyone was on edge, and I could feel that prickle of fear just below my neck.

Because it felt like we were all targets. The young rabbi at the Western Wall. The barista with the dirty laugh. The soldier who still wears braces. The guy who sells the best pomegranates by the Central Bus Station. The mother with two children.

This mother. My children.

But broken down the middle, painfully aware ever since the car accident and my mother's death that I am not invincible, I still went back to Jerusalem.

"And you have to understand something," Musa told me over tea in the middle of that cold December. "When it's quiet for you—for all of you Israelis—it doesn't mean it's quiet for us."

"What do you mean?"

"We live at the mercy of your Minister of Defense," Musa said. "We didn't choose him. We vote in our own elections, but it's all a sham, and our government is even more corrupt than yours. But your government that you choose controls our lives."

"What does that look like for you, like in your day-to-day life?"

Musa sighed. "It means that if the IDF is ordered to raze someone's house because their brother's kid stabbed someone, then an entire family is homeless. It means that the IDF can kick down my door in the middle of the night—because maybe my nephew's best friend's cousin's son was planning an attack. It means it takes me three hours to drive from Jerusalem to Hebron to see my children when it only takes you forty-five minutes. It means that water can be redirected away from my village and toward the settlements if there's a water shortage. It means that my children have never seen the sea, even though they live less than an hour's drive away."

I stared down at my tea.

"I heard a peace activist was shot on the bus," Musa said quietly.

"Yeah. His name was Richard Lakin. And he died yesterday."

"To God we belong and to Him we return," he replied. "But when will it all end?"

I went home that night, back to my kids, and held them until the sun rose in streaks of gold through the cracks in the window.

That was the turning point for me, that wave of violence that held the city I loved best in its grip.

After it began to ebb, I decided that I wanted to live in the Old City because that seemed like the only way through my fear.

"Are you crazy?" people still ask, and I'll be real with you. There's part of me that gets a jolt of satisfaction when they ask me that, because straight up, I probably am a little crazy. And certainly broken by every experience, the cracks filled with gold.

I'm not living in the Old City every day. On the days I'm with my kids, I'm back in our little village next to these rolling fields, in our house that was once a chicken coop (until recently, we lived in a one-room caravan) but is now plastered over and full of art and throw rugs and little glass vases. I have wind chimes hanging from the bamboo lattice outside.

But on the days I'm not with my kids, I'm in the Old City, because it's one thing to understand this place through the thoroughfares, and it's quite another to go behind the walls and see what's hidden, what doesn't meet the eye.

My eyes are open.

Winter

FUN FACT: JERUSALEM of gold is actually beige. Every stone in every building is hewn from the quarries around the City—Jerusalem Stone.

It started in a wave from the Temple Mount—from the heart of this place—where I can picture an old shepherd standing on a hill at dusk and looking out at the Old City, taking it all in—each church, each mosque, each synagogue, each building as one shining being in the distance.

And from each rooftop in the Old City it looks like a sea of beige, except for the little makeshift lean-tos where families might sleep when it's summer, or the laundry flapping in the breeze—the scarves, the *jellabiyas*, the long dresses—except for the crescent moons on the tops of the mosques, or the crosses on the churches.

Jerusalem of beige, where the stones ripple over the hills, the color of seashells and sand, this ragged sea between different worlds.

Jerusalem, too, of black and white, where the faithful and the kind walk alongside the vicious, but where the differences sometimes overlap into grey. Jerusalem of black and white, especially in the Jewish Quarter near the holidays when the ultra-Orthodox gather at the Western Wall en masse, a sea of black and white, singing and swaying, chanting and praying.

God, forgive us our sins.

But there's a rainbow in Jerusalem, and her name is Keshet.

Keshet literally means "rainbow" in Hebrew, and she'll tell you that when she meets you the first time.

"My name is Keshet, and Keshet means rainbow, and that's my mission in the world. To bring color and be a bridge between different people. Every morning when I wake up, I say '*Moda Ani*, thank you God for giving me life,' and then I say, 'Okay, *HaShem*. Use me. Use me to bring good to the world.'"

And that's what she does.

Whether it's delivering food to a sick neighbor, or taking in kids from the neighborhood and helping raise them, Keshet is goodness.

And she's probably the most beautiful woman I've ever seen because she literally shimmers with goodness, and you can't miss her while she walks through the narrow streets; even at dusk, she glows.

There's an unspoken rule in the Old City that separates the quarters. Sure, people have to walk through them sometimes on the way from one end of the Old City to the other, but for the most part, the communities are divided.

That's part of why I want to live here in Jerusalem, in the Old City, and move between the quarters and understand each one, and feel a part of each one as much as an outsider like me can.

"It wasn't always this way," some have told me. Before 1948, the wine merchant in the Cotton Market was Jewish. Before 1948, the Mukhtar from the Syrian Orthodox Church grew up in the Jewish Quarter. But less than a century later, there are invisible walls that people don't cross—except during times of real fighting, and then all bets are off.

But Keshet has two thumbs and doesn't give a damn, and she is a bridge, a rainbow bridge between different worlds, and I admire her, and I want to be like her.

"So you want to live in the Old City? That's wonderful," she tells me. "But you don't get to choose to live in the Old City. The Old City chooses you. HaShem chooses you."

"I never thought about it that way."

"A few days ago, I was in the bathroom, and I heard a tour group below my house, you know, on the way to the Kotel."

"Okay."

"Yeah, and I heard this woman say in English in this New Jersey bray, she's all, 'Wait, are there actually people living here?'"

"That's hilarious."

"So I called down to her while I'm there on the toilet, I said, 'Yes, and we are privileged to be living here in HaShem's backyard!' Then I flushed the toilet. I think I gave her a heart attack!"

That's the funny thing about the Old City. It's actually an old city with walls that let in too much cold in winter, and not enough air in summer, pipes that rattle and get clogged, neighbors who fight over the TV being too loud, or that damn rooster crowing too early, families living on top of one another.

Just an old city, really—except it's steeped in faith, layered in it, and choking on it, *buried* in it, and from a distance you can see it shimmer, which makes it almost impossible to believe that everyday folks just live here and buy their eggs and milk at the corner store and pay rent to surly landlords, and flush their toilets, too.

I hope I am worthy of it.

The Old City is cool in the morning, and still naked before all the shops open up and the merchants cover her stones with scarves and bracelets, kefiyehs and Jewish prayer shawls, before the old guys sit with their cigarettes and cards and spiced coffee. She's quiet, too, in between the calls to prayer, before the Lutheran bell tower strikes noon, while the merchants are still having their coffee.

I'm sitting in a little pocket in the Christian Quarter across from the Greek Catholic school—the door's open and I can see several little girls in red-and-black plaid skirts playing in the courtyard.

I'm nervous because I'm about to do something I promised my mother I would never do.

I am getting a tattoo.

A real live tattoo.

I've wanted one for years, but I've waffled. I've debated. It isn't like my nose ring, which I can take out (and put back in), or my bully button ring, which I *did* take out forever when I was pregnant with my daughter, and my skin stretched tight over my baby bump. Those holes disappear if you want them to. Maybe there's a faint trace of a scar, but you can forget that they ever were. A tattoo is different. It's forever. Even if you laser it off (which *hurts* and is expensive) you can see its shadow on your skin for the rest of your life.

It's also taboo in Judaism. As it is written in Leviticus: "You shall not make gashes in your flesh for the dead, or incise any marks on yourselves: I am the Lord."

(But that prohibition doesn't particularly move me. After all, we circumcise our sons. Why is that kind of gash okay, but a tattoo isn't?)

But I did hear an explanation that was so meaningful and powerful, that it gave me pause.

Apparently, back in the day, the Israelites had slaves who had a mourning custom to cut their own flesh when someone they loved died. With each loss, they would mark themselves, forever changing their skin, a constant reminder of their grief. The Israelites had a different approach: Nothing is forever. Even things as monumental as great loss. Grief—no matter how big and terrible—should not be forever.

We focus on the living, and on the next step.

It's as my mother used to say to me: "This too shall pass." The good, and the bad. And so this explanation still resonates. But I didn't want a tattoo out of grief—I had other reasons.

When my daughter was born, I wanted something to mark that change from being only for myself, to being for my daughter—and then eighteen months and twenty-five days later, my son. I thought about getting the Tree of Life in the sweet dip where my neck meets my back—but that didn't feel right.

When I moved to Israel, I began to think about mermaids—such strange denizens, these liminal creatures that cross borders, that are always Others.

Mermaids are a lot like immigrants that way.

To others, we are both a little familiar, and a little frightening.

To ourselves, we belong in both places, but not really in either.

So yeah, I feel like a mermaid.

(I just don't have the shiny scales.)

My kids know the truth about me, and on dusty nights after long days when my daughter hates her differences—that she isn't like all the other kids, that her mother can't help with homework the same way Shira's mother can, that her mother doesn't always understand what they're supposed to bring or do, and she's stuck having to explain the rules to her mother—she will creep into bed with me and whisper, "I forgive you for not understanding. You're a mermaid. And I am the daughter of a mermaid."

So I wanted a mermaid tattoo.

But not some lame-ass Ariel the Little Mermaid, or some sexy mermaid BS. I wanted something different. I just didn't know what.

I also made a deal with myself—and God, *and* my mother of blessed memory: I would only get a tattoo if I found a tattoo parlor in the Old City of Jerusalem.

Why? Because I love the Old City. I love its angles and its curves. I love its heartbeat and its stone. I also love the idea of getting a mermaid tattoo landlocked within ancient walls that fit between the desert and the coastal plain.

But also—if I'm being real with you—I think the overwhelming reason is I never in a million years thought I'd actually find a tattoo parlor in the Old City.

Jesus sandals? Sure.

A Roman glass pendant? Absolutely.

A Coca-Cola t-shirt in Hebrew? Bought it.

But a tattoo parlor? Something so seemingly modern, and so mundane? No way.

Well . . . it turns out there is.

It was the spring equinox, and I was wafting around the Christian Quarter taking pictures as one does on a cool spring evening when there is perfect balance between night and day. I turned down a street I hadn't been on, made a right, and saw a large wooden sign that read, TATTOOS in COLOR.

I blinked.

It couldn't be.

I walked in and there was a guy behind the counter with rippling muscles, long hair, a serious mouth, and kind eyes.

His left arm was covered in a tattoo of Jesus with a crown of thorns.

"You gotta be kidding, right?" I said. "This place isn't for real, is it?"

"Of course it's for real."

Stunned, I looked around. There was a giant cross hanging on the ceiling. The walls were covered in photos of different men in different shades of sepia, all with the same kind eyes as the man in front of me.

"How old is this place?" I asked the Tattoo Artist.

"Well, we just moved shops. We were in a different place, but my family has been in the tattoo business for seven hundred years. Want some coffee?"

I sat down and drank, and the Tattoo Artist told me how he was born in Jerusalem but that his family originally came from Egypt, and that they've been in the Holy Land for hundreds of years when they first came to tattoo pilgrims who would visit the Church of the Holy Sepulchre.

"Today you get a t-shirt that you came to Jerusalem," he joked. "Back then, you got a tattoo."

Coming to Jerusalem back then was a big deal—you couldn't just book a flight or take a train. People would travel days and days to get to the holy site, and the roads could be rough and violent, and sometimes people died along the way.

"My grandfather was the first tattoo artist in this country to use an electric tattoo machine. He used a car battery to power it, and he used ink made out of soot and wine," he told me, his eyes shining with pride.

"That's amazing," I answered. "Do you have a book of your designs?"

"I have something better than that," he said, and he walked over to a glass case that had three shelves: The top shelf had what looked like a very old tattoo machine. The middle shelf had three wooden blocks—each big enough to fit snugly in the palm of my hand. The bottom shelf had a large book. He lifted the book and handed it to me. "This book was written by a historian named John Carswell. He was walking one day in the Old City when he saw the sign, Tattoos In Color, and he came in and met my grandfather. He was so impressed by my grandfather and the designs that he came back. My grandfather used special blocks carved from olive wood with the tattoo design—like a stencil—and John Carswell included all the designs in the book and wrote about each one. Would you like to see?"

Um, yeah!

The book was a proof copy. It felt heavy, and it smelled like earth and parchment. I opened it carefully. The room was quiet, and my hands shook.

The first page I opened to had this design on it:

Seriously. I can't make this stuff up even I tried.

"Oh my God," I gasped.

"Ah, the mermaid," he said. "She's very special."

She *is* very special, and I felt a shiver move through my body as I looked at her.

"May I take a picture?"

"Of course."

I thought about her every day since that first day—and I went back twice to "visit."

"Are you ready now?" the Tattoo Artist asked at the end of spring, during the last rain fall before summer.

"Not yet," I answered.

"What about now?" he asked again when I went back on a white hot day in the middle of July.

"Almost," I answered.

I asked my dad what he thought.

"No. Absolutely not. What would your mother—of blessed memory—say?"

I even asked my seven- and eight-year-old kids. Their reaction was pretty amazing:

"You have to really think about it," my son told me. "If you don't like it, you can get it lasered off, but it will really hurt."

"He's right," my daughter said. "Maybe you could just get one of the temporary tattoos with a butterfly."

"But it's a mermaid!" I said.

"Mom, we love you anyway, no matter what, but make sure you can live with it. Forever is a long time."

And I really thought about it, and I want it, and I'm ready.

I'm a grown woman, and I want this. I've lived in Israel for six years and I don't see that changing, yet I'm still American, except when I'm in America, and then I'm Israeli.

I can be in both, but I don't fully belong in either.

I'm also embarking on a strange and wonderful adventure where I am actually living in Jerusalem's Old City—a year of living as an inside-outsider, a visitor looking for community, but never really growing roots.

Plus, she's badass: This mermaid with the incredible face, and the looped tale, holding a flower that the Tattoo Artist's grandfather told John Carswell symbolizes fertility, this mermaid with a pair of wings half-hidden behind her arm. This is the mermaid who gives zero fucks.

I want to be this mermaid. Maybe I already am.

A group of pilgrims draped in gauzy scarves turn the corner while I'm waiting outside the tattoo parlor for the Tattoo Artist.

"The President from Italy is still in the Church of the Holy Sepulchre," their guide says in English. "So we will wait a bit before heading down there."

They pass me, a few look down at me and smile. I smile back.

But I'm nervous. I know I want her, but I still haven't decided where I want her to be. Everyone had suggestions.

"How about your shoulder?"

"Your neck would be, like, totally hot."

"What about your leg?"

"Ankle?"

"How about the inside of your forearm?"

I hadn't thought about that.

I look at my forearms. On my left I wear my bracelets—my bangles from Ramle, my silver beads with the Jerusalem cross a priest gave me, and the Lotteria charm bracelet that my aunt gave me.

My right arm is a blank canvas. And as I sit there on the cool stone and look at it, there in Jerusalem, in the holy heart of Abraham's grandchildren, I think of the line: "If I forget thee, O Jerusalem, may my right hand forget her skill" (Psalm 137:5, ASV).

And I know it's meant to be.

From a distance, I can hear the growl of a motorcycle.

It gets louder, then louder still. The stone I'm sitting on vibrates as the Tattoo Artist roars up the steps on a black Harley-Davidson. Of course.

He opens the shop, and we go inside.

"Do you want coffee?"

"Sure."

"Milk and sugar?"

"Just milk, please."

"So you're really ready?"

"Yes."

He opens the glass case and takes out the book.

"I still have the original blocks for many of these designs," he tells me. "But the mermaid—I don't know what happened. Maybe it broke? Maybe it's in a museum? But I will copy the drawing and we will use that."

He flips through the book. There are other pictures that are more religious—the crucifixion, the nativity, St. John the Baptist. There's a small cross. And another one. The Tattoo Artist is wearing a bracelet with silver skulls all around his left wrist. He's added tattoos since the first time I saw him. He now has the crucifixion scene on his left bicep. It ripples.

"Do you do your own tattoos?" I ask.

"Yes."

"Which was your first?"

He rolls up his sleeve and shows me Roman numerals and a question mark.

"What does it mean?"

"It's a date to remind me of something," he says without explaining what he wants to remember. "I asked my father to tattoo it, and he tattooed this one line, and then his hand started shaking and he said, 'I cannot do this anymore. I cannot hurt you.' I said, 'Oh, come on,' and I took the needle and I finished tattooing it myself."

He finds the mermaid picture and begins to sketch. His hands are steady. I am transfixed.

I notice that in the web between his left index finger and thumb is the Arabic letter "nun"—it stands for Nasara, or Nazarenes, a pejorative for "Christian." Islamic State began to mark Christian homes and businesses in Mosul with this letter, demanding that the inhabitants either convert to Islam or die by the sword. This tattoo is a sign of courage, of defiance.

And as his hands move over the looping scales, and each fin, I think about the Christians beheaded on a beach in Egypt not long ago. In fact, I remember that in front of the Egyptian Coptic Church, the Chapel of St. Helena—the same church the Tattoo Artist and his family attend—just behind the Church of the Holy Sepulchre, there is a banner with these men, their heads bowed and their hands bound behind their backs, moments before each was beheaded, one by one, with a swift blade in front of the world.

"I've never done this one," he says as he sketches.

There's accompanying text next to the image in the book. I had read it when I first found her, but I read it again: "It is maintained by a Coptic priest that this design represents 'the bride of the Nile . . .'"—who apparently can be vicious, and needs to be placated with offerings. She also has a track record of luring young men to their deaths. Although sometimes she'll sleep with them and reward them with gold.

I still like her—she has a past.

The Tattoo Artist explains that getting a tattoo is quite spiritual: "It makes something," he said. "Like a pilgrimage or a change. For some, it is like being born again."

He turns to me:

"Are you ready?"

I get up and follow him into the back room. The needles are brand new, still in their packaging. The tattoo machine works. The ink is good.

"Where do you want it?" he asks.

I show him my right forearm.

(Jerusalem, if I forget thee . . .)

He holds my arm in his right hand.

He places the stencil he drew right in the center, in a smooth spot of skin. You can see the vein running below, and above. But the mermaid will rest on an area unblemished. She fits perfectly.

He takes off the stencil, and she's there, and I am in love. I know this mermaid. I am this mermaid. And there is no doubt, no dread, no fear, only a sense of wholeness—of stopping for tea in the middle of a long journey and taking a breath and looking out over something so beautiful that you'll forget as soon as you open your eyes.

He holds my arm.

"Don't move," he says as he turns on the machine. With his right hand he holds the machine. With his left, he steadies my forearm, and my fingers close around his free hand.

The machine hums and he makes the first trace around the tail. I feel warm. I expected pain, but this is different. I feel it, and you *should* feel something when you change your body. But it doesn't hurt exactly. It just is. I feel alive—my *skin* feels alive. Each cell, electrified. And I squeeze the Tattoo Artist's hand while he traces the outline of my mermaid.

Each scale, each fin, then her ribs and arms. The wings. Her flower, her hair, her crown. Her face is somber, a little sad, yet there's the faintest trace of a smile on her lips, as though the tides may change for her, and she could laugh, still.

I love her.

"She's perfect," I say.

The same words I uttered when my daughter was born.

And it's sweet and intimate in this moment, and I wonder if it means something to him:

"Do you remember the people you tattoo?" I ask.

"Many. Yes." The Tattoo Artist tells me about the woman who cried. "'Why are you crying?' I asked. 'Are you in pain?'"

She wasn't in pain. Many years ago, she and her mother and her family had come for tattoos—she was afraid, and she didn't do it, so her mother didn't do it either. "'Her mother said they could come back next year, only there was war, and they didn't. The little girl grew up and never came back until that day. Her mother had died, so she wasn't just getting the tattoo for herself. She was really getting it for her mother."

And then he tells me about the young man who had a lung removed and his heart moved to his back because there was all this space without the lung, and he wanted a Magen David—a Star of David—on his back where his heart was.

I wonder if the Tattoo Artist will remember me and my mermaid, the first time he ever drew this design that came from his ancestor's olive wood blocks.

He may forget, but I won't. Not only because she's there on my right arm to remind me, but because some experiences change you from the inside forever even without ink—and this experience, being here with the scion of the great family of tattooists, is a special stop on that road of living.

"Oh please, you think you're a mermaid and don't fit in?" Harout says to me near King David's Tower at sunset. We are drinking coffee and talking about the ink along our arms. His is covered in crosses, with an eagle and a sword on the right bicep. He rolls his sleeve down again. "Try being an Armenian in Jerusalem. Some of us have been in the Old City since the crusades, like my family. My wife's family came after the Genocide, which your government refuses to recognize, although God forbid anyone ever deny the Holocaust. We speak Hebrew and Arabic, but we aren't part of either community. We're Christian, but we aren't Arab like most of the Christians here. We're outsiders. We're like the Jews when they're everywhere else outside of Israel."

"That's funny and sad."

"Want to know something funny?" Harout asks.

"Always."

"Last month, Papy, my grampa, needed to go to a meeting in the Jewish Quarter with a Jewish friend of his. The Municipality wanted to tear up this road that would have meant ambulances couldn't get through, and it's true that the quarters never really come together, but once they did—the Jews and the Armenians. Us weirdos. Anyway, this woman came to get him from the Jewish Quarter, and Tatik—my gramma—waited at home for him, and she sat there on the couch weeping and praying and weeping and praying. Her face was white as flour, and she just rocked back and forth, her fingers twisting in her lap."

"Why?"

"Because he was going to the Jewish Quarter. She thought he would be killed."

"Seriously?"

"Yeah, that five-minute walk is huge. I tried to tell her that nothing would happen to him, but she's never actually been to the Jewish Quarter, so how could she know that it's perfectly safe?"

He takes a sip of his coffee.

"I used to be religious," he says after he finishes the last sip. "I used to be religious and even sang in the choir and really worried about the rituals, until I really started learning about God. God doesn't want people to fight over stones or tombs or talk to walls. I just want to open my garage and fix cars for everyone in Jerusalem and be a good person, maybe have a beer or two after a long day. God and I have it all figured out."

Jerusalem is not at her best when it's winter and it rains, because the Old City knows many things, but dealing with the cold is not one of them.

And it is cold today. And raining. The kind of rain that turns the streets into pools of silver, the same color as the sky, as it splatters wet and bitter through the holes in the tarps that hang between the buildings.

But one of the few buildings where it's warm inside is the Austrian Hospice.

I'm sitting with Leila in the Austrian Hospice drinking hot chocolate while a Mozart concerto flitters in the background.

The thing about Jerusalem is there's the part you see when you walk through the alleys, and then there are entire worlds behind the stones, like this place, the Austrian Hospice, that you can't see unless you know where to look.

After the wintery afternoon when the Journalist took me to the Old City that first time after all that time, I found this place. It was right around Christmas when another journalist friend told me about the little buzzer in the wall that you can press that opens a door into another world.

And sure enough, it's like going back in time to Vienna, circa mid-nineteenth century, when the world is apple strudel and violin concertos and high vaulted ceilings.

It's the perfect place to be in the throes of a winter storm, which is why Leila and I are here, drinking hot chocolate as one does.

Leila is from Egypt, but she was raised in Denmark, and she lived in New York, and now she lives in Jerusalem and is about to marry a Palestinian who lives in Ramallah, and she works with Syrian refugees in Jordan. Yeah, she's a legit mermaid. We connected online over an article I had written, because she understands what it's like to live between layers that don't always make sense together. She has long, black, curly hair that tumbles wildly over her shoulders, and there are little drops of rain clinging to each strand. She's lived in different worlds, an inside-outsider, too. We get each other, which is why we're friends.

There's a nun at the counter slicing pieces of fresh apple strudel and all is well with the world, except it isn't. We are talking about terror, and about reprisals, and about how two sides must come to the table.

"How can we talk about peace when we have no peace partner?" I ask her.

She pats my hand.

"*Basbussa*," she says to me, touching my hand.

"Wait, what does that mean?"

"It's like 'sweetheart'—'*Basbussa*' is the sweet cake drenched in honey that Arabs love. It's a good thing," she squeezes my hand.

I smile.

"What I want to say is you're right," she continues. "Israelis have no peace partner, because a partnership is based on equality, and the Palestinians aren't equal. Occupation, home demolitions, checkpoints, restrictions, curfews, not to mention corruption . . . you're right, you don't have a peace partner because you're on the mountain, and we are in the valley."

The Mozart concerto changes, and now it's Beethoven. The nun is still slicing the strudel.

"So what do we do about it?" I ask.

"Well, it's a lot easier for you to reach your hand down to us, than it is for us to reach our hand up to you. So what's *your* move?"

"I'll buy lunch?" I wink.

She laughs and shakes her curls. "Oh *Basbussa*, I'm not talking about you. You and I can split the check."

I took my kids to Jerusalem today.

It was their first time. We wended through sinuous alleys, past fluttering scarfs and fragrant spices, past shelves lined with kipot and kefiyehs, past mirrors reflecting a rainbow of fabric and skin, straight to the heart of the Western Wall.

We look like every shopkeeper's wet dream: We look like a trifecta of tourists, the blonde mother and her two blonde children, gobsmacked and ready to pay fifty shekels for a stuffed camel with an "I <3 Israel" saddle (and a label that reads "Made in Taiwan").

A simple "Lo" isn't enough—you gotta break it down with some serious Israeli attitude. Think Marisa Tomei from *My Cousin Vinny* meets Menachem Begin and you get the idea. You have to wave your hands a little, and pop your chin, and for GOD'S SAKE DON'T SMILE, because that'll give you away.

It also helps if your kids speak Hebrew. (Okay, so they're begging you to buy the stupid camel while the shopkeeper leers with a knowing gleam in his eye, but the fact that they're whining about it in one of the two official languages of the shuk is good enough to drop the price faster than Nicki Minaj mid-twerk.)

(Oh yes, I did.)

My kids are Israeli, no doubt. They roll their "reshes" and gut their "ayins," they bronze beneath the sun. They love jahnun and falafel and sahlab and schnitzel. They're impatient and loud and laugh with all their teeth showing.

(And they got their camel—down from fifty shekels a piece to thirty for both. Such a bargain.)

The highlight of my son's day happens when we are near the Western Wall, and we see all these soldiers about to be inducted into the army in a special ceremony. And my son just stands there with his little eyes shining and his mouth open, just staring as the men in their olive green fill the Western Wall plaza, nervous, excited.

There are hundreds of people all around us, and the sun is setting all pretty and peach, and there are mothers beaming but with tears in their eyes while they hug and kiss their sons with pimples on their cheeks.

My son watches the boys (no, men—they're men—but aren't they boys?) and I watch the moms and I wonder what they're thinking.

"I hope you leave Israel before he gets drafted," someone from the United States with loving intentions told me recently on the phone.

It's funny, because I used to want the same thing: "We can move to Israel, but we're getting the hell out of Dodge before our son reaches draft age," I told my husband in between cramming my Old Navy tank tops and hooker boots into the last suitcase we were packing.

I don't feel that way anymore, and I'll tell you something that I never thought I'd feel: After we have reaped the benefits of living in a country where they will never have to worry about tucking their Jewish star necklaces under their shirts, where the rhythms of their year are measured with Jewish festivals, and illuminated by Sabbath candles, it would feel like sneaking out the back door to leave before draft age.

But then I think about Munir, and Leila, and some of the other people I'm getting to know, and I wonder what they think now that my kid, my youngest with the wide smile and the messy blonde hair, will one day be serving in the Israeli military.

I know what I want more than anything, and that's an end to this conflict between cousins, between Arabs and Jews, the promise that their children and our children will be safe, that we will watch out for one another, and take care of each other, like the family we were once, and the family we could someday be.

But I also know that isn't going to happen anytime soon, unless something big changes.

And I wonder if my son will ever have to stand in front of Damascus Gate, if he will be the kind of soldier who asks old men with walking sticks to stop just because they happen to be there on a hot day when everyone is angry, or if he will be the kind of soldier who frisks boys younger than him because they're speaking Arabic, and that's reason enough to stop them and search.

My son has already told me he doesn't want to die in a war. And then, "and Mama, I don't want to kill in a war, either."

And I look at him and I want to tell him that it will never happen, that he will never have to feel the mighty weight of a gun in his hand, and smell dirt and blood and sweat and fear and weigh his life against another's, or stand there terrified and soak himself in sweat and urine, or God forbid, his own blood, or the blood of his best friend, or even the blood of the person he had to kill because it was his life or their life. All this is the stuff of nightmares that are all too real for those of us here who year after year remember our fallen, our sons and our daughters, all of us who have wailed over an open grave or who have held the mothers and the fathers of the sons and daughters buried beneath.

But we live here, and this is part of what that means—this responsibility, this charge—and each year that passes, and each inch he grows, we're getting closer to that ceremony when he will stand by the Western Wall and I'll be standing with the other mothers holding my breath and trembling in dread and in awe at the sight of my little boy in uniform, praying he will come back to me unharmed and whole. And I wonder if he'll still be sleeping with the stuffed camels we bought at the shuk today.

Remember the place I stayed the night I got stoned at Damascus Gate?

I'm there again.

The Grey Man who works at the hotel is the same exact shade as the sky on this cold and clammy day.

He rolls his own cigarettes, and likes Oum Kalthoum.

He smokes a lot, and his eyes are deep-socketed and he doesn't blink. He can also sing—his voice is reedy and warm, and he can hit the high notes, and he does while we sit together in front of the heater near the check-in desk.

I remember him from nearly twenty years ago, when I first stayed there when I was eighteen after that terrible night in Migdal HaEmek.

Back then, the place was different. I found the place by accident, remember? I was lost and wearing one of those peasant skirts that kept hitching in the wrong place, and I was schlepping this big old suitcase that didn't have any wheels and looked like Mary Poppins's carpet bag, and it was the armpit of August, and I was sweaty and panting and had no idea where to stay or what to do, and that's when I met Gideon with his guitar and his weed, and I followed him all the way through Jaffa Gate, past the bread man, and the shop with all the icons, and I followed him past the man with the lemonade and the soldiers leaning against a building in the shade, and we made a sharp turn and another and another, and past the scarf guy with the scowl and the rotting teeth, and up a cramped and fetid flight of stairs into a room that was made of sky.

But all these years later, and the place has changed.

Jono and Rachel are gone. Dead? Jail? Left the country? No idea.

And now the Grey Man was there, and only him.

All the folks smoking hookah pipes and drinking coffee are gone, too. There's only one rug left and it's threadbare.

The walls aren't blue anymore. They're the color of chalk.

I don't know what I expected, but maybe if I'm being honest with myself, I expected to climb back into that big blue room the same color as the sky.

It's also dark out, and so the Eastern window looks out on blackness, with a few lights—the gold dome shines leaden, and a few mosques are lit with green lights. It's still beautiful, but you have this feeling like you showed up too late, and everyone's gone home.

"In Arabic, we have a saying that the mountain and the mountain never meet," the Grey Man says when I hand him my Israeli passport as he draws on his cigarette. "But the people on each mountain can meet if they want because the world is small. And it is nice to meet you."

"It's nice to meet you, too."

He gives me a good price for my favorite room, knocking one hundred shekels off it. It was the blue room, the one with the domed ceiling and the view of the old walls, the one with its own little bathroom—grungy, but usually with hot water.

The toilet flushes for real, and that shouldn't be taken for granted.

That, my friends, is a luxury in the Old City.

"When you come back tonight," the Grey Man says to me, "I will give you something to eat and we will talk."

It's winter. A bright and blue December, and we haven't had much rain. Fires have ravaged the hills and forests just a few weeks earlier, and finally, *finally*, the sky opened just enough to soak the earth and turn it green again.

It's funny how little attention the earth needs. After a summer that stretched grey and dry, one day of rain and a little more overnight and the leaves shimmered like emerald and jade, and little white blossoms peeked out behind the rocks.

Winter is my daughter's favorite season. "Mama, the winter makes me feel cozy," she told me, "and I like the white flowers that have no real name."

So it was like that—grey skies again, restless wind, a few stars showing through at night, and a little sun against the window.

I guess I should tell you that after I checked in, I went out drinking.

Because I know you're wondering.

I don't remember walking back to the Old City, and suddenly the sky is clear and the moon is sharp, and it hurts to look up.

I stumble up the narrow steps into the room I had fallen in love with when I was eighteen.

The blue swirled all around me, I was caught in the sky.

The Grey Man has kebab waiting and Oum Kalthoum playing just like he said, and the little space heater is on and cheery, and we sit and eat and talk about his kids, and about growing up in the Old City, and about the old days when there were tourists, and people stayed in this hotel—when there was music and bright rugs and the room smelled like roses from the hookah pipes.

I think about my mom, and the room she stayed in all those years back, and I take out the picture of her and Benny Sharon from my wallet of her from the Old City, the one I always carry.

"This was my mom when she was in Jerusalem," I say, and my eyes well with tears.

"I want to show you something, but it's over there," he says, pointing to another room. "Can you come with me?"

And I wonder if maybe he has something from my mother in there (again, I had been drinking), or maybe she actually stayed here, in that room where he wants me to follow, so of course I go because in Jerusalem anything can happen.

And in the little room that smells like jasmine and old socks, the Grey Man who gave me my room for a discount because "I am like a daughter," pours oil on my head and pulls my dress over my shoulders. He rubs my back. He squeezes my breasts until milk flows out of them, and he says to me in a rough whisper, "you've been used, but not used up." He tries to kiss me, and I turn my head away and say "no."

"I can't hear you," he says, and he squeezes harder while the milk drips onto the floor, pooling around my feet.

It smells like blood, and salt, and dirt and sea.

"No," I say again, and he doesn't stop. "Please don't."

And there I am and I'm waking up on that rumpled bed in Migdal HaEmek.

I'm wiping my own blood from my head while I run through Damascus Gate.

I am keening over my mother's body.

I'm frozen. I just stand there while he kneads me like challah dough. I don't kick him. I don't push him away. I don't scream.

He pulls the dress down lower, while he reaches under my skirt, and he sees the marks across my belly—the lines and scars from two big babies, from swallowing the moon two times back to back.

"You're a mother," he says, his eyes huge and round, seeing me for the first time as I am. I can see myself reflected in them, hunched, an old crone, milk dripping down her breasts and into little rivers over each squiggle across my skin.

"No" wasn't enough.

But I was a mother, and he stops.

I start shaking, and my stomach lurches, and my head pounds, and I don't have the words for what is happening, except "no."

"Please no."

I pull my dress up over my belly and breasts, and he goes to close the little button at the back, and I actually say to him, "No need, it's okay, but thanks."

Stupid, stupid, stupid.

Like it is an ordinary evening, and he's just offered to carry my bags or give me another serving of kebab. He looks embarrassed, and I feel sick, and I want to tell him it's okay, except it isn't okay, and I feel sick and I just want to shower everything off me—the oil, the scotch, my foul, foul skin.

Back in the room, I lock the door, and turn on the shower full blast, and get under the water, and it's bitter cold.

And I am freezing, shaking, wracked with sickness, but I can't throw up. The room smells feral and rotten—like the stink of an animal when it knows it's going to die, and I realize the smell is coming from me. From my fingers, my legs, the folds in my skin.

There is no towel. So I grab a blanket, and my hair clings to my face, and I can't stop shaking.

It is so cold, and Jerusalem doesn't know what to do with herself when it's cold. The stone walls and the domed ceilings are perfect for a hot day in summer, but when the winter comes, there's no corner, no crevice that's safe from her icy grip without a heater.

But, there was a little metal space heater next to the bed, and I plug it in.

The room plunges into darkness.

It must have blown a fuse.

Are you fucking kidding me?

And I am naked, except for a blanket wrapped around me.

And freezing.

The Grey Man pounds on the door.

"Please don't come in."

"My darling, I will fix this for you—I want you to feel safe and warm."

Moments later the light comes on.

"Did you use the heater?" he asks. "Sometimes, it doesn't work."

"I'm okay, don't worry. I won't use the heater."

"I will bring you another one."

He knocks again, and by this time, my fingers are numb, and my face, too. My arms and legs are stiff branches.

I stagger to the door. I let him in.

He plugs in the new heater, and I crouch next to it, and feel the blood return to my arms and legs and face and hands. He sits next to me and puts his arms around me, like the way my mother held me, like I was a baby.

I shrink into myself, deep into my skin. "I'm more than my body, I'm more than my body, I'm more than my body," I say in my head over and over, while I recoil from his touch.

"My love, my darling," he whispers in my ear. "You'll be okay."

My skin crawls and I want to throw up.

"I'm okay," I say. "I need to sleep. Please let me sleep. I need to be with my children tomorrow."

And he leaves. And I lock the door.

"Something terrible has happened," I say out loud, but I don't have the vocabulary to say what it was. Everything is grey. He stopped—finally—even though he didn't before. He left when I asked him to.

But my stomach seizes, and I want to tear my skin off with my nails—my stupid red nails—pull my hair out, tear my face off.

"Something terrible has happened," I say again.

I look at my phone. 2:54 a.m.

Outside was even colder, and I am still soaked through, and the heater is still warm, and that is the only true thing I know in the world right now.

I don't leave.

Here's why: Everything is grey.

The front door is locked—the Grey Man bolts it at midnight—and I can't just walk out without asking him for help.

He knows about this book I'm writing, the one you're reading right now. He knows I am living here half the week to write about Jerusalem. All it would take is a few whispered words to his sons, or to his sons' wives, and my reputation would be ruined here.

"The writer, she's a liar." Or, "The writer, you cannot trust her." Or, "The writer, she's a whore."

And also, where would I go at nearly 3:00 a.m. when the moon was just a wink, and the air biting and bitter cold?

If I stay just a few more hours by this little heater, I'll be safe.

No, I won't call the police, either.

Here's why: Everything is grey.

He did stop. Eventually.

Maybe I wasn't clear enough.

Maybe I should have hit him or pushed him or bit him or kicked him.

Maybe I should have screamed.

They would make this an issue about a Palestinian man assaulting an Israeli woman, and that has nothing to do with it.

It did not happen because I'm an Israeli and he's a Palestinian.

It happened because I am woman and he is an asshole.

I didn't call the police, because they would have said what many of you might be saying to yourself right now:

"You were drinking."

Like that's an excuse.

"You were too friendly."

Like *that's* an excuse.

"You should have left."

When I couldn't.

I won't call the police, because if I do, my living in the Old City will be compromised. What Palestinian man or woman would talk to me as openly as they have if they know that I got one of their friends or neighbors or uncles or brothers arrested?

And I don't have the words for what happened. I can smell him, and I can feel his oily hands still on my skin, but I can't articulate what he's done.

"Something terrible has happened," I say to myself a third time, and I curl up under the wet blanket, next to the heater on the floor, and I fall asleep.

And in the morning, the sun rises, like it always does, and I pack my bags, and walk out the reception looking straight ahead all the way back through the shuk toward Damascus Gate, and I buy a bottle of water because I feel sick, and I sit down on the stone ledge next to the place where I was hit in the head with a rock that one summer, and I watch a Border Police Officer with zits and braces stop a man with a cane and his son who are walking in, and the guy in uniform pats down the father while his son watches with tears in his eyes.

I look away.

I get in a taxi and go home to my children.

After the night with the Grey Man, I went home back to the moshav, sick as a dog. I showered under boiling hot water with the strongest soap I could find. For nearly an hour I stood there under the pounding spray until my skin turned red, just like it did in the hours after the thing that happened in Migdal HaEmek that I can't remember.

I got out of the shower and wrapped myself in a fluffy green towel, leaned over the toilet bowl, and puked my guts out. My vomit smelled like zatar, jasmine, and rotten meat.

Stupid, stupid, stupid.

I lay there curled by the toilet, my face pressed against the tile. I lay there until my stomach heaved again and I sat up, emptied my guts over and over, until I fell asleep.

I got up again and showered until I smelled like shampoo and soap and nothing more.

That night, I went to sleep and I dreamed about my grandmother, and I dreamed she was pushed off the roof by her lover, but instead of landing splat on the stone, she flew.

I woke up and decided to fly, too.

I went back to LA to see my family.

So, this time last week, I was on a four-lane freeway with about a million other cars moving slowly as one, toward downtown LA. LA is familiar. It's a world away from the Grey Man in the blue room. It's familiar and it's safe, and I am safe and it isn't too cold, and I can sleep.

In LA, I am vanilla lattes.

I am strawberry margaritas with a light ring of salt, and a side order of fries (please and thanks). I am champagne brunches with my BFF, henna tattoos, and dinners with family.

In LA, I am my mother's daughter, and in between champagne brunches and sushi lunches, in between happy hour and fro yo at the mall, I am looking for her everywhere.

Do you know what I did after my mom died?

I got really, really high.

Well, technically, first I got really, really low.

There was this bag of pills, see: pink hearts, yellow moons, orange stars, buried in her underwear drawer, to the right of her black lace slip, underneath the potpourri. OxyContin, Vicodin, and a few other names I couldn't read through blurry eyes.

(They had just taken her away. "Kiss your mother goodbye," my father told me. And I touched her feet.)

You could still see the indent of where she had spent the last two weeks in the bed she had shared with the love of her life. The bed by the window, next to the purple roses growing just beyond the screen. Her marriage bed, the bed she nursed me in, her death bed, too, that final resting place. Her feather weight still left its mark right there on the pillow, on the left side where she had always slept, next to the end table with her reading glasses, and the light still on. Ruth Rendell's latest book was bookmarked. She never knew the end.

I could still smell the GAP Dream perfume I had sprayed on her only an hour before. The scent lingered on, that fragrant ghost, near the dresser, against the walls, by the window, behind the door.

I drank a pill with dusty wine—"Two Buck Chuck" from Trader Joe's, a new bottle from the big case she and my dad had bought six months before, a new bottle she would never taste from the case she would never finish.

I wouldn't let it go to waste.

(Cheers! Cabernet goes great with Oxy! Here's to you! *Salud*! To life!)

I drank it down—pink, I think—not caring which, not caring what, not caring how it would feel or what I'd wake up to, if at all.

I just wanted to be her.

So I sprayed GAP Dream on my wrists and behind my hair, that fragrant ghost all up on me.

I found her cigarettes—hidden from my dad, and from her parents, from the hospice workers, and the oncologist, hidden, only I knew where, behind the Woody Allen video cassette tapes, just next to the Ken Burns she never finished watching.

And I smoked until I stank beyond GAP Dream, like dried leaves, like late nights, like coffee breaks, like her.

And then: outside the room, closed in with others who were grieving.

(What kind of God lets an eighty-five-year-old mother bury two children in two years? What kind of God lets a family break in half when the linchpins are removed? What kind of God lets a girl get so low that she'll do anything—anything—to make the frightened child deep inside her stop from screaming, "help me, help me?" Mommy fixes everything. But Mommy isn't coming.)

So I went outside, high and low, and from the top of the hill I saw a VW Bug bopping along, chugging with intention until it stopped in front of me.

A man hopped out, sprightly spry, despite the web of wrinkles on his face, the silver dust of hair across his knuckles. He tipped his jaunty cap.

He came with lilies. I hate lilies. The smell of death begins with lilies.

"You really shouldn't smoke," he said.

I coughed.

He laughed.

"My mom just died," I said these words for the first time. Ugh, how strange they felt upon my tongue, against my teeth, and through my lips. “My mom just died,” I said again, these words a second time, how bitter was their taste, like chemicals and cigarettes, and perfume rank.

“My mom just died,” I threw the cigarette on the ground, watched it burn a wilting leaf beneath the tree. Mashed both hard with my bare foot.

“I am looking for magnolias,” he said, pointing to the tree, the tree my mother loved, the tree that made her stop and take a second look at the little brown house at the bend of the road when she went looking for a place to make a home.

He popped the trunk of the bright blue car, and with a creak and a groan it lifted up, the same color as the sky. He pushed it open all the way, a tumble of blankets, of boxes, potting soil, and a trowel, a bag of seeds, and a vase. And a folded step ladder that somehow fit inside the tiny space. He pulled it out and shook it once, and it unfolded like a staircase.

Up he stepped into the leaves, high above the cigarette smoldering, high above the waste.

“They are beautiful, you see,” he called down to me, his arms outstretched to catch the blossoms. “They are beautiful even though they die.”

He breathed in deep, the branches shook.

“They’re smooth and lovely, look! Like a woman in her blooming. But they too fade, and wither. They too, will disappear. But come here, and you will see: There are seeds—lots of them. So many seeds, they’ll blow away, beyond the tree, beyond the street, and a new tree will grow someday, as lovely as the one before. So they never really vanish even when they’re gone, because their memory lives on.”

And he came back down, his arms full of branches, full of leaves, and full of flowers. He came back down and drove away.

“But keep the stepladder,” he said to me before he disappeared. “Sometimes, we need a new perspective.”

I'm in the taxi on the way back from Jerusalem, after being home a week, and the driver's name is Raed. He's young and he says to me all the things I want to hear about peace, about coexistence, about how we all love the Land and belong here together.

"We all have to live together," he says.

"You're right," I answer. "But tell me something: When you go out with your friends, do you ever go out with Jews?"

He sighs. "It isn't easy in Jerusalem. The invisible lines in the city divide us and have conquered us. We don't meet each other. Even if we are sitting at tables next to each other at the same restaurant."

I remember just last week thinking that. At a kosher nargila place with Palestinian and Muslim friends, we were the only mixed table of Jews and Arabs. The other tables were split accordingly.

"Why is that?"

"Because the Jews are afraid to mix with us."

"Why do you think that is?"

"Because they're afraid we'll fuck their women and marry them and have babies with them."

I start to interrupt.

"Wait," he says, and he holds up his hand. "I had a girlfriend—a beautiful Jewish Israeli girl. She was even in the army. I had no problem with this. I brought her home on some weekends and she would stay with me. My parents took it fine, even though she was working at a checkpoint near my cousin's village. They didn't care. She was nice, so it was okay. In our culture, it's fine for me to marry someone who isn't Muslim. Okay, my sister can't—she has to marry a Muslim—but men can marry Jews, Christians, it's fine."

"Because Islam is passed through the father, right?"

"Yeah. It isn't that way for Jews though."

"I know. My dad isn't Jewish. My mom is. So I'm Jewish."

"Right. Okay, so I go out with this girl and it's fine with my family, but her family? Wow. They didn't speak to her. We weren't going to get married or anything. I liked her, she liked me. But they hated the idea that she went to sleep with me at night and woke up with me in the morning. And her parents weren't even those crazy extremists Lahava assholes who beat up Arabs! They vote Left—Avoda bullshit. Meretz Shmeretz, they're all happy to be Left wing and eat our hummus and talk about coexistence until their kids are playing with our kids, or their daughter is fucking one of us. Why?"

"Fear."

"Racism. And I'm a nice guy! I met her father; I shook his hand. I went to Shabbat dinner at her house, and he wouldn't look me in the eye. Do you know how that feels?"

"No. I've never been treated badly because of my skin color or my religion."

"It's like that all the time. And it makes me angry. And it makes me not want to even try to talk to people from your side because you've drawn lines and you've made sides—okay, not you, but most Israelis, when they look at me, they see a dirty Arab. I'm sorry but I have to say the truth: Don't they remember what it was like to be a dirty Jew?"

I think about how his sister can't marry a Jewish guy, either, same-same.

"I saw something on TV I'll never forget," he says. "There was an attack—one by Damascus Gate. A cop was stabbed, and the guy who did it was shot. There was blood all over. Everywhere. Bright red—really red. All over. And I couldn't tell where the Jewish blood stopped and the Arab blood began. It's all the same color. We all bleed the same color. It's all the same. So why does it matter so much where we come from? We all are born the same way and we die the same way, too."

He turns off the highway and down the quiet lane. "It's nice here," he says looking out at the fields. "But I bet there isn't a single Arab who lives here, so what are you teaching your kids that's any different?"

I'm back on the moshav with the kids, and oh man, I really messed up tonight.

The kids are getting new beds tomorrow.

Bunk beds.

I guess you don't know this, but for the last forever, when the kids are with me, they sleep together on a futon in our little house in the village where we live on my nights when I'm not in Jerusalem.

It started because the landlord gave us a futon and we were poor, and then it turned into this thing where it was cozy and sweet, and she'd end up with her foot flung over his stomach, or he'd end up with his arm across her face, and usually I'd end up on the futon with them, too, sometimes holding one, or both, or neither, and it was sweet.

The thing is, my kids haven't had it easy. Their father and I split up when they were babies—my daughter was three and barely out of diapers, and my son wasn't even two. In the beginning, they lived with their dad in the house we used to live in, in the bedroom we built out of Ikea furniture and things from Home Center, the one with the lilac walls (I chose the color), and the pictures we hung.

I didn't really have a place. I stayed with friends—I sublet an apartment over on Ussishkin for a few weeks. Then I got this place over in some strange little pocket in Tel Aviv where the whole entire world smelled like cholent and laundry detergent, but I couldn't take the kids there with me because their lives revolved around the kibbutz where my ex lived.

It took time—but eventually, we found this caravan in a big yard under a fig tree with a futon in the living room where my kids and I slept.

The first winter there, when the roof leaked all the time and I taped plastic bags to the ceiling, when I washed the same plates over and over again because we only had two, when I hung old family photos on the wall as if we planned on staying in the same place for a long time, we would all fall asleep together on that futon, and we learned how to be a family of three on our days together.

The walls were cardboard with a coat of plaster, but we stayed mostly dry in the winter and cool in the summer, and it was home.

And then the landlord knocked on my door one day and said, "You'll have to move, God help you," because apparently our caravan wasn't legal, and can I just tell you? My stomach fell, because I didn't know where to go that would be close enough to the kibbutz, and the idea of moving while those cardboard walls we had nailed pictures on were torn down made my breath catch in my throat.

But then the neighbors in the back—the ones behind the wall with the vines that bloomed with bright orange flowers in the winter, the ones that had three proper bedrooms and a real kitchen and space in the living room—moved out, and, "*Be'ezrat Hashem*, with God's help you can move in there," the landlord said, and so we did.

The futon came, too—tucked into a corner in the big bedroom, and they slept there that first night.

That was the night the Gaza War started for real, when we had air raid sirens for the first time in our region and we ran to the bomb shelter, like we would night after night for weeks after that.

That was the night we became real Israelis—the low-frequency hum of a vacuum cleaner is the same sound the siren makes when it starts up, and it sends our pulses racing through our veins.

That was the night that makes my kids line up their shoes by the door—even to this day. Like sleeping together on the big old futon. Except they'll keep lining up their shoes, and they're getting bunk beds.

They share everything, my kids.

Stomach flu, bad colds, head lice for starters.

Warmth and companionship, too, and sometimes, they'll chat in the middle of the night when they're both asleep because they're sharing a dream.

Because that's the thing you have to understand about kids who have divorced parents:

Some days, they're with their dad. Some days, they're with me. But they are always together.

But then my kids—my wonderful, wonderful kids—can be total assholes sometimes, and present a united front against me:

"*Mama*, you can't punish my sister!"

"How can you get angry at him, Mama?"

Which is exactly as it should be.

And they still want me to tuck them in, and lie next to them on the futon right in the middle, while I tell them the story about Laughing Boy, or we sing "Come As You Are" by Nirvana or "Umbrella" by Rihanna. That's our jam.

But they're getting bigger. He still sleeps with a stuffed camel under his chin, but he also won first place in a judo competition. Her legs are so long now, and she comes up to my neck. She spends time brushing her hair.

And they see the differences that each day brings even if they can't articulate it, and I know this because lately they've piled their stuffed animals between them, as though to separate the futon into two special beds.

So it was time, and my dad and my dad's credit card and I went to the furniture store, and we got them. They're white and pretty, and you can separate them into two beds if you want.

But even if we keep the bunk beds as they are—which is the plan—it'll still be a separation. She's on the top, he's on the bottom. Unless they decide to change for one night. But they won't share a futon any longer, side by side.

And here's where I messed up.

It was their last night in the big old futon.

When I said something about that, my daughter started breathing fast, and she said, "This is hard for me because change is hard for me."

I *did* hug her.

But then we all went to bed churlish.

My son fell asleep within two minutes, but my daughter stayed up, heaving heavy sighs and rolling her eyes and shooting down my feeble attempts to fix things.

And I didn't really try to fix things after that. I didn't stay in bed with her.

We should have had some sort of ceremony in that futon to honor the family we were—the struggling wild family in the caravan that was broken down, the asymmetrical misplaced family with the mother that spoke no Hebrew. The Americans. Except not really.

We should have talked about it—about who we were, and who we are now.

In Judaism, there are so many rituals—we light candles for the end of the week, we light candles for the start of the new one.

And we should have done something to honor this change, too.

We aren't the same family that could all fit on that mattress comfortably for a full night's sleep. Even if we tried, we couldn't. Their legs are longer and their bodies fill more space, and it's time.

She's going into fourth grade, and he'll be in third.

They do homework now, and they take the bus, and they walk alone sometimes, and their world has stretched beyond these walls and beyond our village and it's time to change.

But I let that change happen without anything to mark it—no song or ceremony or bedtime story about the little family that slept together through the winter storms, and the rain of rockets, and so much uncertainty.

Because maybe that change was so soft and gradual, that this is just like shedding skin cells, and being exactly the same, but different.

But still, I felt bad—and I wanted to wake them up and tell them how sorry I was for their cleaved life—for the small caravan with the leaky roof, for all the hours I work, and the mac and cheese dinners, and everything I've fucked up including that night. But I let them sleep through the night as sweetly as they could together . . .

And I crawled in next to them, and we woke up like that, as we were back when we started all over again, as I try to put all these little pieces back together.

Don't ask what I am doing sitting on the ground deep in the heart of the Christian Quarter at sunset, dressed in grey, my shoulders bare in winter, and my eyes shimmering. The old nun doesn't ask. She just tells me, "The ground is no place for a woman to sit."

I say, "I'm just tired."

And I guess that's the short version, even though she didn't ask. I *am* tired.

I chose this country eighteen seasons ago, right before a dust storm roiled across the land, right before the rains came. And we shared these dark times together, this land and I—a winter that would not quit, sicknesses that rocked my family until we broke, then homelessness; I was a mother without her children for half a year until I found my footing and could walk again.

But I am tired, and a little lost, and cold, even when I know these paths, and know these stones by route, if not by heart, even when I can walk with my eyes closed from my doorstep through the fields—with a quick step to the left around the giant cistern built centuries ago—all the way to Highway 40.

It's the newness—even on this ancient land, it's new to me. I hear it never goes away, the newness, the sense of wonder, of miracles, each moment its own tiny universe.

It's new, even when there's a "routine" to follow, even when you know you need to be at the bus by 7:09 a.m. to take the kids to school, and then you'll wait by the south gate for a ride to Ramla to catch the bus to Jerusalem at 9:40. You can get coffee for five shekels if you arrive by 9:30, if not, then too bad, you'll get it at the Central Bus Station, like always. For each time, the world opens up a little more, as you get to know it—texture, depth, nuance, like finding a hidden staircase in a crumbling building that takes you to a room with clear windows overlooking the crown of an ancient city. I remember how that really happened once for real and by accident.

I found this stairwell up, up, up to a roof high above Jerusalem on a day too hot to bear, when tempers flared, during the war last summer when everyone else was tired, too. And there, high enough in the clear blue nowhere, the city was laid out below me like a mosaic of metal and stone. The only sound was the wind around me, a roar, and then a whisper, then the beating of my heart.

I didn't know what to expect, but I never expected *that*.

Every day, another miracle, and then, that sense of wonder, and another universe unfastens.

But now I'm tired. I want home, its warm, strong arms around me. I want to close my eyes for once, and not worry about missing something, because my heart will finally be quiet, no longer searching; it's made its choice, and it's been chosen, too.

I'm also tired because the Grey Man breaks my sleep this winter. He's there in every dream, and now I hate the smell of jasmine. Last night, I dreamt that he and the boy from Migdal HaEmek were waiting for me at Damascus Gate, and then my mother came to me and said, "I wanted you to meet someone nice," and she stared at me with big deep eyes that turned into two black pools of mud and tar, and I woke up soaked in sweat and tears. Even when I'm awake, I'm afraid of him. I avoid all my favorite places in the Old City, in case he can read my mind and find me.

I don't want to think about that terrible room in Migdal HaEmek, or that night at Damascus Gate, or cats that "disappeared," or how I watched my mother's last breath fade into nothing, or the Grey Man.

I don't want to be a mermaid today. I want to go home, and grow roots somewhere, but I don't where that is, and I am tired.

So that's why I am sitting, against hard stone in the Christian Quarter, deep in the cold winter sunset.

"I'm just tired," I say again.

"So come with me to the convent," she says. "You can rest there."

And because my heart is way too loud against the stone, because it hurts, because it's searching, and because this *is* a place of miracles, it's the obvious choice to stand up, dust myself off, and follow her.

Inside, we sit, the nuns and I.

We sit on high-backed chairs like thrones without the sides. Jesus's face beams down at us from each wall.

The television's on and the nuns are watching *Seinfeld*.

Wait, what?

I blink and look again. They are literally watching *Seinfeld*.

One nun asks me if I have lost my way.

Another asks if I have a place to sleep.

A third asks why my eyes are shining.

"I'm just tired," I say, and I look down at my feet covered in the dust from each step I've taken until this moment: "And I still have a ways to go before I get home."

Sometimes, on your way home, you have to say, "Yes."

Like tonight, when I was walking out toward Jaffa Gate, and I had just gotten off the phone with a friend in California, and I'm here, and this is the first time I've mostly forgotten about the Grey Man, except sometimes I think I see him, but I want to be there, and the world feels way too vast and big to wrap my arms around.

It was a hard news day, too. An attempted stabbing. The attacker was shot dead while clutching a knife. LA and my mother's house are a million light years away from inside these walls, and I look around from the middle of "God's Back Yard," and it just feels so torn up, gutted, and gaping.

And on my way out of the Old City, through gilded shadows, the moment stretches and Musa calls, "Wait!"

I turn around.

"You're wearing too much black. Let me give you something with color."

I look down: black dress, black tights, black boots. Since the night with the Grey Man, I wear a lot of black. Maybe so he won't see me.

"Yes."

So, he gave me this tiny ring he fashioned in thirty seconds with Eilat stone and wire, cobalt blue, emerald green, with a smudge of white across the surface, wrapped in silver around my finger, this tiny remembrance that looks like the world from way up high.

And I'll look at this every day and remember: We all live here together. And the world can be small if you let it.

You know, faith is a funny thing. You can starve it and choke it and leave it out in the sun, you can drown it, or bury it in a cold stone tomb, but it endures.

Not only that, but it sticks to the stories you tell, and you pass it down to your children, and to your children's children.

You can see it in strange glimpses through little windows—like the Catholic woman who lights candles in dark closets. She doesn't know why she does it, but her mother did it, and *her* mother did it, and *her* mother did it, and it turns out that she's the descendant of Spanish Jews who were given a choice: Flee for their lives from the only home they had ever known, or convert. And while they changed their religion, they didn't really—and they lit their Shabbat candles, and ate unleavened bread during Passover. They just did it in secret—in closets, and behind closed curtains. And so that secrecy became part of the ritual.

I never really thought about it, until I started noticing the Russian pilgrims that waft through the Old City. It's easy to spot them: They stick out because, unlike the Koreans in their matching shirts, or the Indians in matching saris, or the Texans in their matching Trump hats, the Russians are a mixed group and dressed accordingly. The guys either have shaved heads and prison tattoos, or look like Baryshnikov.

The women are different, too. The ones who came of age around the fall of Communism look like fashion models in their leggings and gauzy scarves and stilettos, and they pick their way over the ancient stones like sexy giraffes. The other half look like a misplaced mah jong table of Baba Yagas with their flowered kerchiefs knotted tight beneath their chins, and their cheeks soft as sweet dough, and the same clunky shoes left over from their days standing in the bread lines.

They all wear tiny gold crosses.

The priests wear sunglasses left over from that one time a big old case of Ray-Bans and Levi's jeans was smuggled in back in 1987, and they sneak cigarettes when no one is looking.

The nuns scowl and elbow the young women in the ribs. I've seen them elbow the priests, too.

Why is all this special? Because for generations, under Communism, Russians were cut off from faith. Remember Anatevka? The shtetl from *Fiddler on the Roof*? Faith was strong there and it did things to people.

Remember that scene when the Christian Orthodox men reach across this great divide to dance with Tevye and the rest of the Jewish men in the pub and they all sing "To Life!"? It was a rare moment when the Christians and the Jews of this little make-believe community came together and celebrated as one.

And then remember when those same men who danced with Tevye and his friends came galloping in during Tzeitel's wedding, and pillaged the shtetl, and broke the candlesticks and killed the chickens and probably raped some of the young girls, because that's what always happened? And remember when the Jews of Anatevka had to flee at the end, scattering throughout the world: Lazar Wolf to Chicago, Tevye and his family to New York, Yente the Matchmaker to Jerusalem?

Communism would eventually wipe out the remaining Christian Orthodox community of Anatevka just as they wiped out the Jews. Communism was the great equalizer. Except not really.

But the thing is, faith sticks—from Anatevka to Chicago, or New York, or Jerusalem, or through the long grey years for the Soviets who were once devout Christians, in bread lines and in gulags, in cinder block apartments . . . faith never left.

The churches and synagogues lay fallow, except in secret. But faith never died.

And you can see it here in Jerusalem, because no matter the season, there are always Russian pilgrims. Whether a thick summer, or a mean winter, whether the red poppies are growing through the cracks in the earth after the last rains, or the first rains hit sideways as the wind whips across your face and the leaves skitter off the trees, whether we are living through calm, sweet days where the kids sleep at night, or the rockets are falling, they come.

And some days, I look like I'm one of them.

I have a scarf the color of a moth's wing, and just as thin, and I wear it over my hair sometimes, and when I walk into the Church of the Holy Sepulchre—especially when I wear my sunglasses, and try not to smile too much—I can pass as a Russian pilgrim.

Even without my scarf, I can pass as a Russian pilgrim, and one Friday night, in the middle of the night, while I ate baklava in the place I'm staying, a man with pale skin and paler eyes who had walked in on me in the shower earlier that afternoon, grabbed my arm and said something to me in Russian.

I had a choice: Get up, run for my room, and lock the door, or download a Russian script on my phone and click over to Google Translate.

When in doubt, always Google Translate.

This is what he wrote:

"Will you please give me the honor of attending the Orthodox Mass at the Holy Church with me?"

At one in the morning.

Under a thin slice of moon.

With a man whose name I didn't know who had seen me naked hours before and covered in soap, and whose arms were covered in crosses that followed the sinews of his arms, and crossed over his veins.

They were poorly drawn—the colors brackish and faded in places, which means they were probably made in prison.

I'll tell you the truth. I almost said no. After the Grey Man, I've been a little more cautious about who to trust, but I also don't want to miss out on that feeling where the world opens up a little and the light comes pouring in. So, I went anyway, my head covered in my pale pink scarf, my arms and legs covered by a long dress and jacket. I wore my Jewish star tucked under my dress.

But it's complicated for me, for reasons beyond the Grey Man, beyond that dribbly voice in the back of my head that maybe this isn't a good idea.

And when he asked my name, I replied, "Esther."

Esther is not my real name. Not even close. It was my great grandmother's name. Not the one who kissed a stranger on the roof. My other great grandmother.

My great grandmother who fled her shtetl in Belarus in the middle of the night, like Tzeitel and Tevye and Lazar Wolf and Yente the Matchmaker.

Esther told her stories to her children, who told them to their children, who told them to me: She whispered of the earth shaking beneath the galloping hooves of the Cossacks army while she hid in an old well down the road from the house her father's father's father was born in.

"But maybe it was only three men; still, it felt like thousands," she would say.

She was a young woman with long hair, and soft breasts that the Cossacks would have split in two if they had found her hiding in an old well.

They didn't find her, and she escaped on a boat across the sea with her husband who would read aloud to her from the Communist Manifesto in Yiddish.

What she didn't know as she stood by the side of the ship and vomited into the wind was that a baby had already taken root.

"Surely, it's just the waves," she told herself as the boat lurched across the Atlantic. "Surely, it's just the stink," she said to herself while she slept inside the belly of the ship, her lips salty, her shivering body pressed against her husband's, cramped in the ship's hold that smelled like sweat and shit and old potatoes.

When they arrived at Ellis Island, the young man with the bad skin and rotting teeth who sucked a cigarette through thin lips couldn't write their last name, so he gave them a new one: Singer.

And she was sick all over her dress. "Surely, it's just this new place, so far from my mama and papa."

But by the time she got to Chicago, and her stomach was sweet and round, and her breasts swollen and her nipples dark, she understood why she was still throwing up even on dry land in her new apartment in West Rogers Park.

That was my grandpa growing inside her—the first of his line born in America.

They say she gave me her Russian bones—a little nose with a wavy bump in the middle, her cheekbones that curve beneath deep set eyes, her wide mouth and straight teeth. I have her same breasts and the curve of her hips.

But my colors belong to my father, who isn't Jewish. My eyes come from a fishing village off the coast of England. My hair, from the shire. My skin, from the Pyrenees. So unless you can see beyond my colors, you won't know that I'm from Great Gramma Esther's shtetl—except I am.

I don't think I'm the only Jewish person who thinks about this, and when I was little and learning about the pogroms my family endured, and the Holocaust, too, and all the times my grandparents were told, "No dogs or Jews allowed here," I used to ask myself, "Would I have passed?"

Or would they have seen the history of my family shining in my pale eyes—or—would I have spoken up and said, "Take me, too"?

I never asked my mother with her flashing black eyes and brown skin she got from our Baghdadi ancestors, because she wouldn't have passed. Nor would she have pretended to, even if she could have.

It's one thing to walk into the Church of the Holy Sepulchre during the day when everyone is taking selfies by the tomb, and the tour guides are droning on in every language—including Hebrew—when Mr. Nusebeh is dozing on the low bench, and the air hums with shouts and murmurs.

It's another thing to go in the still of the night, when the only sound outside is your footsteps over the old stones, and when you come inside and the stones gleam gold from the light of the candles, and dozens of pilgrims are standing in rows—except for the old ones who sit on a thin wooden bench, or the nuns who are on their knees while the Greek Patriarch chants, "*Kyrie Eleison*. Lord have mercy."

But I go, and I stand there, because faith is a funny thing. And surrounded by the great grandchildren of the people who terrorized my great grandmother, I stand my ground, respectful and in awe of their faith.

And I realize what we share, and what we share is big. They waited for nearly one hundred years to pray freely, too. Because we Jews have also endured as a people and a faith for thousands of years. Through diaspora, through wars, through pogroms and Holocaust, through persecution little and large, we are still here, I am still here. I take out my Jewish star in the Church of the Holy Sepulchre, and close my eyes and pray.

I guess I should tell you about where I'm living now.

It's the place on the seam between the Christian and the Armenian Quarters—it's on a quiet street that you have to know about in order to find. The hostel looks small from the street, but it's one of these places that grew over time.

Basically, it's like M. C. Escher moved to Jerusalem and got really baked and had to build a house out of stone and glass.

There are two sets of five flights of stairs that wend and bend through the narrow space around the corners and past the windows where the light gets brighter, the air thinner, leading you through each level of the building, all the way to the top where I sleep in a room made of plywood and glass. On the window ledge, there's a copy of the Koran—even though this place is in the Christian Quarter.

And through the window there's a view of the Old City that brings me to my knees. Especially at dawn, when the sun rises over the Dome of the Rock, and the city turns pinks and gold, when the muezzin echoes off each stone and the church bells peal. I stand out on the ledge sometimes, the wind in my face, and the stone behind me.

Back in my room, there's a big bed with flowered sheets and an elaborate wrought iron headboard that makes me wish I had a pair of handcuffs.

The downstairs was built seven hundred years ago, from rocks hewn in mortar. There are curved ceilings and cozy nooks where people sit with water pipes and pretzels, their computers plugged in and hooked to the free Wi-Fi.

One night, this guy named Christos played bouzouki, and everyone danced.

Another night, the common area was empty, except for me and the glow of my laptop screen.

The downstairs smells like cotton from the wall hangings, and wool from the Bedouin rugs on the floor, and sandalwood from the carved tables, and stone from the everything.

It also smells like Windex, which makes no sense because there are no windows down here.

Everything smells like stone in Jerusalem, beneath the coffee, or the zatar or the cardamom, or the stink of raw sewage, which happens too. Beneath the smell of human sweat, and dead cat, beneath the perfume we put on before we go out—the Jews toward the Moshava, the Arabs toward Salahadin, everyone down Jaffa—beneath the soap we use to wash the day off our hands. It's there. Breathe deep if you can take it, beneath each layer of living here.

Because that's the thing, and you'll get it if you live here: Jerusalem is built on layers, and each layer is true.

Over by Damascus Gate to the north, just before you enter the Old City, after you pass the guy who sells hot corn and yummy Nutella crepes in the winter, you can see to the left several feet below Damascus Gate, there is a smaller gate.

Actually, my friend the Archaeologist told me that this little gate is the reason that Damascus Gate's Arabic name is Bab Al Amud—the gate of the column. It got its name because when Suleiman the Magnificent rebuilt the walls of the Old City and built Damascus Gate in the sixteenth century, you could still see the remnants of an earlier Roman gate that once was the entrance to the Cardo.

Back in the second century, this Roman Gate was built by Hadrian, and *it* was the entrance to the Old City, the Cardo running north and south, past the Church of the Holy Sepulchre to the remains of the ancient temple. This main artery through the Old City was the place where people sold fruit and glass and silver pieces, where merchants argued, and mothers jostled screaming babies, where young men would walk in sandals—the place where all roads led.

Now, it's several feet lower than the current gate, and almost hidden behind a metal railing and a pile of garbage, and old stone stairs. But it's there, and you can see it if you know to look for it.

There's a sign that says it's under excavation, but I have yet to see a single archaeologist come out. But once, the gate was open, and I stepped over the pile of paper cups and plastic bottles and soda cans and Bamba wrappers, and I went inside where it smelled like water and stone, and the stillness of an old tomb where the bodies have turned to dust.

But I haven't been able to get in since, because the gate is locked again.

Also, the last time I stood over it, I saw a rat the size of a small child scurry down the steps.

Above the Roman Gate—high above it—are the ramparts, where you can walk along the walls and see the Old City spread below on one side, and see East or West Jerusalem on the other depending where you stand.

And if you make it to the south end of the Old City, and the air is clear, and the sky is blue, you can see Jordan stretching grey and pink in the distance.

But sometimes you can't walk on the ramparts because they're blocked off and IDF snipers are waiting there, the barrels of their guns sticking through the crevices where Suleiman the Magnificent's army once shot arrows to protect the city from invaders coming from the north.

Because the day before the snipers, a young mother—a police officer—was stabbed in the neck. Or maybe a soldier, or a woman from Nepal waiting at the bus stop.

Damascus Gate is an area where anything can happen; it's one of the main gates from East Jerusalem, where old women sit cross-legged in the sun and sell ripe figs, where ultra-Orthodox Jews enter the Muslim Quarter in their black hats and black suits to get to the Yeshiva or the Kotel, where tourists waft down the steps into the shuk speaking French or Italian or Russian, where young guys speaking Arabic with gelled hair are frisked and searched without any reason other than the fact that they're young guys speaking Arabic, where you won't see any Jewish birthright groups because they're warned "it isn't safe."

It's the same place where I walked that night I was eighteen in a long skirt and a tank top and got hit with stones.

It's the place where the tension is as thick as the scent of Nutella and hot corn and the stink of raw sewage mixed together, wafting up toward the ramparts.

The next time you're there in the front plaza, look down at the Roman Gate, and you'll see the roots of the city, and how it grew from earth and stone, or a rat darting through the shadows, and then look up, up, up, to a wall hewn in gold when the light hits just right, and it is wow. But if you look up on the wrong day you might be staring into the barrel of a gun.

Because Jerusalem has its layers, from its bedrock that smells like moss and stone to its turrets—actually, even higher—all the way to the sky where our eyes turn when we pray, and wait for a sign that the messiah is coming.

If you walk through Damascus Gate and into the Old City, and pass the women selling sage, and the guys drinking coffee and smoking cigarettes, the road splits into two right next to the man who sells strawberries by the falafel stand.

Go left and you can find the best pizza in the world, where they bake soft dough with egg and meat and zatar and tomato in a wood fire oven built into a crusader wall. Go right, and you'll pass the kenafe place, and the guy who sells bootleg Turkish hip-hop—and porn, I hear—and the money exchange booth where the surly man behind the counter hands out copies of the Koran in English (the same one on the window ledge of my little room on top of the Old City).

Keep walking along this artery, and when it ends, hook a right, toward Muristan Square.

Muristan is this open air plaza in the middle of the Old City where old men sell bread, and little boys play the same five sharp notes on wooden flutes, and the pilgrims waft past in their robes and scarves, and the tourists take selfies next to old men in kefiyehs.

It's one of the prettiest spots in the Old City, actually—intricate stone carvings along the buildings decorated with flowing scarves with little coins sewn on them. (Don't look too close or you'll see "MADE IN CHINA" on the labels.)

Muristan is one of the few open spaces where you can stretch your arms from side to side without knocking over glass candle holders, or hitting someone in the mouth. It's a place you can feel the rain or the sun or the wind on your skin, where you can go when the narrow alleys start to close in on you, where you can BREATHE air above the stone.

But keep walking; don't stop there because you'll get pulled into one of the restaurants where you'll eat the smallest and most expensive hummus in the world. And for fuck's sake don't tell me you know a guy who says he has the best value for your shekel. Because He. Is. Lying.

Muristan is always full of tourists, and you'll get the Disneyland version of the Old City there. So put your wallet away.

And keep walking.

But look down for a minute while you walk, and I'll tell you something that you won't believe: You're walking on top of an ancient crusader hospital.

I couldn't make this up even if I tried.

There, below Muristan Square—yes, right there, under your feet—are the ruins of Knights Hospitaller built nearly one thousand years ago.

Because space in Jerusalem can't just be measured side to side—you have to think in four dimensions to understand all its layers.

The Fabric Merchant's shop is the best place to see these layers.

It looks like any other shop, and that's its magic: it's one of those places like the Roman Gate that you don't see unless you know how to look for it. The metal door is half open. The walls are painted chalk white, and there's a tiny window covered in shimmering fabrics.

The Fabric Merchant has the biggest smile I've ever seen. The kind that crinkles his eyes until they disappear. He always has coffee waiting, and the place smells like cardamom.

Still, you could easily walk in, glance around, and walk out without ever discovering the truth about this place. But if you look down by the counter near the door, you'll see the glass floor, half-hidden beneath the shelf where fabric piles up in a rainbow of silk, cotton, and cashmere.

The place is built on top of a crusader church—they found it when the Fabric Merchant wanted to renovate the shop his family has run for three generations.

"Can you turn on the light below?" I ask him.

He flips a switch, and the darkness beneath the glass floor sputters to light and I can see a corner of the old skeleton of a church looming in the depths below like a sunken ship.

"Can you open the floor?" I ask.

"Anything is possible," the Fabric Merchant winks as he unlocks the latch.

He pulls on the handle. It opens with a moan.

The air beneath wafts up into the shop, and it is clammy, and I think of graves and rain, and the bedrock that holds us all.

I reach down into the dark space and feel the bones of the old church against my palm. I sniff, and it smells brackish—like moss and old things, maybe like fresh blood—but how could it? There is nothing living down there.

Is there?

And just above the Fabric Merchant's shop is my new favorite roof where I like to sit when I don't want to be seen. It isn't the usual flat stone roof with the overlook, the kind you have to pay ten shekels to visit. This roof is made from broken red tile that wobbles beneath my feet when I climb it. Most people don't know they can climb it—just the Old City kids from the Muslim Quarter, and a few artists. You can only get to it from the Roof of the Four Quarters on top of the shuk, which offers a sweeping view of the Temple Mount and the Church of the Holy Sepulchre, and a Yeshiva ringed in barbed wire, and the shuk. The roof got its name because it's the place where the Four Quarters meet: Christian to the northwest; Muslim to the northeast; Armenian to the southwest; and Jewish to the southeast. Separate but touching, this is the spot where all roads meet.

And like Muristan Square below, this roof of the Four Quarters is one of the few places where you can feel the sun, where you can stretch your arms, where you can breathe. And at sunset when the sky turns from blue to gold to peach to plum, you can watch Palestinian kids dancing Darbuka and ultra-Orthodox kids going off to daven, and it's beautiful and it's sad, because they're the exact same age and they pass each other like the other is a ghost.

But just behind this roof is a wall with barbed wire, and next to it is a metal fence, and if you scale the fence, you'll be on the roof by the Fabric Merchant's shop, and from this steep red roof where the tiles slip and fall and shatter across the Muristan stone if you don't hold your balance and your breath as you walk, you can see to the south a building like a layer cake—stone and wood and glass and light, the highest part on the seam between the quarters. It shimmers and breathes. And that's where I'm living.

And from here, and there, from the roots and the sky, the Old City keeps growing with stone on top of stone.

Jerusalem is built on layers, and there are things we do not see.

But if we know how to listen, we can hear.

Z. lives in the Muslim Quarter, but he used to live in Queens—he wears baggy pants and a backwards Yankees hat. He says "yo, yo" a lot, even when he's just arranging the wooden camels on the shelf of the store his family owns on Al-Wad Street.

He is built with smooth arms, and a broad chest, and flicks his cigarette with more swagger than a Kanye rant.

"I needed a big city, yo—just for a little while," he tells me when I ask him why he left Jerusalem for six years. "I needed some anonymity, you know what I'm saying?"

I've been here in the Old City long enough to start to recognize the rhythms of this place, and long enough to know I'm recognized, too.

"Nah my sister, you just got here—you don't know how bad it is. There is nothing like living in the Old City long-term. I mean, this stuff goes back generations, when our grandparents and our great grandparents were all on top of each other. Just smell the air sometime. Bread and spices and shit when the pipes burst, and sweat, even in the winter. And even behind the walls—they may be made of stone, yo, but you can hear everything. And I do mean *everything*. Every time you flush your toilet, the neighbor hears it and knows what you threw down there—paper towel, toilet paper, if your wife has her period. And then every time your wife starts in on you about how you're always working and never make time for her or take her places, your neighbor will come over and offer advice. There's no privacy! And don't even *think* about having sex with your mouth open in this place."

"Really?"

"Yeah. Really. It's bad. That's why some people drive out to the hills outside the Jewish settlements to do it—especially the teenagers."

"Wait, *what*?"

"Yeah, look—sex is taboo in our world. I mean, I swear everyone is thinking about it, but we don't talk about it. And if you aren't married, you can't have it. No way. Even being alone with a girl in a car is a problem. You know, I don't like to talk smack about my own, yo, but that can get you killed if you're a woman. So sometimes Palestinian couples will head out to the settlements and get it on there, you know what I'm saying?"

"With one another?"

"Yeah. Naw, they aren't getting it on with Jews or anything. They just want privacy, to be alone, you know? And it's safer out there. Even with the soldiers and the checkpoints. They might get arrested, but they won't get shot by some crazy older brother. See, teenagers are teenagers, and they see things on TV from Europe and America, and yeah from Israel, although they won't admit it, and then they see the Jewish teenagers holding hands and doing stuff, they want to, you know, do it too. They're teenagers. You were a teenager. I was teenager. I got lucky and went to New York for some of the best years of my life, know what I'm saying? But most people don't have that kind of money or a rich uncle, so you do what you have to."

Hooking up—whether it's sex or close to it—outdoors is a rite of passage.

I remember the spring before I went to Israel for the first time, and I told my parents I was just going to 7–Eleven for a Slurpee, but instead, I snuck around to this little patch of grass and gravel behind the apartment buildings over on Charnock Road a few blocks away, where Matt was waiting for me. He was sixteen, and drove his mom's blue Volvo, and I climbed in the backseat with him, and then on top of him, and he slipped his hands up my skirt, his mouth on my neck, my hands in his hair. He pulled the left strap of my tank top down, and my bra strap with it, and left a purple rose on my left breast.

We never got caught.

But if I had been, I would have been grounded. Not killed.

"Okay . . . I get it," I tell Z.

"Yeah, but if you're planning on having sex outside, don't think too loud about it, because people can hear that, too."

I get the privacy thing. When I moved to Israel six years ago with my husband and the kids, we lived on a kibbutz.

People ask me all the time what a kibbutz is, and you can Google it and get a lot of different answers, but I'll give you mine: A kibbutz is one part Club Med, two parts mental institution. Israeli intelligence ain't got nothing on the kibbutz where generations have lived and loved and worked and fought and slept together, where Moti isn't talking to Shaul because their great grandparents were both in love with the same woman.

People notice when you get a new shirt, or cut your hair, or when you're wearing new deodorant. People know who is having an affair before the affair even starts, or who is getting divorced before the marriage is even finished.

I tell Z. all of this and he laughs. "Yeah, but you're forgetting something. You got those fields, you got all that space. You have your Israeli ID and your passport and you can go anywhere. We're stuck. Want an insider tip if you ever want to have sex here?"

"Always."

"Do it during call to prayer. The muezzin is loud, yo."

Later that night, in bed in my little room with the mermaid blue walls deep in the heart of the Old City, I kept my ears open for hours. But I didn't hear a sound.

I guess I should be honest about something, even though it's hard to admit it.

I'm lonely here.

I love my life—the wildness of it, the freedom. I love being a mermaid and being able to dive into different worlds. I want to go places and see things and talk to strangers. But the thing is, I also dream of growing roots, too, maybe not some*where*, but with some*one*.

I had a boyfriend for a while after my husband and I split up—a nice guy, but he liked his couch and sports news more than he liked me, and our relationship died quietly of old age four years after it began.

I've been alone for a while now, and I like it, but I also miss curling up next to someone at night—someone I love, who loves me, too.

And Z. gives me a great idea.

"You should try Tinder, yo!"

Tinder: the dating app founded on the laws of attraction and proximity. It's usually for hookups, but you never know. And it occurred to me that I could do something even more with it.

What would happen if I stood on the Galitzia roof where the four corners of the Old City come together—my favorite roof these days—and see who's using Tinder within a small radius?

Orthodox Jews?

Palestinians?

Christian pilgrims?

Tourists?

Why not?

"Besides," my mom told me before I went to Israel that summer I was sixteen, "you might meet someone wonderful."

It was late afternoon when I decided to do it, and the Old City was peach and gold.

And so, on the roof named after the region in Poland where my Great Gramma Sarah came from, I swiped right for the first time.

The loneliness cuts deep here.

When I was a kid in LA, I didn't think about it much, but now that I do, now that I live here, in Israel, now that I'm a mermaid, I remember there were these mothers who would always stand in the back during school-type things—book fairs, or the holiday concerts.

They were the ones who spoke funny, who mixed up words, who wore jeans that were a little too tight, and had hair that was a little too big. One had green eye shadow, another clackity shoes, and they didn't talk much, and when they did, it sounded strange, like big round rocks rolling down stairs, da-dum DUM, or like a river washing over bamboo reeds, hwish hwish, or like the wings of a hummingbird, fweee fweeee.

When their kids were around, they would speak to them in Spanish or Farsi or Mandarin, but when they were alone, they'd stand in the back, arms clasped or folded, or hands in their pockets, and it's not like they could even talk freely to one another, and they'd just stand there. My mom and the other mothers—Susan and Eileen and Marikay and all of them—were nice to them. It wasn't that they were left alone on purpose, it's just, it was hard to get beyond the pleasantries, and the smiles. Because the short hand of shared language and culture my mom and Susan and Eileen and Marikay and all of them took for granted, these women just didn't understand.

The distance was too vast between them, the distance of growing up in the same kind of boxes on the same kind of grid and watching the same kind of TV shows and eating the same kind of hamburgers with fries, of knowing what all the words say without having to read them letter by letter, sound by sound. Versus being from somewhere else, a place of mountains and smoke, or green rice fields, or blue fountains, or cold bread lines, or dirty sand, a place that when you said where you're from, you're met with the quick head tilt and the vague, "Oh, that's nice." Or, "Oh, what was that like?" and then you're reduced to explaining your childhood in three sentences or less. Or worse: "Why did you come here?" and then you're stuck explaining about the Revolution, or the drug lords, or how it felt watching your mom give blow jobs for a roll of toilet paper, or whatever it is that made you give up the comfort and ease of your language and your own box and your own grid for someone else's.

I never thought about them much, those other mothers, those different mothers, those mermaid mothers, but now living here, I think about them all the time.

I think about them and I want to find them, and I want to get down on my knees and wrap my arms around their legs and beg them to tell me how they did it, how they survived. Day after day, year after year, how they did it, how they lived through the loneliness, how they continued on feeling stupid all the time, how they raised their kids to be so foreign from them, to speak like the others who ignored them.

Because it's true, I can speak Hebrew. I can spend the whole day in Hebrew. I can spend the whole day and even find my way back home again and order a fucking glass of whisky in Hebrew.

But I'm not smart in Hebrew. I'm not funny in Hebrew, I'm not *interesting* in Hebrew, except maybe as a novelty and a, "Oh, why would you leave America?" or "What do you think of Israel?" and then I have to hurry up and say it all before their eyes glaze over, and I'm just standing there with my strange feathers and fins, my funny weird voice, and the quieter I am, the louder the difference, and the conversation turns into something that I can't follow, and so I sit there with my hands clasped, drowned bird, flailing fish.

Disappeared.

No one.

Exactly three weeks into the darkest December that I had ever known, my dad called to tell me that the war was ending, and it didn't look good.

(Just nine months before, when my mom was planting her begonia bulbs in the garden, my dad would say, "And here we are, the allied forces of chemotherapy pounding the hell out of the Nazi cancer cells. We are on the beaches of Normandy, and we will win this.")

My dad is a World War II history buff, and when shit gets real, he switches to metaphor. And I guess there ain't nothing more real than your wife fighting cancer.

Well, apparently the front lines had now shifted: "The cancer just dropped a series of firebombs. Sarah, you better come home now."

So I took the train to the airport on the darkest day of the year four days before Christmas to say goodbye to my mom.

Now, airports are funny. Not funny-haha, but funny-strange. (And sometimes funny-sad.) People who would never in a million years share the same space at the same time are thrust together for all sorts of reasons as they hurtle toward their gates clutching their Starbucks gingerbread lattes: Maybe a warm winter vacay lying topless on a beach in Cancun. Or a snowy ski weekend in Vale. Or a romantic getaway to Paris. Or a wedding in Connecticut.

Or . . .

Look. I know I couldn't have been the only one walking through the airport to fly home to say goodbye to someone for the last time. But it sure felt that way.

Because when you're smiling, the whole world smiles with you. But when you're teetering on grief's slick and icy ledge, then you are all alone with no one to catch you.

And you know what made it even harder and made me feel even more alone? In December, the airport looks like Santa Claus blew himself up smack dab in the middle of the terminal. Everything is red and green, and there's tinsel and colored lights and reindeer shit everywhere, and Christmas music is piped in against your will on a steady loop when you are sitting at Gate 23 and texting your dad to make sure your mom is still alive.

Man, it sucked Santa's balls.

And in that moment, I hated Christmas.

Hell, let's be real: I was always kind of a Grinch when it came to

Christmas. I never wore red and green. You would never in a million years catch me wearing a Santa hat. And this one time, I even yelled at my high school principal for allowing a Christmas tree to prominently decorate the main office without so much as a menorah for religious parity.

Well, are you ready for a slice of irony with a side of figgy pudding? Now that I'm living in Israel, I miss Christmas.

I miss the holly wreaths, and the red and green everythings. I miss gingerbread lattes from Starbucks.

Hell, I even miss "Jingle Bells."

It comes down to this: Once Hanukkah is over, December in these parts is really depressing. The blue and silver decorations have been packed away. Everyone is suffering from latke fatigue, and ain't no one going to fry up nothing no how.

(Ditto for jelly donuts.)

The candles have long ago burned low into a puddle of rainbow wax. And as we've reached that critical mass moment of darkness, and we stand in the shadows of the Winter Solstice, I remember those long weeks that passed too quickly those years ago when I last saw my mom.

I'm lonely and I just really, really miss the lights.

So, feeling this way, I am doing the only reasonable thing I can on December 24. I have found one of the few places in Israel that is covered with lights, less than a half day's walk from the birthplace of Jesus, and I am spending Christmas Eve in the Christian Quarter.

It's cold, and I'm wearing my winter coat, the green one with the hood, plus two scarves wrapped around my neck, and the stars are shining, and the entire world is covered in long strings of rainbow lights—the same ones they hang in the Muslim Quarter during Ramadan—lights that blink and flash like the sign outside a brothel. And there are silver bells hanging from the awnings, and a fat old pink Santa on a plastic sled dangles from one of the roofs, and my friend is out there in the cold stomping around in his Santa suit ringing a gold bell and shouting, "MERRY CHRISTMAS!"

in Hebrew, Arabic, and English, and everyone is pink-cheeked and merry AF.

And it's cold out, but there's mulled wine, just like Christmas parties back home in LA, and now it's midnight, and I'm at mass in one of the Catholic churches, and I'm sitting with a beautiful woman I met on Tinder, because why not, and she has long black hair hanging down her back, and we are holding hands.

I don't know why we're holding hands, except she's warm and she smells like vanilla, and I want to hold her hand, because I just do, so I am.

I'm also crying, because there are priests and nuns from all over the world—from the Philippines, from Nigeria, from Korea, from Mexico, from the United States, from Italy, from France, from Paraguay, and they're on the stage and everyone is singing, and the tiny candles gleam from the church walls, and it's warm inside.

These are dark days, and the priest speaks in English for all assembled about the refugees in Syria, about opening our borders and our hearts, because that's what it means to be a good Christian.

"Let us pray to the Lord," says the priest.

"Lord, hear our prayer," replies the congregation in unison.

"That Jesus, born of Mary and protected by Joseph will strengthen family life with respect and love and sustain those separated by war and traumatized by natural disasters and feeling the pressures of poverty and mistrust.

"Let us pray to the Lord."

"Lord, hear our prayer."

"That Jesus, first visited by poor shepherds, will have in his care those living in poverty, and lead those who have more than they need to share with those who lack basic necessities.

"Let us pray to the Lord."

"Lord, hear our prayer."

"That Jesus who became a refugee as an infant, will be close to refugees around the world who have little hope for their future, mindful of asylum seekers denied residency.

"Let us pray to the Lord."

"Lord, hear our prayer."

"That Jesus, whose birth was heralded with songs of peace, will move hearts to negotiate for peace wherever there is violence, especially in places like Syria, Iraq, Afghanistan, and the Holy Land."

I'm Jewish, and I love being Jewish, but I love faith, too, in all its forms. And I don't fit in anywhere in the Old City. I'm not Muslim or Christian or Armenian, so I'm an outsider in those three quarters. And I'm not an observant Jew, so I'm an outsider in my own quarter, too. Different with my tank tops and my nose ring and my mermaid tattoo, a woman with no real status behind the walls, no family close by besides her kids. But the beauty of not fitting in anywhere is that you can go almost everywhere, so I do. And I've gone to church.

And after eating little meringue cookies and hot chocolate with little pink marshmallows, we walk back through the cold and sleepy streets of the Old City holding hands, warm in the cold, the only sound our footsteps and our breath, and it makes sense to move toward her as she turns toward me, and smell her hair, and run my fingers through it, cold and soft and shining in a million lights, and I kiss her.

I feel her body soft against mine. This isn't my first time kissing a woman, but it's the first time I've wanted to kiss a woman so much that I'm thrumming with it, spilling over. Maybe it's the lights, maybe it's the fact that it's taboo here in Jerusalem—two women in the middle of the Muslim Quarter, our mouths open, breathing the other in. But I want to feel her against me, skin to skin.

So I take her upstairs to my little room with the purple windows, and she tastes like salt and wine.

Spring

It's still cold in Jerusalem, but there are tiny flowers growing in the cracks in the stones, because it's also almost spring, and outside the Old City, the almond trees are like brides again.

Spring is that in-between time, between the long bare nights of winter and the long hot days of summer, between blossoming trees and parched earth. And spring is many things—renewal, hope, a little blooming, and as the sun gets warmer and higher in the sky, we know that the long, dry days of the dusty summer stretch before us.

I'm thinking about this while I munch on a piece of fresh bread with the Mukhtar of the Syrian Christian Orthodox community.

"My father was Ottoman Turkish, so I am Turkish. I was born under the British mandate and my birth certificate has Queen Elizabeth's father's name on it," he says. "In 1948 when I was thirteen, I became a citizen of Jordan. I still have my passport. In 1967, I became an Israeli resident. They won't give me citizenship but I am a resident. And I am a Palestinian.

"I am like the mayor," he says proudly. "And in 1967 when Israel took over all of Jerusalem, Mayor Teddy Kollek came to my store to see me. We became friends, and he used to visit all the time, and he told his secretary that if I ever came to his office she should kick down the door and let me in, even if he was in the middle of a meeting with the Prime Minister!"

He smiles, and arches his eyebrow.

He has a huge photo of himself with Teddy Kollek in front of his shop, and he beams.

"Now *he* was a real mayor," he says.

His eyes are gleaming, and he purses his lips, and I know he is too much a gentleman to say something nasty about the current mayor.

The Mukhtar of the Syrian Orthodox Church is also a tailor, and he's been working in this little shop with the yellow walls since the 1950s.

"I was here under Jordanian rule, and I am here under Israeli rule, but all that matters to me is God's rule."

He has silver hair brushed with Brylcreem, and he wears a natty maroon vest over a pinstriped shirt, and black slacks. While he stitches and measures, he listens to music in Aramaic—it's his first language, and the one Jesus would have spoken while he walked the same streets where I drink my coffee, and where the Mukhtar buys his bread.

Once, he tells me, his hair was blacker and shinier than the sewing machine he would work over, stitching mantels and scarves and suits, dressing the people of the Old City—Christians, Muslims, and Jews. He still does, but he also sells souvenirs, including a linguistic tree of the Semitic languages.

"I did my hair just like Elvis, and all the women of Jerusalem used to come to admire my hair," he winks. "Some of them still do."

He looks hopefully out the window.

I'm having a five-shekel coffee with Keshet in the middle of the Cardo, the original Roman road, the one my ancestors walked on before our Temple was ransacked and burned, except for a few stones and the old retaining wall that we Jews touch with faithful hands to this day.

It's almost Passover, and the whole entire Jewish Quarter is in a frenzy, cleaning the bread crumbs from every corner, from every nook, from every crack in every wall or in between the stones or tiles on the floor. Year after year on Passover, we tell the story of our slavery in Egypt, and how God, with the help of Moses and Aaron and Miriam and Tsiporah, delivered us from the house of bondage and into the promised land. "Next year in Jerusalem," we say at the Seder year after year, and I think about what that means, how Jerusalem is literally this physical space, but how the word "peace" in Hebrew comes from the Hebrew root word "wholeness."

I'm sitting on a broken piece of a Roman pillar. And all around me, the world feels broken.

And I'm angry at Jerusalem today because sometime in the middle of the night, a bunch of young guys from the Jewish Quarter went stamping though the Muslim Quarter, banging on walls and doors and singing loud enough to wake the babies who cried long into the night after the boys had left.

In the morning were the words, "*Mavet l'aravim,*" "death to the Arabs," scrawled on a few doors.

My eyes are burning and my hair stands on end, I am thrumming with anger and I'm staring down every young man who passes in a yarmulke, wondering if they woke up Abu Ibrahim and Um Ibrahim's youngest son, the one with asthma, frightening him and making him struggle to breathe all the way till sunrise.

Keshet puts her hand on my arm. "Sarah, remember something," she says. "For every misguided foolish child out there banging the walls and waking up those poor people, there are ten mothers telling him to stop. Rest assured, these boys will be punished. If not by the police, then by their mothers."

"I hope you're right."

"Oh please. The families in the Muslim Quarter are our neighbors, and this is not how you treat neighbors. Give us Jewish mothers some credit." We get up and head back to our houses to clean away the bread and dust before the holiday.

One of the most important days in Israel is today, Yom HaShoah, the day we commemorate the Holocaust.

And one of the most terrible sounds in the whole world is the siren on Yom HaShoah. It's the sound of every mother and daughter and father and son, every sister and brother and lover and friend screaming from that miserable maw of humanity, that sound mixed down into one keening wail.

But one of the most moving sites in the whole world is what happens in Israel during the siren on Yom HaShoah. The entire country grinds to a halt.

We put aside the grievances, the stress. Coffee cups are placed down mid-sip. Arguments end mid-sentence. A joke breaks at the punch line. Even the children stop playing, their bodies eerily still on the playground, stiller than the trees that grow deep into the ground, branches swaying against the sky. Every car pulls to the side of the road. And we stand. Together.

And every year I want to be where I don't just hear it, but I see it.

So I can feel.

Last year, I stood in a cafe, and I stood with everyone, because everyone stood, and while the siren blared, the cappuccino machine hissed, because you don't turn off the machine when the siren stops—you just stop. You stop and you stand, and nothing matters but those terrible moments when you're hearing that sound, shaken. And you remember.

The year before, I was in a building near a highway, and from the high up windows, I looked down, and saw each and every car pull to the side of the road, and the doors open, and each driver and each passenger, stand straight and silent. I remember crying when I saw that. Israelis never agree on anything—and yet, on Yom HaShoah, we move as one.

This year I stand at Jaffa Gate.

I am curious to see what happens in an area where both Palestinians and Israelis share space, if not conversation.

And Jaffa Gate is that nexus point. It's the gate facing west, over the hills and forests, across the fields and to the sea. Back in the day, if you walked out of Jaffa Gate and headed in a straight line, you would hit the port city of Jaffa where the waves crash on the rocks and merchants and pilgrims would arrive seasick and weary to take the road back again to Jerusalem.

It's the entrance to the Christian Quarter, but if you turn right, you'll hit the Armenian Quarter, and many Jewish Israelis—both secular and observant—use it as an entry point, too, as do Muslims. There are souvenir shops run by Palestinian guys who sell yarmulkes and IDF t-shirts, next to a place run by this Greek Orthodox guy who sells crosses and icons. Just around the corner is a place with gorgeous Armenian pottery. Inside the gate, sometimes there's an angel playing the harp. It's the gate where the roads really meet.

And I know a lot of the people hanging out there, like Zaki who sells bread, and Ali the cop from Daliat el-Carmel, and George who plays Motown's greatest hits and sells black coffee with cardamom and pomegranate juice, and all the soldiers who keep changing, but who are always there.

And I want to be here to see what happens, on this day when the Israel I know and live in screeches to a halt.

Who would stop?

Who wouldn't?

How would I feel if the people I know didn't stop?

So I wait. I sit down on the cobblestone street before the siren because I want to stand to be seen making that active choice to go from one way to another—from a place of easy rest, to a state of total attention.

And the siren wails and I stop and I stand, and I look around. The Border Police stand beside me. The men in yarmulkes stand, too. The mother with the sheitel and the baby carriage stops mid-step, frozen.

Four little kids with yarmulkes and sidelocks were running toward David Street, and they stop, little trees rooted to the ground.

It takes the tourists a minute to figure out WTF is going on. I see them look at each other, baffled, like, "Oh shit, we got front row seats to the Zombie Apocalypse," but their guide explains and they stop.

Nuns and priests waft past me, talking.

Women in hijab, too.

The old men playing backgammon—including Abu Ibrahim—keep rolling the dice, and a taxi drives past and curves around the Tower of David.

And across the way, my friend Harout from the Armenian Quarter checks his phone, and takes a picture of me standing there, a statue in jeans and a tank top, and decorated with bracelets from his cousin's shop.

I feel a lot of things.

And I let myself feel them.

The Holocaust is part of my identity. I didn't live it personally, but it's in my DNA, as are thousands of years of persecution we have endured—throughout Europe, and the Middle East, and the Americas, too.

My optimism comes from a history of survival. My sense of the absurd and the macabre, too. Because I am alive against all odds.

I go between the Jewish and Muslim and Christian and Armenian Quarters because after surviving all of this, I am free and strong, and I will live that way or die.

I criticize the government because we did not survive thousands of years of persecution to put up with bullshit from our own leaders. I fight for human rights and demand equality for everyone *dafka* because #NeverAgain cannot just be about us. It means never again for anyone else, in any gradation, from prejudice to full on persecution. No.

And the siren reminds me of all of this, and it reminds of such a great loss. A systematic, mechanized, *modern* genocide—on purpose, planned, and meticulously carried out against the Jews—as well as so many others.

And the Holocaust is bigger than Israel. It's bigger than the Jewish people. It is a horror almost beyond reckoning, and yes: I want the world to recognize it.

And yes, I want my friends to recognize it.

So after the siren, I walk up to Harout.

I can still hear the echo of the siren, the little hairs on the back of my neck are still standing.

"Good morning," I say to him with tears in my eyes as I think about all those people—all those millions of people—who were murdered.

He reaches out, and I shake his hand.

"Good morning," he answers.

I start to speak when he hands me a black coffee and says, "Tell me something, Sarah: Why was there a siren just now?"

And a sound that is half laugh and half sob tears out of me, and my eyes fill with tears again, because really, he just didn't know.

And a new wave of sadness washes over me because here in the place that is holy to us all, where the Old City comes together, we all live in different worlds.

"Oh right!" he says.

Maybe next year he'll remember.

"You know, it's the day we commemorate the Armenian Genocide," he tells me.

I had no idea. Maybe next year I'll remember, too.

My mom used to tell me about how she would watch the old guys play backgammon downstairs from where she would stay in the Old City, and I guess maybe I'm looking for her there—for her ghost, which I've been looking for really in earnest since I started living in the Old City.

She isn't there, but the guys playing backgammon are.

It's funny, these big old guys sitting there and smoking, their ragged laughs from too much nargila and the occasional spliff after the mosque, history under their fingernails, and they sit there playing until their wives call them in like little boys.

Or at least that's what it looks like to me—my Arabic isn't good enough yet unless I'm cursing someone for cutting me in line, or bumping into me at the shuk, but I catch enough to get the gist, and the rest is up to my imagination.

Usually, it's the woman they call Um Ibrahim who summons the boys. She's badass. She's got a stern but rosy face and black eyelashes that cover laughing eyes; even when she's scolding the men, you can see them glitter. Okay, *especially* when she's scolding them.

She's tall. I've never seen her hair because it's hidden beneath her hijab, which is usually grey. When she was born—in Jerusalem, she says with pride—Um Ibrahim had had another name, but I don't know it, and I don't know her well enough to ask. Maybe it was Suha, or Rania? Maybe Amal? I guess I'd have to see her hair before I could ask her that—it's an intimate question . . . *Who were you before?*

Because now she's Um Ibrahim, which literally means, "Mother of Ibrahim," because when her first baby was born—the baby who is now the guy with the kefiyeh who sells the wooden flutes inside Muristan Square—they named him Ibrahim. Ibrahim is the patriarch—and father of Ishmael—who was the ancestor of the Arab people. If this baby were born just a few hundred meters away in the Jewish quarter, he would have been named Avraham or Abraham, the patriarch—and father of Isaac—who was the ancestor of the Jewish people.

Cousins.

Abu Ibrahim and I are friendly, and have been for several months now, but there's a distance between us. Maybe because I'm a woman, maybe because I have no real status here in the Old City, but I've never been invited in behind the heavy wooden door to the home he shares with Um Ibrahim and their nine children.

Still, there's this wall between us, a separation between their private life, and who they are on these streets when we pass by. And while we smile to one another, and say hello, we haven't gotten beyond the barrier.

"It's late," Um Ibrahim shouts as her mother must have shouted and as her mother's mother must have shouted to the men from generation to generation to generation from the window. When the men ignore her—which they always do the first time, because that's how it's done—while the pale smoke rises, and the small plastic dice clickity clack over the lacquered board, she comes down, hands on her full hips.

"*Yalla*, the dishes!" she says pointing a long finger at Abu Ibrahim.

Abu Ibrahim sighs and tries to hide the package of sunflower seeds he's been eating.

"Oh, don't think you can hide those from me," she says. I could hear you cracking them all evening from all the way upstairs. And you've got pieces of shell on your shirt!"

She wags her finger.

"*Yalla*, Abu Muhammad, I'll tell your wife you're smoking," she turns her gimlet eyes on her brother-in-law, while her own husband Abu Ibrahim sighs again and heaves himself off from the little chair that bent under his weight.

He sits there every day. The chair is used to it by now, I'm sure. It's a game they play, the chair made as it is by Samir in the Christian Quarter, and Abu Ibrahim, every day a little more so, made as he was in the Muslim Quarter sixty-seven years ago. Just a little more sweet kenafe, a few more creamy pistachio cookies, a little more tahina and hummus with fava beans, and always wiped with lafa. Abu Ibrahim sits and plays and smokes with the guys. And the chair beneath him suffers patiently through it all.

I like Abu Ibrahim. He runs this jewelry store near Muristan Square, right around the corner from the Church of the Holy Sepulchre.

We met each other over shining remnants of Rome and Byzantine, and ancient Israel, too, the leavings of ancient markets and dynasties turned to rubble. Old coins and glass beads are now crafted into necklaces and rings. It's funny—Jerusalem is this wild creature that empires have fought to the death to dominate. They wage wars over her stone and earth and even sky, and what happens? The empires crumble. Yet Jerusalem endures. And we are left centuries later wearing the remains around our necks—Roman glass pendants, or ancient coins rimmed with sterling silver.

And it makes me wonder what will be left of us when it's all over but the shouting.

But back to Abu Ibrahim. It was in his shop. It was a cool spring evening, and the sky was pink.

He's got this display case in the window, and it has beautiful pieces of jewelry, and old coins lined up, and beyond it, I could see antique furniture, and a large man sleeping in an elaborate chair. It was the kind of move my dad would pull—find a spot that's comfortable and close his eyes and before he knew it his belly was rising and falling like the tides, a snore or two escaping. It happened once in synagogue, and my mom kicked him until he woke up with a grunt.

"We have beautiful pieces," the man in the armchair said with his eyes still closed.

"Didn't mean to wake you!" I said.

"And it was a beautiful dream—gardens and a fountain, and a tree with sweet fruit," he sighed. "Buy something and it'll make waking up worth it!" he rubbed his eyes and coughed.

He heaved himself up and lumbered to the counter. He wore a red shirt tucked in and a bow tie and a grey cap that matched his hair and thick moustache. His eyes were amber and webbed with wrinkles. He told me his name was Abu Ibrahim.

He offered coffee—the spiced black kind with cardamom and sugar, the kind they grind in front of you at the stall next to the place with the wind chimes and old watches.

"You will insult me if you don't take it," he told me.

"You are welcome, you are welcome," he said as I drank.

"Thanks, this is really good."

He took a cigarette out of his pocket, and lit it. Lucky Strike. Same kind my grampa smoked back in Chicago. He closed his eyes, and he looked younger through the smoke, his wrinkles softened, his eyes closed.

"Don't tell my wife," he said. "She doesn't like me to smoke."

(My grandpa used to say the same thing.)

He coughed, a ragged sound that shook his big shoulders and made him hunch. "Don't tell her about that either. She worries. Do you worry about your husband?" he asked me while he took another drag.

"I'm divorced."

"Ohh. I am so sorry!" he said, looking older, the same look my rabbi gave me at my mom's funeral, when he held my hand and looked deep into my eyes while I stood there shocked and shaking over her open grave. "I am so sorry."

"Oh, no, it's cool," I said. "It's fine. It's better actually."

"No, it isn't good to be alone," he said.

I hear this a lot. Especially now that I'm living here half the week in these ancient walls where most women my age are married, big with baby, or nursing, or both, or yelling after toddlers who run down the alleys, or all of the above. And I'm . . . not. I have my son and daughter with me half the week back in our house near these rolling fields. We have our garden and our wind chimes from the Old City, and macaroni and cheese and ice cream for dessert. Every two weeks we're together for Shabbat and we light our candles and sing "Shalom Aleichem"—a traditional song welcoming the Angels of Peace.

It's funny, the importance of belonging. When I first came to Israel and lived with my husband and our kids on the kibbutz where he grew up, people would come up to me in the kibbutz convenience store and ask "*Shel mi at?*—Who do you belong to?"

"It's like they're asking me 'whose bitch are you?'" I told my husband when I got home after the first time it happened. "It's like I only exist because of you and your family, and if it weren't for you I'd disappear."

"Whatever. Did you get toilet paper?"

So day after day until they got used to seeing me around, I would answer: "I'm married to so-and-so," while wishing the whole time I had the presence of mind to say, "I belong to me."

But here? In these walls? Wafting around? Sometimes wearing a hijab in the Muslim Quarter, sometimes with my hair uncovered, I guess it's the opposite and I only belong to me.

I've felt this way since moving to Israel several years ago. I don't quite fit in anywhere, which means I can go almost anywhere, between the quarters, and also between walls and into different worlds, like a mermaid.

But that's hard for people to see, especially when nearly everyone in the Old City is defined by who they belong to—Um Ibrahim is the mother of Ibrahim. She is the wife of Abu Ibrahim. She cooks the best makloubeh in town, or so they say.

I'm just Sarah. Sarah with no husband, who has two kids she only sees half the week, who has a toaster oven and makes a mean Cup-O-Noodles in the microwave.

Maybe that makes people uneasy, but I keep hoping that will change and I'll be invited in. Abu Ibrahim still looks at me with sorrow even now, even still, and I can hear him thinking: "It isn't good to be alone."

"You are tourist?" he asked me on that day in his shop when we first met. And I guess that's how I look in my long white sundress with the scarf around my shoulders and the brown leather Jesus sandals.

"No, I actually live here."

"What do you do?"

"I'm a journalist!"

"Ah, a journalist! You are very busy I am sure," he says. "It's terrible what is happening here in Jerusalem."

"It is," I say. "It really is."

I've learned in moments like these that you can push. You can ask questions and lead the conversation down a certain path: the struggles, the tourist industry in the Old City going to shit, the relative who couldn't get through the checkpoint to work on time and the shop that went bankrupt, daily humiliation from the same exact young soldiers who protect the Israeli Jews but stop and search the Palestinian shopkeepers without any explanation. Some stories are told in anger—usually by the young guys with their hair cut like soccer players (shaved on the sides, and poufy on the top), the guys who smell like Davidoff Cool Water and drink in secret when no one is looking. Other stories are told with resignation, by their fathers, tired and grey, who watch their sons walk through the Old City with fists clenched and look the other way when they smoke weed or drink too much in an effort to forget—until they wake up and remember with a headache that gnaws them through the day.

All their stories are true and sad. And the fathers were once angry sons, and one day—*inshallah*, God willing—the sons will be fathers, resigned to the realities.

I've also learned in moments like these you should sometimes sit back and wait, and let them tell their own story, which is what happened when I met Abu Ibrahim.

"You cannot look at the struggle for Jerusalem from one direction alone," he said to me that evening in his shop while wrapping up the coins. "Just like a coin—it has two sides."

He handed me a small coin, worn and gritty—you could see that it was once bronze, but was now black and white.

Time does that.

I held the coin between my right thumb and index finger. I turned it over.

Constantine on the front, and . . . hard to tell what it was on the back.

"We can't expect only you—only the Israelis—to meet our needs," he said. "We have to find a way to understand you, too."

He drew a breath, deep and long, and sighed. "I love this city," he said to me, his arm outstretched toward the sunset, toward the shadows, toward the stones, and toward the people. "I love this city," he repeated, and he coughed, as a man with a yarmulke walked by next to a woman in a hijab, as a group of pilgrims all in white floated down the road, as three soldiers spoke with two police officers near the Lutheran Church, as two children ran toward the man selling bread at the entrance of the square, as an old man shuffled past the window.

He pointed to the coin in my hand. "Time does things," he said. "This too, shall pass. And this too, shall endure."

And he turned to me, and sighed again, a wave of breath, floating, falling, free.

"I love this city. And so do you."

He was right. I do. I love this city.

Which is why I'm here in the throes of it, "alone" as he would see me, yet very much a part of things.

It's late, and I have to get to the other side of the Old City by the Western Wall before it closes. Watches and cell phones are meaningless here. The day and night is measured in prayer time—the call of the muezzin echoing off the stone, the church bells peeling from the steeples, the groups of men and women davening at the Western Wall. Time is measured in cups of coffee and the crispiness of the semolina on kenafe, it's measured in how much hummus is left at Abu Shukri on a Thursday, or how fresh the bread is by Jaffa Gate on Monday. It's measured in the hands that knit yarmulkes and stitch kefiyehs and polished brass candlesticks.

It's measured when Um Ibrahim stalks downstairs and sends the old men home to their wives. Which means it's very, very late.

It's been a long day. I'm still wearing the leather Jesus sandals I wore when I met Abu Ibrahim a few months ago, and my feet hurt. There's a real gym in the Old City. Built inside the ancient stone, the elliptical machines and treadmill look so strange. I've never seen women go in—at least not yet. But I don't need the membership because the Old City itself is where I get my exercise—I race up the Nun's Ascent, then the steps pitching back toward the shuk. Sometimes, for no reason, I pretend I'm being followed like in a spy novel and I run, my scarf flowing . . . I like the drama. The thing is, these days, sometimes there's actually a reason to run—stabbing attacks even within the walls of the Old City, two blood stains in the shape of two men—two fathers. They were murdered not far from where Um Ibrahim is yelling at these old guys playing backgammon, and sometimes I feel the teeny tiny hairs on the back of my neck stand up, and I look around, and see only shadow. Then I run for real.

Today, I only ran once. And that was really only for the artistic effect of flying past a group of tourists from a church group standing outside the Austrian Hospice.

But I am tired.

I was underneath the tunnels of the Old City, this long stretch of stone that touches the heart of the Holy of Holies, a place where private donors have paid thousands and thousands of shekels to pad the ceiling so folks won't bump their heads as they walk beneath and touch the base of Solomon's Temple. And there at the end, in a cistern where our voices echoed as we spoke of history and faith near the ancient ruins, I leaned too far and dropped my sunglasses. They disappeared with a plink and three ripples, gone.

These were not just any sunglasses, but the pair my mom gave me the summer before she died, the pair she bought at ROSS Dress for Less, that she wanted me to have. One of the few things I still have of hers, thousands of miles from where she took her last breath, I wear them every day there's sun, and when there isn't, I check to make sure they're still there. They're so old they're back in style, but that isn't the point—I wear them because I remember how she wore them, and it's something we can have in common even now, even still. But now, this pair is at the bottom of the cistern. Cheap plastic, and metal, but with so much meaning—my mom chose them, and in one of those rare instances where her taste and mine aligned, they were exactly what I didn't know I wanted.

I want them back, and the soldier guarding the tunnels said to come back at closing and he'd help me find them.

Soldiers tell real time, and closing is at 10:00 p.m., and I know we are close to that already since Um Ibrahim has come down and shouted for the men to go back home to their wives and the dishes and the bills they need to pay.

And the men know it's late, too. Abu Ibrahim yawns and pats his belly. Ramzi, the guy to his left, rubs his eyes and pours water over the smoldering nargila coal. It goes out with a hiss. He dumps the coal on the ground, pulls the glass bottom base away from the tobacco holder, and pours the dirty water down the grate nearby.

"You're still the worst backgammon player that ever lived," he mutters to Abu Ibrahim. "Even if you beat me."

He packs up the board, and puts the small dice in his pocket. I wonder why he doesn't leave it in the board and why he carries it, but I don't know him well enough to ask. Like Um Ibrahim's name, there are questions that you can only ask when you know someone, and I know them on these streets, but not behind closed doors. Not where the quiet truths exist and just are. I know them behind nargila smoke and hijab and the "*Salaam Aleikums*" and the shops, and they know me as the journalist, the woman who doesn't belong, who shouldn't be alone, but is.

The men are all standing at this point. "You shouldn't be alone," Abu Muhammad tells me in Hebrew. "A journalist like you, you know better, even with your little red string around your wrist," he laughs and points to the piece of yarn I got from the Western Wall earlier that day.

It's meant for luck. I've never had one before, but this morning on my way to the tunnels, the man who sells red string just outside the Western Wall stopped me—he stands there every day, in his black coat and black hat, shivering sometimes in the winter, sweating in the summer like today, and normally, I walk by in a blur when he asks for tzedakah—a donation—in exchange for a blessing and a reminder in red worn around the wrist. Except this one time, on my way to the bottom of Jerusalem, I looked up long enough to look into his eyes, and I said to him, "I just don't have the money to give you."

"May you be healthy!" he said to me—"take it, take it." And he murmured a prayer for me, for my health, for happy children, for love, and for—with God's assistance, always—enough money some day to never worry about such things.

And he handed me twenty strings.

"I can see you need the blessings."

So, I have the blessings, but lost my mother's sunglasses, now at the bottom of the cistern, and I think in a flash that maybe I'll fish it out with all the red string he gave me.

"Do you want a string?" I ask the men as they pack up.

They laugh, and I head off, down Al-Wad to the Western Wall to the tunnels.

And now that the men have gone, it's even later. And the air is thick and still, and I'm alone.

And can I just tell you? I am scared. I feel the darkness, fast and deep, now that the big old men are gone. Abu Ibrahim is washing dishes, and Abu Muhammad is hiding the smell of smoke from his hands with cologne, and the night smells like stone and ripe strawberries.

Shadows stir, and a cat slithers past, a bag of bones, against my legs.

His hiss.

My gasp.

And our echo.

He skitters away, and I am alone, except for his shadow that climbs the walls.

Remember how I said I sometimes run for the drama? Not this time. This time I was running for real.

I think about the two fathers who were stabbed just a few twists and turns away, how they lay there in the middle of the day; the blood stains in the shape of two bodies are still there on the ground.

I think about the two old grandmothers who were walking on the promenade and how they were stabbed, one in the chest, one in the back.

I think about standing by Damascus Gate with my own blood dripping on the stones.

I think about the Grey Man.

I think about how alone I am in this moment. If something happens, who will find me?

I don't want to think this way, but when it's night and you're alone and there are strange echoes tilting off the walls, the mind teeters.

I can smell my sweat, so strong it fills my nose and my mouth. It's rank and sour, the same smell I remember from Damascus Gate when I stood there with my hands covered in my blood, the same smell when I was stuck in that little room after the night with the Grey Man.

My left sandal flies off my foot, but there's garbage on the ground, and I ain't no Cinderella, so missing half a beat I slide my foot back in and twist my ankle. I have these thick Polish ankles—"peasant ankles," my mom would call them. But even though they're thick, they're weak, and I yelp in pain while I stumble, and I hear breathing. Mine? Or someone else's? The cat is gone. It's only me, and maybe someone else, and I'm alone, except I'm not, I can feel someone behind me to my side, in front of me, and I run blindly.

"You shouldn't be alone," Abu Muhammad had said.

Am I alone?

I stumble down the flight of stairs.

A shadow looms against the wall, towering over me, big and fierce. My feet stop and so do theirs, and a scream rises in me, and I turn to face the form that cast the shadow on the wall, my firsts clenched. I was ready to bite and kick and scream and claw like I did in words that morning on the train, because right now, all I can remember are the stones against my skull when I stood by Damascus Gate, and the smell of my own blood, and the writing scrawled on the wall in crimson paint, and I remember that terrible moment the night before I woke up with no memory but couldn't forget . . .

A little girl stood there in the doorway of one of the old houses with the marmulk stone. She must have been my daughter's age, river-rock eyes, just like my daughter. She's trembling.

"You scared me!" she said. "You scared me!" she said again. "You scared me!" she said a third time, as she turns around and slams the door.

And I wonder if my daughter is asleep by now, in her top bunk with the neon stars she pasted on the walls to light the way.

"I'm sorry, I'm sorry, I'm sorry," I chant back to the empty street as I sink to my knees, my ankle throbbing, all alone on an empty step.

Another door opens, and a woman calls out to me, "You, the journalist! What are you doing?"

It's Um Ibrahim, her sturdy body edged in gold from the light behind her. "Are you hurt?" she calls to me.

"I twisted my ankle," I say. "I dropped my glasses in the Western Wall tunnel today, and I need to go get them."

"You crazy woman! You'll get them tomorrow. You shouldn't be alone out here, it really isn't safe. Tonight, you'll stay with us."

And she opens the door a little wider and the light spills out against the long stone ascent, and I get up, and walk toward her.

I didn't get my glasses—my mom's glasses—they're still there at the bottom of the cistern, but I'm okay with that. Because I had tea instead with Um Ibrahim, and we ate little almond cookies, and we talked about our mothers. Hers used to sit just outside Damascus Gate selling whatever was in season.

That's one of the things that I love about living here—we don't get whatever fruits and vegetables you want all year round, like in the United States. It isn't like LA where I'd drive a block and a half to Trader Joe's and find whatever fruits or veggies I want whenever I want them. Here, to everything there is a season and when you go to the corner store or the stalls by Damascus Gate, you get what the earth gives you. During the summer, fresh mangoes—sweet, ripe, golden beauties, juice dripping down your chin when you eat them. Before that, strawberries, red and pert. In winter, bitter greens. Almonds after the first rains. And in the fall, juicy figs and bright red pomegranates, split open into tiny jewels.

Here, especially in the stalls by Damascus Gate, you have to be grateful for the gifts you have when you have them . . . and still know that when they're gone, they'll be back again when the earth turns around the sun at the right time in its right pace.

I also learned Um Ibrahim's name: Amal. It means hope.

By now, I'm learning Jerusalem well enough to have a routine.

Hummus in the morning at Arafat Hummus where I sit wedged in between the Waqf officials who oversee the Temple Mount. When I've gone there as a tourist, they stand legs akimbo, grim-faced. But over warm hummus? We're friends.

Coffee at this little place by Herod's Gate in the Muslim Quarter where it costs five shekels, and the men play cards inside, and the whole place smells like cardamom and the inside of an ashtray.

I visit my favorite roofs, thinking of my great grandmother.

This time, the place I usually stay with the big purple windows and the view of the Old City that makes the whole place look like a crazy mosaic jigsaw puzzle is full. There's a group of journalists from Belgium staying there. There's Jan and Boudewijn, both tall and blonde and gorgeous and from Brussels, and they've got this group of writers and photographers with them, and that's part of the Old City, too—people from abroad (mostly Europe) who come out of real fascination to understand the conflict on the ground.

And here in Jerusalem where faith and insanity overlap, where the streets are overrun with scorpions and the righteous, this is ground zero. Which means, people come, eyes open and fascinated, to see the cosmic struggle play out against the stones and sky.

The Israeli/Palestinian conflict has shifted over the years—it's always been chimerical with many sides and facets—like that story about the seven blind men asked to describe an elephant, and each guy touches a different part. ("An elephant is broad and rough!" "No, an elephant is smooth and sharp at the end!" "An elephant is sinewy like a rope!")

But lately, the conflict has become just as much about faith as it is about anything else.

It wasn't always this way—the Old City used to be much more secular.

My friend Mary who is a Palestinian Christian journalist living in the Old City explained that it used to be unusual to see a Palestinian woman with her head covered. They wore jeans, she said. It was easier to run and throw rocks in jeans.

But that's changed—not just on the Muslim side, but on the Jewish side, too.

There used to be this crazy night life scene in the Old City—artists and writers, Arabs and Jews, everyone just hanging out and getting high and hooking up. But that wildness turned inward, turned nasty, and lines were drawn with barbed wire, and the reckless abandon of the Old City around the time my mom was there disappeared during the First Intifada. And as folks became more religious, the city changed.

And since the place I usually stay is full of journalists trying to understand Jerusalem in eight days, I had to find a new place to stay.

I did, although my room is really just a glorified supply closet with a single bed and a little sink I had to pee in when the communal toilet backed up after someone (yeah, okay, me) tried to flush a tampon down.

The place is run by a guy named Abdullah, and I'm sitting with him, now.

Some people take up a lot of space, even when they're short, and that's Abdullah. If we were to slow dance together—which we won't—at least I don't think we will—he'd bury his face in my armpit.

But instead, he's making chicken soup in the tiny kitchen of the hostel where I'm staying, and I'm leaning against an old stone wall, painted over in mermaid blue.

But he's this thrumming force of energy in the kitchen—moving between the stove and the spice rack, shaking, tasting, scowling, shaking, and tasting again.

Abdullah has black hair, the same color as shoe polish. He has grey sideburns, and he wears a natty grey moustache. He has a mouth that turns down around the corners easily, and it takes great effort to turn it up into a smile. I've seen it happen for a split second once—I blinked and it was gone.

Cell reception sucks in the Old City. It's like, the closer you get to God, the worse the network and the harder to communicate with humans. But I'm trying to check email.

My dad sent a "*Gut Shabbos*" greeting—he does this every Friday.

The Times of Israel Daily Edition's headlines have gone out—there was another attempted stabbing.

My artist friend Woolf who is 96 and lives near Paris sent me another rendering of Jerusalem. This time, he took a photo I sent him of the roofs over Muristan Square and turned it into a pastiche of paint and newspaper clippings. I smile, knowing that through the thick stone wall on the other side are those same rooftops. I'm actually *inside* the building where I took that picture a few weeks before.

And I am also tired—the Old City is heavy today, each stone weighted by history and memory, and I feel it on my skin as clear as I felt the needle etch the mermaid into my right arm. Some days, it isn't like this, but today it is. Maybe it's the stabbing nearby? Or maybe Jerusalem is just in one of her moods.

Abdullah shakes his finger at me.

"No, not like that," he says, and he motions for me to lean forward, and he squeezes a small hand-embroidered pillow that's between the small of my back and the wall.

"That's better," he tells me.

Abdullah turns back to the stove and stirs the soup—he tastes it. He scowls and he mutters something that sounds like, "your mother's vagina," in Arabic. He adds a dash of salt and a sprinkle of pepper. He tastes again. He shrugs and hisses, "you son of a bitch." He adds something green to it that looks like weed, but probably isn't. He stirs and tastes again.

"Okay," he says.

It smells amazing.

He ladles soup into two plastic bowls—one he hands to me. "You look too tired and you need your strength," he tells me.

What *is* it about chicken soup? My mom used to say that chicken soup can cure everything from a bad cold to a broken heart. She would make it whenever I was sick, or sad, and she added a lot of dill and celery. Her soup was always *her* soup, and it always helped.

I taste Abdullah's soup. His helps, too.

There are no recipes for chicken soup. If you find one in a cookbook, it's bullshit. Don't believe it for a second. Chicken soup is about intuition and memory—it's about what you tasted at the kitchen table on a rainy night when you were seven years old, or when you lay on the couch propped up on fresh pillows and your mom brought it to you on a tray. It's about what you ate in the glow of the Sabbath candles, with your family, safe and warm.

Chicken soup is also an inheritance.

My soup has a lot of dill in it because my mom's soup had a lot of dill in it, which means her mom's soup had a lot of dill in it, and *her* mom's soup had a lot of dill in it. From generation to generation, chicken soup is a legacy as sacred as bequeathing land or gold.

And I can tell you the best compliment I got in my entire life came from my ninety-two-year-old gramma the Passover before she died. We were all sitting around the table eating the soup I had made for the family dinner. My mom had died, and my gramma had stopped cooking after she buried her oldest daughter, so I said I would do it. I started cooking the soup the day before. As the meat cooked in boiling water, I skimmed the fat floating on the top. I added parsnips, carrots, onions, leaks, and a lot of dill. Just like I remember my mom doing it. I made the matzo balls in the soup, small and hard, just like my mom did it, too.

My gramma tasted it, and closed her eyes. When she opened them, they were shining, and the years softened around her face.

"Oh. I'm still here," she said. "For a minute I thought I was back at my mother's table eating her soup."

I felt like I might break open then—both of us, sitting there, my gramma and me, both of us desperately missing our mother's tables and our mother's soup.

Anyway, I guess Abdullah's mother made her chicken soup with a lot of onion and black pepper. It's good.

"Okay," he says to me while bouncing on the balls of his feet. "While you're eating, I want to tell you about a fundamental difference between us."

"Okay . . ."

He wags a finger at my nose, it barely touched the tip.

"You trust people!" he snorts. "You walk in here with your scarf and your bags and your blondeness, and you smile and trust people!"

"Okay, that's true. I believe in giving people the benefit of the doubt," I say as I think about what that's meant in my life—waking up on that dirty bed, getting stoned at Damascus Gate, and the Grey Man in the foul room that smelled like a dying animal.

"Ah, but I am older than you, and I. Trust. No one."

He takes out a ten-shekel piece from his shirt pocket and slams it on the table in front of us.

"Look at this!"

I pick up the coin.

"You are looking at this coin, and you believe it! You believe what it wants you to believe. If you were selling chewing gum or cigarettes or sahlab downstairs, and I gave you this coin, you would take it!"

"Sure."

"You would be *wrong*!" He jabs the space in front of us with his finger, and his eyes dance.

"How come?"

"It is counterfeit!"

He takes out another coin. It looks exactly the same to me as the first.

"Open your hands!" he orders me. I place my hands open in front of him. My left, and my right. He places one coin in each.

"Close your eyes, and feel the difference."

I do just like he tells me. One coin feels slightly heavier than the other—I feel its density. It matters. The other coin, now that I can compare, feels a little lighter. But when I place them side-by-side on the wooden table, it is actually a hair or two thicker than the first coin. I rub each surface with my thumb. The heavier coin feels smoother—the edges softened by other hands. The lighter coin is rough, almost like I can scratch off the palm tree in the middle with seven leaves and the two baskets with dates, and the state emblem and the words "for the redemption of Zion" in ancient and modern Hebrew letters.

The cool thing about Israeli shekel is it's modeled on the ancient shekel that peopled used back in the day. Even the name "shekel" is the same name for the currency they used in biblical times—it's even in the book of Genesis. Hebrew words all contain a three-letter root, and the root of "shekel" is based on the root verb "weighing."

The shekel may have referred to a weight in barley.

I Googled it—and I learned that back in the day when the patriarchs and the matriarchs were milling around, the shekel may have been worth 180 grains.

The ten-shekel piece and its evil almost-twin that I'm holding in each hand are Israeli New Shekels—but they bear the traces of those ancient coins that were used thousands of years ago.

"Now look at this coin!"

He points to a tiny mark on the heavier, smoother coin. I look closely just to the right of his shiny fingernail at the little emblem for the State of Israel with the word "Israel" written beneath it in Hebrew.

"Do you see that? This means it is a real coin! Now look at the other one!"

There is no emblem. No "Israel."

"This! Is! Fake!" He snatched it from my hand and slammed it down on the table. My chicken soup ripples in the bowl.

"Don't spill!" he says, and he grabs a napkin and wipes around the bowl even though there's nothing on the table.

"Don't spill and trust no one!" he says again.

I take another bite of the soup. "It's really good."

I close my eyes for a minute, and think about my mother's dinner table.

She did this once—lived in the Old City—years ago, in 1967, after the Six Day War, when the Israeli army crushed the Jordanians and took control over all of Jerusalem, when Jews could return to the Western Wall for the first time in decades. I wonder if she ever lived here.

"Okay, I know the soup is good. It is my mother's soup. Now, let's talk about you. So you are writing this book. And I want to tell you a story about me. You know, I am a Muslim. I was educated in a Muslim school here in the Old City. I prayed five times a day, with my father and my brothers—my brothers are scum, now. Except the one who is dead. We never speak ill of the dead even though he was a liar and a *thief*!"

Abdullah nods and sways.

"I will explain to you why I trust no one," he says, rocking on his heels.

"So, I was a Muslim, and I trusted my teachers. I listened to them when they told me gay people are disgusting! They are taboo! I believed them!"

I put my spoon down and watch him. His hands shake. His little grey moustache quivers.

"I believed this all my life, *all my life*, I swear to God. And then so much time passing, so much time believing, so much time listening to the things the imam told me about the sins of men, and what they do, and I grew up—but it took a long time. I work many years here and learn many people's stories, and they all sank in like water through the sand. I was the sand. The truth was water. Do you know what I am trying to tell you?"

"No," I say. I don't blink. And I can feel something happening in the room as the soup simmers, and steam rises, as Abdullah moves from left foot to right, as the light shines off the mermaid walls.

Little kids from the Jewish Quarter on an afternoon in late summer.

The best part of this winter afternoon was when the ultra orthodox family on David Street greeted all the Arabic speaking shopkeepers with a hearty Yiddish *Zei Gezundt!* "Be healthy!"

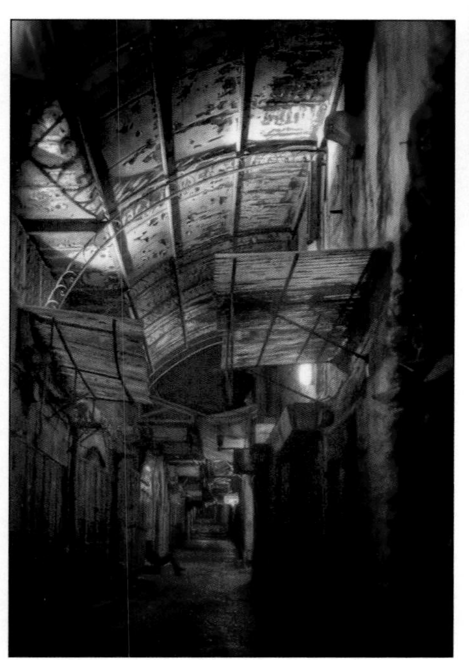

In this little part of David Street, a few hundred steps from Jaffa Gate, the whole world smells like saffron and old coins.

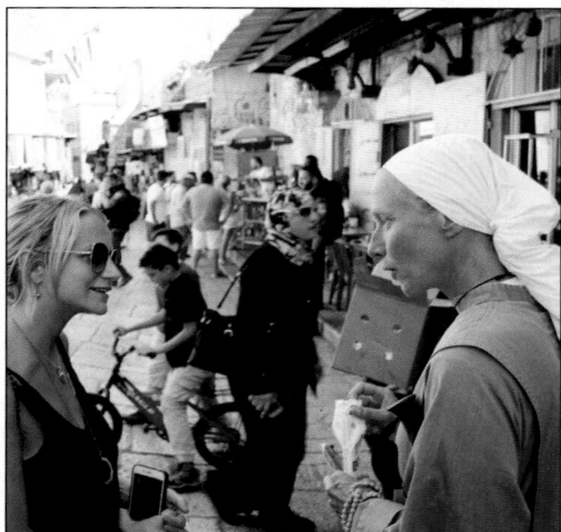

On a hot day in the dregs of summer, a group of us stood in front of the Austrian hospice at the intersection of Al-Wad/Ha-Gai Street and Via Dolorosa and handed out (kosher) popsicles to anyone who would accept. Why? Because it was hot out. And we may come from different cultures and religions, we may speak different languages and see the world through different eyes, but we are all a sum total of chemical and biological processes, and we all get hot. *Top photo by Oren Rosenfeld. Middle photo by David Abitbol.*

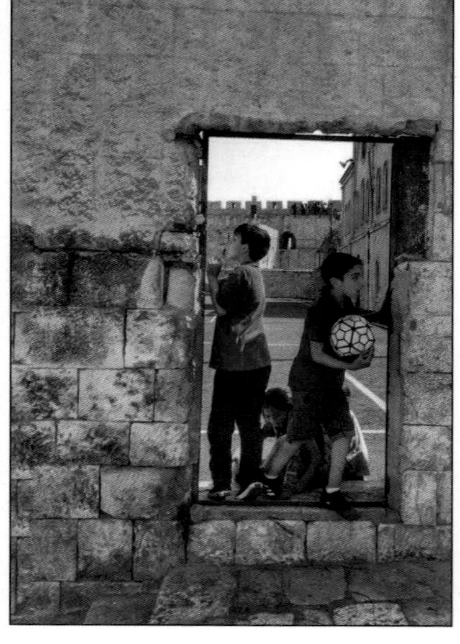

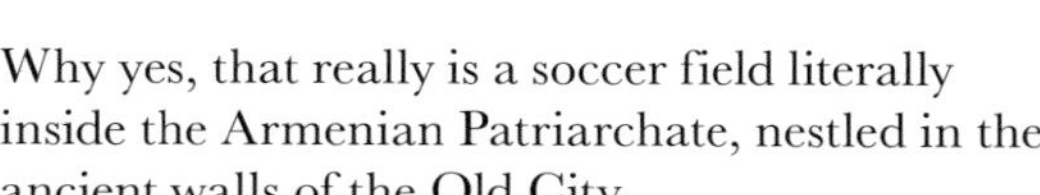

Why yes, that really is a soccer field literally inside the Armenian Patriarchate, nestled in the ancient walls of the Old City.

Here on the Galitzia Roof where the Four Quarters of the Old City meet, you'll see Jewish, Christian, and Muslim kids playing—but I've never seen them play together.

Two brothers walk arm in arm up Via Dolorosa in the Muslim Quarter on a late afternoon in the middle of summer.

Christian Pilgrims from all over the world come to pray at the Church of the Holy Sepulcher, and it gives me goose bumps when I hear them singing hymns.

Jaffa Gate is special to me because it's the entrance to an area that feeds into all four quarters and you see a real cross section of people. It's where I imagine that back in the day the spice traders and the beggars, the whores and the holy men, the healers and the warriors would arrive weary and spent from their long travels over the sea to Jaffa Port and then on the long road to Jerusalem where they would arrive here at this gate and sink to their knees.

When it's Christmas in Jerusalem and you can't find your reindeer.

The area around Damascus Gate is fraught with tension between Arabs and Jews, but if you look for moments of connection, you'll find them. The air smells sweet like citrus and greens.

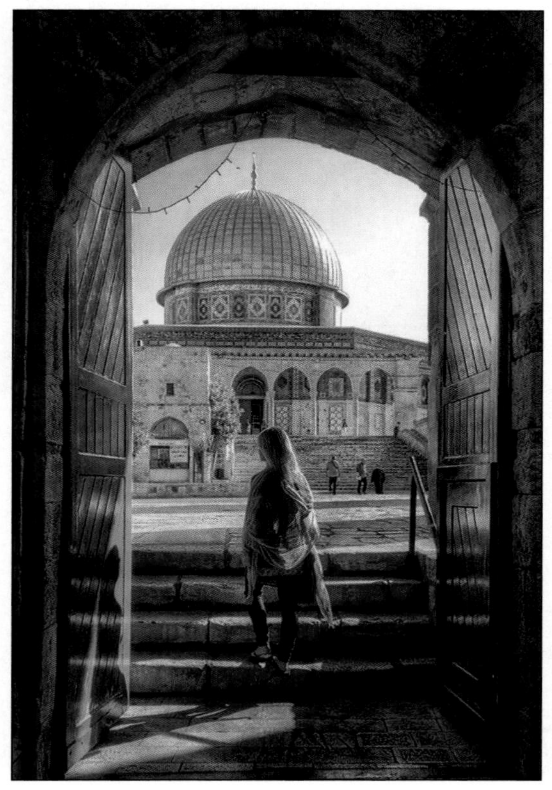

After nearly oversleeping one morning, I stood in the tourist line by Robinson's Arch, handed over my Israeli ID, and promised the soldiers and police in Hebrew that I wasn't there to pray. ("I accept the status agreement Israel signed with the Waqf, besides stones aren't holy—people are.") They let me though. I watched the Waqf administrators feed the birds and cats. I made friends with a black kitten and wanted to take her home but we are already feeding 11 cats and a hedgehog and there is a limit. I accepted a string of bright blue prayer beads from one of the old men standing by Haram al-Sharif. I hung out with Israeli and Palestinian peace activist friends as the sun rose higher. I felt no need to pray, even silently, because that morning my prayers were already answered. *Photo by Aia Khalaily*

This is one of my favorite photos in the whole entire world—the warmth and friendship between the sisters makes me smile.

This is my favorite spice merchant in the Old City—100 grams of zatar for 3 shekels? The best. I love how it smells here—like standing in my grandmother's kitchen.

The Butcher's Market smells like blood and sinew, and on a hot day I hold my breath if I walk through it. But sometimes, there's a welcome whiff of citrus.

Just inside Jaffa Gate, and look: I made a new friend!

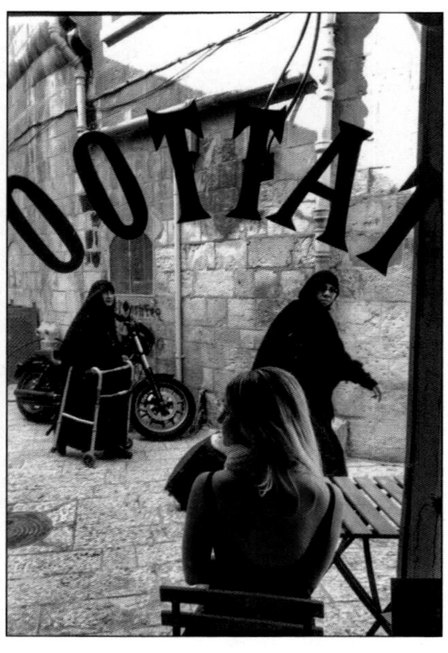

Hanging out with the Tattoo Artist while he inks another friend of mine, and yes that *is* a Harley Davidson in the Old City. *Photo by Bernice Keren*

Jerusalem is a layer cake in stone. While I walked down Habbad Street past the shops and bread stands, toward Arafat Hummus, I looked down at the ancient street below. This is the Cardo, and it runs north and south, and 1500 years ago, it was Jerusalem's Main Street right through the "heart" (cardo—like cardiac!) of this ancient city.

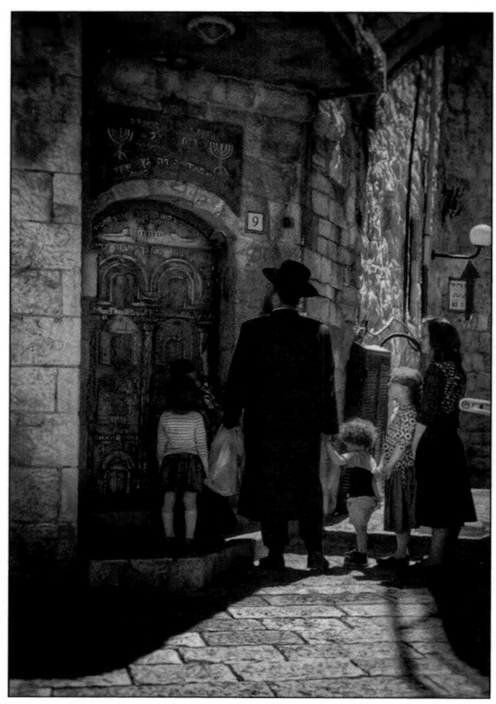

I have a thing for cool doors, and this one in the Jewish Quarter with the gates of the Old City carved on it is one of my favorites. This gorgeous family seems to agree.

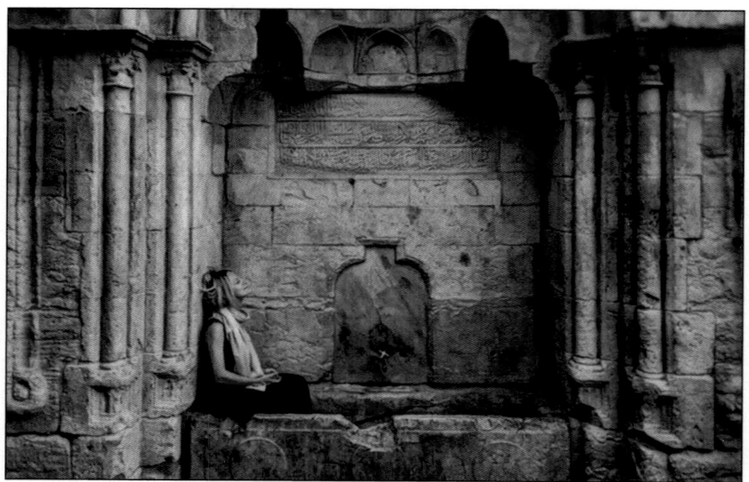

The Archaeologist says this structure is named Sabil Tariq Al Wad. Which makes sense because it's on Al-Wad/Ha-Gai Street—my favorite street—in the heart of the Old City in Jerusalem. The basin was built in the 16th century by Suliman the Magnificent, who reused earlier stones built by the Mamlukes and Crusaders. It also includes an ancient sarcophagus as a water basin. In which I am sitting. Which is maybe a little creepy. *Photo by David Abitbol of Jewlicious (used with permission)*

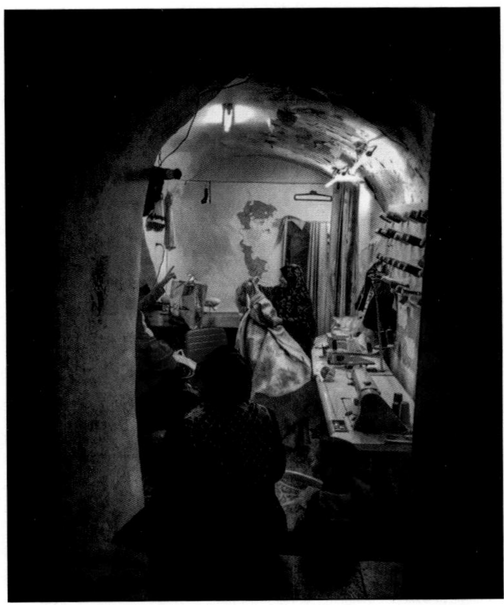

I was walking past the seamstress in the Muslim Quarter at dusk—these women were sighing and smiling over a freshly made dress in soft peach satin. And it made me laugh to see this little boy scuff his feet and mutter under his breath and try to pry his mother away while she and the others gazed at the dress. My son would do the same. Young Grasshoppers have much to learn.

Just inside Damascus Gate, there are these women sitting on the stone and selling the fresh growing things from the village outside of Jerusalem. The thing about it is you can tell the seasons by what they're selling. In the winter, it's bitter greens. They bring almonds after the first rains. In the late summer, there are juicy figs. And today, it's sage and mulberries. And it's the best.

This is St. Mark's street on the seam between the quarters. It's just above David Street—a loud and clanging place—but because of the thick stone, this street is nearly silent. Down the path is the metal staircase that leads to the roof of the Four Quarters—my favorite roof in the world.

There is a special staircase through the Ethiopian section of the Church of the Holy Sepulcher that leads to this little roof where members of the Ethiopian Coptic community have their homes, and I love this blue wall.

Here lies the remains of Hezekiah's Pool (Hebrew: והיקזח תכירב, Brikhat Hizkiyahu), also known as the Pool of Pillars, or the Pool of the Patriarch's Bath (in Arabic: Birkat Hammam el-Batrak كرطبلا مامح ةكرب).

Once it was filled with sweet water—the bottom hewn from stone, a reservoir that nourished the Holy City. It was fed from the Mamilla Pool just outside of Jaffa Gate, one of the three reservoirs constructed by Herod the Great during the 1st century BCE by an underground conduit which still exists, even now. And now it's empty, desiccated and fetid in the summer. In the winter when the rains come, it smells like copper and old moss. Plastic bottles and Bamba wrappers float in shallow pools.

But that blue door though. That blue door right there, do you see it? I want to go through it. That door is everything.

I was sitting on the Galitzia roof where the four quarters meet, and I made a new friend. *Photo by Karen Brunwasser.*

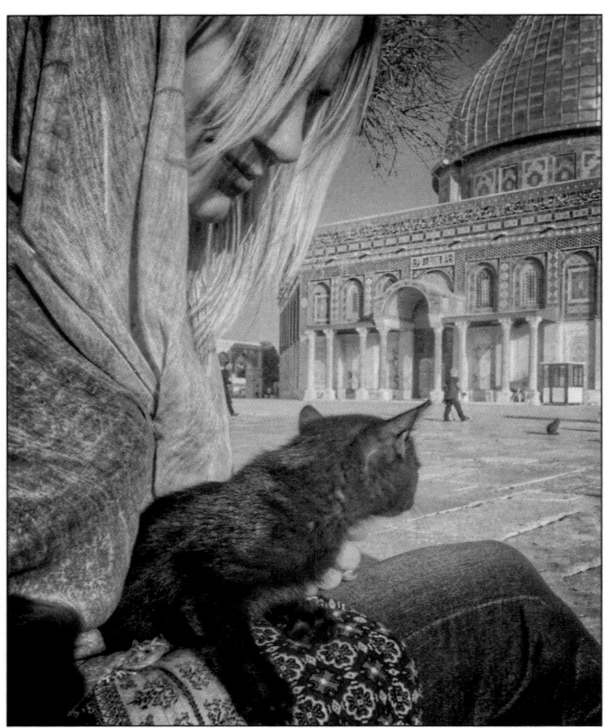

Each morning there are these guys who put bread and scraps of food out by the Dome of the Rock and the cats come and feast.

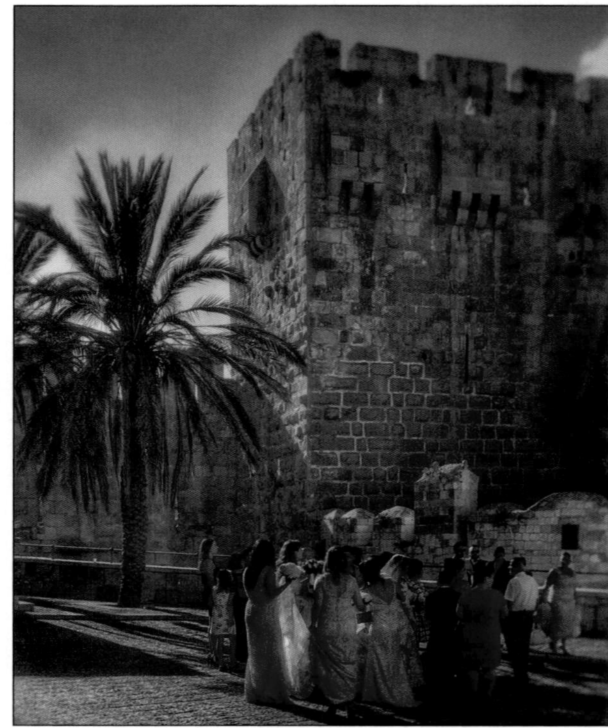

Family and friends from the Armenian Quarter gather near David's Citadel to celebrate an upcoming wedding. I love all the pretty dresses.

A Jewish family just inside Jaffa gate heading toward the Jewish Quarter.

A Muslim family just inside Damascus gate inside the Muslim Quarter.

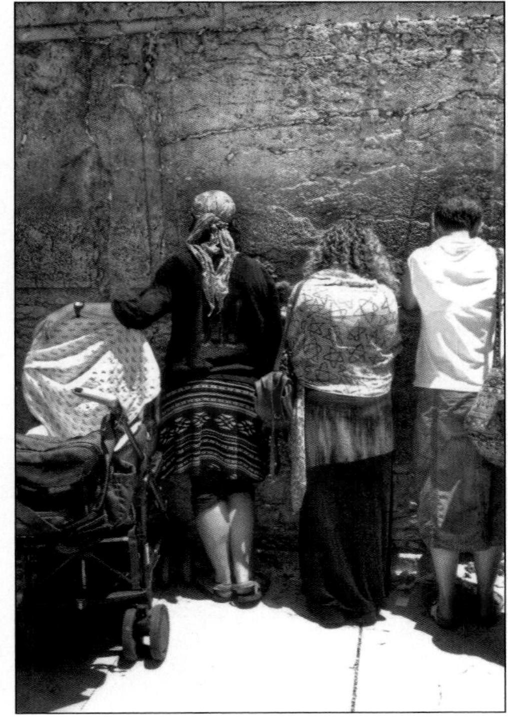

On the 9th of Av (in the summer) Jews from all over the world come to the Western Wall to mourn the destruction of the First and Second Temple in Jerusalem. According to Judaism, it is the saddest day of the year.

I took this picture (on the left) during a time of escalated violence in Jerusalem when there were frequent stabbing just outside Damascus Gate. Can you spot the military sniper? But sometimes, Damascus Gate looks like this (photo to the right).

A beautiful night during Ramadan—the fast is ending and the streets are steeped in the fragrance of chicken and rice and saffron. Contentment.

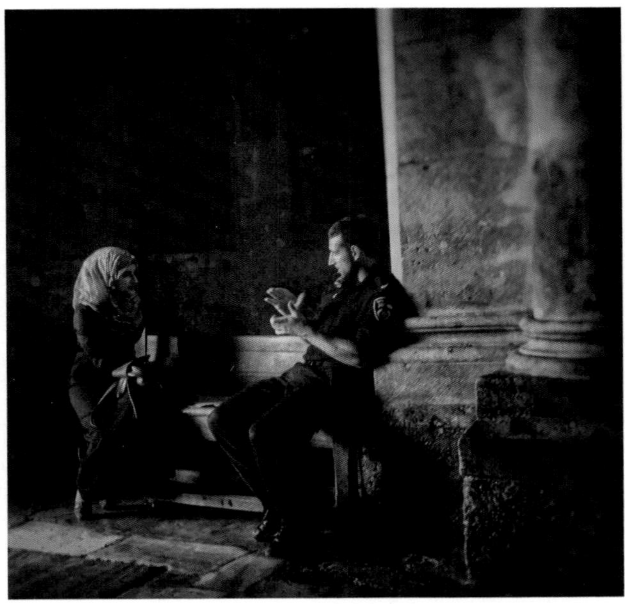

Late afternoon in the church of the Holy Sepulcher, and the light is perfect.

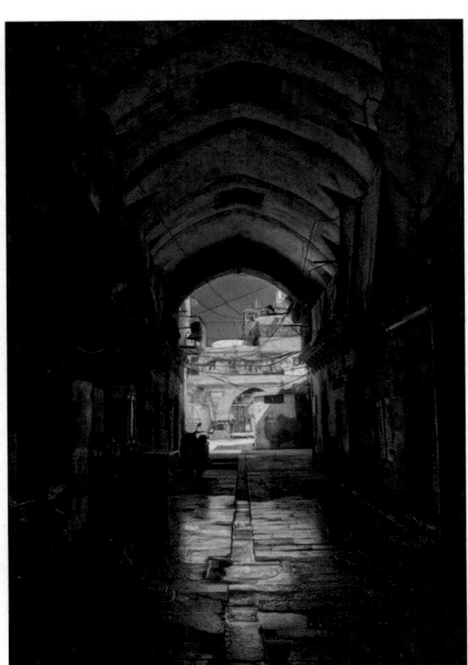

A rainbow of laundry hangs to dry on a hot summer morning in the Muslim Quarter.

There are giant hollyhocks literally growing out of the roof where the four quarters meet. The mural in the back over my shoulder was painted by Israeli and Palestinian peace activists.

This little slip of Western Wall is tucked away a few hundred paces from the Wall we know in pictures. It's tucked away from partitions, and from politics, from selfie sticks and self-righteousness. And here, away from the crowds and all the tsurus, here I feel something stirring through me when I place my palms on the stones: the steady beating of my determined heart. *Photos by Rob Eshman (left) and Ralph Buck (right)*

The best was when I showed my favorite roof to my kids.

My daughter imagines Jerusalem.

"Well. I turned sixty. Such a birthday is sixty. I turned sixty and I woke up, I swear to God, on that first morning, and I said to myself, 'Maybe I don't hate gay people so much. Maybe they are not so taboo. Maybe I am actually gay!'"

I dropped my spoon. The soup rippled again.

"Don't spill! This soup is too good to waste," he says. "So yes, I am gay. I go to the LGBT center in West Jerusalem, and I talk to people and I make a lot of friends, and I like to go clubbing in Tel Aviv! We can go sometime!" he dances a little to show what he can do.

"Wow," I say to him. "That's amazing. But, Abdullah, you just spent the last few minutes telling me not to trust anyone, and how to tell if someone is trying to cheat you out of ten shekels. So how am I supposed to know if what you are saying is true?"

"Ah!" he says as he turns off the soup, turns to me and smiles for more than the blink of an eye. "Everything about me is the truth. After all the lies I have heard, and all the stories fed to me, I live the truth. Except for my hair. I dye it dense black—you know, for the boys. But that is all. My hair is the only thing not true about me. The rest you can trust."

I think about Jerusalem and her rooftops, and my mother, and I think about the others who are struggling to understand this place earnestly. I think about the mermaid on my arm and what she means, and I think about my children and the life I'm giving them. I think about all the leaps of faith I've taken, and the ones I've seen others take, about the things I've lost and the things I've gained. . . . And I'm glad for every misstep, for every mistake.

So I trust him.

The next day is bright and sunny, piercing blue, and I walk through Muristan Square with my coffee and one of those twisty bagel thingies with zatar. My cousin's husband has just died suddenly out of nowhere—one minute he was driving and the next he was slumped over the wheel of his truck.

I know what it's like to lose someone I love, but when my mom died, we had time to say goodbye—we had time to hold her hand and kiss her face and measure each breath and listen for any words she might murmur in that halfway space where she hung between worlds.

My cousin didn't get that, and she's grieving, and she's hurting, and just thinking about the pain she's in makes me want to curl up into a little ball.

I can't be there to make food and hold her hand or do the laundry or clean her house. But I can do the only thing I can from here, from Jerusalem, from this spiritual epicenter. I can pray. And since my cousin is Christian, I am heading to the Church of the Holy Sepulchre to light a candle for her, and for her beloved, to pierce the darkness the only way I can.

But instead of that timeless scene of candlelight and stone, there is something different happening in the Church of the Holy Sepulchre.

There are fluorescent lights in the main room, and there's dust in the air, and the squeal of drills and the clanging of hammers fills the sacred space and drowns out the singing. The candles are still burning, and the nuns flow past dressed in white, but, there's also Yossi with the drill.

Maybe you don't know this, but for centuries the different Christian churches have been fighting over the Church of the Holy Sepulchre. It gets ugly, even bloody.

They literally fight over inches of stone—over who gets to light the fire, and who has the right to pray in which corner. And people have died over it, too. Look carefully, and you'll see blood, indelible in the stones.

But recently, the different churches have pulled together to restore Jesus's burial shrine. So now the church is a mess. The sound of hammering and buzzsaws fill the church. There is scaffolding and the smell of paint, instead of incense.

"I wish there wasn't this mess," I say out loud to myself as I walk inside.

Two Border Police Officers I know, Gal and Idan, are standing nearby and hear me say this.

"What are you talking about?" Idan says. "This is the first time in a long time different Christians have agreed on something and worked together. The Church has never been so beautiful."

"Nu? What are you? A tour guide? Stop Jewsplaining."

But it is true. The church *is* beautiful. They're fixing and rebuilding and making it stronger, and I think about my family, and my cousin, my heartbroken and hurting cousin and how her life must seem in ruins now. And I light a candle and hope that she, too, will find the courage to rebuild.

It starts out like our usual afternoons together. My daughter is hot and sullen (so am I).

It's been a long day at a desk, learning for the first time while sitting, looking at a chalkboard, getting used to these new rules, the culture of first grade.

Her backpack is almost as big as she is—bright pink with the Little Mermaid on it. She struggles to put it on, so many books for first grade. And burdened with so much homework, now, already.

There are things she'd rather do, like build a pirate ship out of Styrofoam, tinfoil, and duct tape, or ride her bike down the dusty road and into the fields, or watch TV—and there are things I'd rather do, and things I *need* to do, too—but with a sigh she heaves the backpack to the floor, unzips it, and takes out her reading homework, and with a sigh, I sit down beside her while she opens her book.

I think about this song my gramma used to sing to me, a song she learned from her mother. This was my Great Gramma Sarah, who kissed a stranger on the roof in the Old City, and it was a Yiddish song that spills out of a primal feeling, a dark and shining shard of memory that isn't mine alone—a memory from a time not long ago at all when we ran from the Cossacks, when we hid from the Nazis, when we were vulnerable, but defiant. They might smash our holy kiddish cups. They might burn our holy books. But we would keep learning our holy language, so that we, in turn, could pass it on to our children as the greatest legacy of all.

A fire burns on the hearth and it is warm in the little house. And the rabbi is teaching little children the alphabet.

Remember, children, remember, dear ones, what you learn here. Repeat and repeat yet again, komets alef-o.

Learn, children, don't be afraid, every beginning is hard. Lucky is the Jew who studies Torah. What more do we need?

When, children, you will grow older you will understand, how many tears lie in these letters and how much crying.

When, children, carry on the exile, in torture, you will gain strength from these letters. Look inside them!

Learn, children, with enthusiasm, as I instruct you. The one who learns Hebrew better will receive a flag.

"*Kamatz Alef Ah*," my daughter says in Hebrew. My little girl, born in exile, is learning the language of our ancestors, the language that has sustained us as a people until this moment, right now, today.

My little girl born in exile has returned home to learn the language of our future.

And suddenly, it doesn't feel like a burden anymore, these hours spent learning.

We are here, my children and I, by choice, in this complicated, crazy, wonderful country. We are here, by choice, a link in the chain from generation to generation. We are here, by choice, a living testimony to all who have come before us, and a place marker to all who will come after.

And learning how to read the language that has sustained us throughout too many years in exile is not a burden. It is a blessing as sweet as the apples and honey we will enjoy together to welcome in the new year.

"Blessed are you, Eternal One, who has given us life, sustained us, and brought us to this moment in time," I whisper.

And I bend over the page, with my daughter, and we learn together.

Summer

BOUDEWIJN, THE BELGIAN journalist, and I are heading out of the Old City for a drink at my favorite restaurant, Crave, near the shuk. It's the watering hole—well, more like a wellspring where people from all over Jerusalem come together to eat really good food, listen to really good music, and hang out. Boudewijn and I are on Jaffa Street. (If you walk out of Jaffa Gate and hook a right and just head straight, you're on Jaffa Street, a two-day walk to the port city of Jaffa. This is part of the ancient road that connected Port City to Holy City.)

Boudewijn and I have just crossed that invisible line between East and West on the way to Crave, where almost everyone is speaking Hebrew and English all around us.

The last few weeks have been tense—more stabbings, more arrests. Jerusalem has her rhythms, and you shouldn't get too comfortable when it is comfortable because it will change in one little heartbeat.

"You know, Sarah," Boudewijn says. "It's funny, I swear I've seen some of these same guys before," he says, gesturing to all the young men walking around and laughing with their friends. "I've seen them up Saladin Street, and in Silwan, and in the Old City, and they look so angry and so old. They really look old. And also, a little scary. But right now they look like funny, flirty, silly kids. They could be my younger brother."

I think back on the Waqf officials I see eating hummus each morning. They're grim and tense when they're on the Temple Mount and working and I avoid them, but when I see them hanging out and dipping their pita into the warm paste, they're the guys I sit with and say "good morning," to, and "what's up?"

What is it about Jerusalem that does this to us?

I love Jerusalem best in the morning when she's still naked, before the shops are open and the scarves and jewelry cover the stone. And I like to watch her wake up and get dressed while I drink my jasmine green tea from the balcony overlooking Jaffa Gate. Or earlier still, from the Western Wall, when sacred time meets sunrise, and Jews and Muslims pray together although separately behind their glass walls at the brink of sunrise.

The Jewish prayer, the Amidah, at the Western Wall reaches that moment when the voices are lulled and people stand in silence while their faces press against the ancient stone, and the call of the muezzin echoes from Al-Aqsa in one shared space, but separate, and the sun crowns over the ancient stone as the birds take flight.

I love Jerusalem when the streets are cool and empty, when cracks in the stones look like veins through skin, pale blue and thrumming, when the Old City opens its eyes.

We all wake up the same way. There is no difference in how we groan and turn off the alarm clock, or how we press our body against the person next to us, or how we pee and wash our face and go to the bathroom and make coffee and eat a simple piece of bread and cheese. The nuns at the Sisters of the Rosary, and Um Ibrahim over by Damascus Gate, and Michael Malconian who paints tile next to the Armenian church, and Reb Mottle, my friend who hands out the red string by the Western Wall—they all wake up the same way. One eye, then the other. Maybe a smile, maybe a sigh. One foot, and then the other, touches the floor. Our mornings are so similar, but behind our walls, how would we know this?

But Jerusalem is never fully naked. Even when the stones are bare, there on the ground, she is covered in trash, in the leavings of all four quarters from days of living. Ismat's cigarette butts, or Nadim's pomegranate rinds, or Reb Mottle's empty water bottle, or Michael's dried up tubes of paint—it hurts to see the place we all call holy treated like this so carelessly.

I mean, come *on*—we all say she's ours, so why don't we take care of her?

My kids go to a school where they teach the students about taking care of the environment. Every afternoon, they have to pick up trash around the schoolyard and water the vegetable patch and feed the chickens.

And my son and daughter are really into it, and they take it seriously. Once when I was sitting on my porch at sunset smoking the one cigarette I give myself every week, my son came over and wagged his finger in my face and said, "Nu, nu, nu, Mama, don't leave a cigarette butt on the ground. That's hurting the environment."

I didn't have an ashtray with me, so when I was finished, I ground it out on the ground, took a sip of Goldstar, and closed my eyes. It had been a long day—hell, it had been a long year. But the cigarette felt good, the beer felt good, and the sound of the birds was so sweet.

I heard the sound of a throat clearing.

"Hmm hmm."

I ignored it.

"Mama?"

"Yeah, baby?" I opened one eye and my son was glowering at me.

"Mama, you left your cigarette butt on the ground."

"Don't worry, I'll pick it up and throw it away when I go inside."

"Do it now, please."

"Dude, I'll do it later."

"No, you are hurting the environment. Do it now."

I had a choice. I could pull rank and be all like, "I'm the grownup and if I want to leave a freaking cigarette butt on the ground, I will until I'm good and ready to throw it away."

Or, I could concede that my son was right. Because he *was* right.

I bent down, picked up the cigarette butt, and threw it away.

"Done. Now, I wish you would show as much enthusiasm for cleaning when I ask you to straighten up your room."

Half the week, we live like this in our little village. The other half of the week when they're with their dad, I'm here in the Old City.

I haven't brought my kids to stay with me here yet—for many reasons. The first one is there's a fine line between being crazy and being stupid, and maybe it's a little crazy to live for a year in the Old City during these days of great tension when the calm here dances like an angel on the head of a pin. But I don't mind being a little crazy. That's part of what it means to be a journalist—you take yourself to the edge, close enough to look over and feel your heart stammer, but with enough sense to know when to back off.

Bringing my Hebrew-speaking kids to live with me full time in the Old City when the emotional temperature of this place can go from freezing to boiling isn't crazy. It's stupid. And I don't want to be stupid.

Still, I want them to see this place. I want them to understand this space in a way that gets under their skin so they can grow with its complexities instead of being afraid. As the news gets scarier and scarier, I need for my kids to see and understand that there are other kids just like them in all four quarters of the Old City, who go to school and share snacks and take judo classes and skip rope and collect stickers and draw in little sketchbooks.

So I spoke with Abu and Um Ibrahim over the first Iftar dinner when Ramadan had ended for the night, and the moon was a fingernail sliver in the sky.

"I want to bring my kids to visit," I said to them. "And I have an idea. I want the kids to come with me and clean a little bit around Jerusalem. A friend of mine has this initiative called Cleaning the Hate where everyone who loves Jerusalem is encouraged to show that love by cleaning up garbage."

I waited. And I wondered if their eyes would roll so far back in their head that they'd swallow them.

"*Wallah!*" Um Ibrahim said as she took a bite of maklouba. "That's really nice. Your kids are actually going to clean up garbage?"

"Yes. Do you think Yusef and Luba could come with us?"

"They don't speak Hebrew or English."

"That's okay. We'll manage."

I waited. And wondered if they'd say no. Did the idea of their two youngest Palestinian kids and my two Israeli Jewish kids cleaning up the garbage lining Al-Wad street seem . . . ridiculous? Offensive? Even dangerous?

But I've learned in moments like these to wait. Sometimes I talk too much and try to fill in the spaces of silence with explanations and apologies, when that only builds a wall.

"Let the game come to you," my mother used to say. "Just wait and let the game come to you."

So I sat there and ate my maklouba.

I took a sip of water.

Um Ibrahim said something to Abu Ibrahim in Arabic staccato. He shook his head.

I ate another bite.

She said something even faster, her voice pitching a little higher. He sighed.

I drank a sip of water.

She pointed her finger at him, and he rubbed his eyes.

He murmured something back, and heaved himself up from the chair.

"Okay."

And so here we are. We spent night in the Old City together, the kids and I. We got back to Jerusalem when it was dark, so they haven't seen her except in fluorescent light and shadow, and I want them to really see her when she wakes up, the way I like her best.

The call of the muezzin wakes them up at dawn.

"That's pretty!" my daughter murmurs as she turns over and goes back to sleep.

"Oof, turn down the volume," my son groans, and he buries his head under the pillow.

I look at their sturdy bodies in bed with me. I kiss them each on each cheek, and their breathing slows, rises and falls, rises and falls while Jerusalem lifts with the sunrise.

We get out of bed for real when the room turns pearly grey. Like little kids all over each quarter, they rub their eyes, and clear their throats, and fight over who gets to pee first, and brush their teeth, and eat bread with Shahar chocolate spread and I have my coffee. We sit on the balcony and watch Jerusalem get dressed.

This is the first time they've seen her like this and their eyes shine. "Why is he wearing a dress?" my son asks as a priest walks below our balcony.

"Why is she wearing a towel on her head?" my daughter asks as a woman in a long purple robe floats past with an elaborate pink-and-gold turban on her head. Abu Muhammad is below and he looks up and waves. I smell fresh bread that they sell by Jaffa Gate, and George walks by carrying a huge wooden plank laden with it on his head.

"Look babies, that's the same bread we're eating!"

"No, it isn't. Because we ate our bread and that bread is still there," my son rolls his eyes.

"That isn't the point!" my daughter says. "Why do you have to argue about everything?"

"Because that's part of being Jewish! It's how we learn!"

A guy in a knitted yarmulke tosses a paper cup toward the trash, it misses, and lands on the ground.

"Oof," my daughter says. "I see we have a lot of work to do."

"Are they nice?" my son asks.

"Who?"

"The other kids."

"Yeah, they're great," I answer.

"How old are they?"

"Yusef is ten and Luba is eight."

"Like me!" says my daughter.

"Oof not fair. Why aren't they *my* age?" my son asks.

"Do they speak Hebrew?"

My daughter is drawing. I look over at the page and see she's drawn herself and her brother and two other kids—the boy, taller than both, and the girl her exact same height. The two girls in the pictures are holding hands.

"No, they speak Arabic—and they might understand a little Hebrew and a little English."

"How are we supposed to know what they're saying?" my son asks.

"It doesn't matter. We're there to clean, and *doing* something important is sometimes more important than talking," my daughter answers.

He sticks his tongue out at her, she sticks hers out at him, and we head downstairs into Jerusalem at her best.

Some days with my kids are great, and some days suck. Like today, when the rooster living in the Muslim Quarter—as loud and obnoxious as the one who lives two houses away in our village—wakes me up with his crowing when it's still dark, and an asshole mosquito is all like, "Catch me if you can, suckah," while I'm trying to go back to sleep, but by the time I smash him dead against the wall the call of the muezzin ripples across the Old City, and by the time I finally fall back asleep, the alarm clock's beeping, but then *the kids* don't want to wake up. And when they do, it's a WWF-style wrestling match to get them into clean underwear, shorts, and t-shirts, and their too-tight sandals pinch too-pudgy feet that have somehow (overnight it seems) grown too big, and, well, crap, I don't have enough in the bank to buy new ones at least 'til next paycheck, which is eight days away. And my daughter is scratching her head, which means the lice are back, and there are no clean pairs of Spiderman underwear to take to preschool for my son, and the milk tastes funny, and the Cheerios were left open so they're stale, and we're out of toilet paper, and "Mama! It's Number 2!!!" and the kids can't find that one special doll hidden in the mass graveyard of stuffed animals on the floor, and then it's an epic fight because they want the same doll, because, of course.

Yeah, it's been a long day, and it isn't even 8:00 a.m.

And you know what? I miss my mom.

I dreamt about her last night, and I can't remember what it was, but all I know is it made me sad, and I just miss her.

My kids are grouchy, too. They're dragging their feet, and even though it's only morning, it's hot out, and we're sweating, and they're thirsty and they're hungry, and "Mama, my toenail hurts" and "Mama, you never buy us chocolate milk," and I turn around and snarl, "*What do you want from me?*"

My daughter tosses her head and storms in front of me toward the gate when we see Abdullah. His hair is glossy black, "dense black," even the sideburns, so it must be date night. Maybe that's why he's in a good mood.

"Good morning! Good morning!" he says to us. "How are you?" he asks my kids by name.

My kids shuffle their feet and ignore him, and this is where I start to lose it, because "Kids, when someone you know asks how you are, you look them in the eye and answer them and make sure you always add 'and how are *you*?' because no child of mine will act like a selfish asshole who doesn't treat others with the same dignity and respect given to them."

Abdullah bends down to their level and he looks my daughter and my son in the eyes.

"How old are you today?" he asks.

"You know that already," my son says. "I'm seven, and she's eight."

"No," Abdullah asks. "How old are you *really*?" He smiles and rocks back on his heels, and my kids shift their weight from one foot to the other.

"Three," my son answers.

"Two," my daughter answers.

"Well, that explains it," Abdullah answers. "And it's hard to be two and three on a hot day like today."

My kids smile.

He turns to me, wags his finger and winks. "And you, Mama? How old are *you*?"

"Thirty-five."

"No . . ." he says long and drawn with a twinkle in his eye. "Just like your son and daughter aren't seven and eight today, I don't think you're really thirty-five today. How old are you *really*?"

"Fine. I'm six."

"Well, I think the best thing to do when you're two and three and six is have ice cream on a hot day."

"But . . ." I interrupt, because it's still morning, and we have to catch the light rail back to the bus, and we have a long walk ahead of us, and it's hot, and suddenly, I am very, very tired, and *oof,* the walk seems like it'll take *forever*, and I'm *six years old*!

But by the time I opened my mouth to answer, Abdullah had bought us three cups of sorbet and a bottle of water, which is exactly what my mother would have done for us if she were alive, and suddenly, I'm six in a good way, but still a grownup, happy and giddy—my mother's daughter, and my children's mother—and having a great morning with my kids.

It's Friday—a Shabbat without my kids—and I'm eating maklouba in the middle of Muristan Square with Fadi in a restaurant near the fountain that's lit up with blue lights.

Leila brought me.

"It's so good," she tells me. "My friend Fadi works at this restaurant and he makes maklouba, and when the restaurant closes, all his friends come there to eat. Want to come?"

Um, yeah!

Maklouba is amazing. It is chicken and onions and celery and carrots cooked with rice in a big old pot, and when it's done, you take the pot, flip it over, tap it, and remove it from the rice. Some joke that it's one of the pillars of Palestinian identity, along with resistance, struggle, and connection to the land.

We showed up at the restaurant after closing that first time. Fadi was waiting for us outside—he's about our age, and he and Leila greeted each other in Arabic. She's Egyptian—but she speaks Amiyah—Palestinian street dialect. Fadi is from Ramallah, but he's been working in the Old City since 1997.

He speaks Hebrew if he has to, but he prefers Arabic or English.

"My Hebrew is actually good," he says. "But it's the principle of the thing."

He brings out maklouba and plates for all of us.

"What do you think we are?" Leila laughs. "Tourists? *Americans*?" she pushes the plates aside. "*Halas*, enough. Just give us forks."

We dig into the mountain of chicken and rice and veggies and OMG it was delicious.

The restaurant is hewn in stone, like most of the buildings in the Old City. "When was it built?" I ask Fadi. "Well, this part is Byzantine," he tells me. "But look down here at the base—do you see? These are Romans. Over here is where they tied their horses."

Fadi is an archaeologist and a total history nerd like me, and when he sees my eyes light up, he brings out this box of things he's found sifting through Jerusalem's layers: coins, or beads, a statue of a tiny goddess, and even an Egyptian scarab.

"They're all from here," he tells me. "From right here in the Old City."

That's how friendships start, I guess—a shared interest like old things and old stories. And good food, too.

❖

It's another Friday night, and I'm back again at the restaurant with the fountain, only this time Fadi and I are joined by Mahmoud.

Mahmoud has a broad face and bright green eyes and hair clipped short, the color of steel. He doesn't smile.

Actually, we're sitting in his restaurant, so I've seen him often. And I've never seen him smile.

"I won't shake your hand," he tells me when we meet. "It isn't because you're a Jew or an Israeli, so don't be offended. I won't shake your hand because you are a woman . . . because I am a Muslim man, and we do not shake hands with women that are not our closest relatives or our wives. You know this custom, no? You have it in your own religion."

We do. And over the years of living here in Israel, I've learned when it's okay to shake hands and when it isn't.

He sits down. "Fadi says you are someone who listens."

"I try to," I say.

"Fine. So I am going to speak on behalf of everyone I know here in the Old City because you need to know the truth. Are you ready to listen?"

"Yes."

"Are you sure? You won't like it."

"I'm sure."

I put my fork down and look at him.

"I know Fadi won't speak Hebrew, but my English isn't as good as his, so I will speak it so you will understand me. Until you learn Arabic and then I can understand you."

I nod.

"Everyone on this street in the shuk will smile at you and sell yarmulkes and your IDF shirts and welcome you and say, '*Ahlan WaSalaam,*' and serve you tea. It is our culture to offer hospitality. We learned this from Father Ibrahim. You call Avraham. Are you with me so far?"

"Yes."

"But you have to understand that there is something deeper here for us, and it makes us angry, and that anger is there underneath our smiles and our mint tea," he rubs his face between his large hands and he sighs.

He drops his hands and looks at me.

"Listen: We are not killers, we are not thieves. We don't want to hurt you. But we do have a story, and that story is we were here first, and you took our land and you kicked us out of our houses."

He's staring at me now, and his eyes are boring into mine. The room is silent.

"My father built our house in Bakka. Just south of here. He built it with his own hands, with stones he found, and he shaped each corner with his hands. And he planted fruit trees in the front. And in 1948, the Israelis kicked him out of his house and he fled to Jordan with my mother who was pregnant with me. He had to keep her safe, so he took her and they ran away. But after the war, he came back, and his house was still there but it was gone. Jews were living in it. His house. The house he built. The house he built for my mother and for me, and for my brothers. I want my house back. Do you understand?"

"Yes."

"After he died, I went to the house, and an Israeli was living here. 'This is my house,' I told him. 'No, it is my house,' he told me. 'My family has lived in it since 1948.' 'And my father built it before 1948,' I told him. 'I'm sorry,' he said, and he shut the door. He's sorry. That's all. But what will that do? Will he leave the house my father built? Will he leave the house I was supposed to be born in? Will he leave *my* house? *My house*!"

Mahmoud's voice breaks, and his eyes are shining.

Fadi stares at his hands.

"Are you still listening to me?" Mahmoud asks. "I want my house back. That's all. I want my house back. Do you understand?"

"Yes. I do."

And then, for the first time, he smiles. And then he lets me see the tears spill over and down his face. This big, gruff man with grey hair and grandchildren. He's sitting there and crying in the restaurant he owns, and I can see him as he must have been—a little boy moving from place to place, the key to the house his father built hanging from his mother's neck. A little boy yearning with his parents for those fruit trees and those stones and that piece of land that was theirs just weeks before he was born.

And I do understand. I do. Because part of being Jewish is knowing what it's like to yearn for our homeland. And year after year after year since we became a People, we've been telling the story of how we were slaves in Egypt, and how with a mighty hand and an outstretched arm God delivered us out of those dire straits and into the Promised Land—the land of our ancestors. Those same deserts we walked, and the wells that nourished us, the fields we tilled and the homes we built, we have been yearning for this for thousands of years—and even still, when all around the world we say at the Seder, "Next year in Jerusalem."

And it's the same for Mahmoud, too.

During the Seder, at the peak of celebrating liberty, it is our custom to pour out wine when we read the Ten Plagues so as to diminish our joy as we remember the suffering of the Egyptians.

And next year on Passover, I will pour wine for Mahmoud, too. Because while I celebrate being free in Jerusalem this year, he isn't. And he is yearning for this as much as I am.

Musa sits on a low stool and strokes the skinny cat next to him. The cat's name is Kitty, and she is brown and grey, and she reminds me of the cats that I watched "disappear" in the bathtub that terrible night. Kitty has peridot eyes that are half open, and she vibrates beneath his hand and nuzzles his wrist. She kisses his thumb, then curls up again, while he scratches behind her left ear.

"She's sad," he says. And he looks sad when he says this.

"Why?"

He rubs beneath her chin.

"I just gave away her kittens. She had five of them—each as beautiful as the moon, but I can't feed them. Once her milk was gone, and she started biting them, it was time for them to leave."

"I'm sure you found them good homes, though."

"Yes—my nephew's daughter took one, and a Jewish family over in Talpiot took two, and the others went to some of the neighborhood kids . . ." He looked down at the cat as she dozed beneath his fingers. "They all went to good homes, but she doesn't know that."

The cat opens her eyes.

"She only knows that she had her babies, and she loved them, and now they're gone. She's always sad the first few days. The first few days are the hardest."

"Have you thought about fixing her? You know, so she can't have more babies?"

"Yes," he said while the cat stretched and then curled again beside him. "But then she wouldn't know the joy of having more again."

My mom loved cats, and she always had one sitting with her in her office when she worked. She called them "her familiar." My mom was mystical like that—she was also my muse. When I went away to university, and I had essays to write, my mom would help me write them. I'd tell her the assignment and she would hang up the phone to think about it, and then she'd call at one or two in the morning after her late night cigarette in a cloud of smoke and inspiration, and I would stagger groggily to the computer, turn it on, and type out her notes.

It was like when I was little and she would wake me up in the middle of the night smelling like cigarettes and patchouli, and we would drink tea and eat cookies on our porch in Venice while the fog horns moaned out at sea. Except we were six hours drive away on different ends of the state, and so much of my life I kept secret from her. But not my school assignments.

It was how we stayed close, even though she was dying, and I was pretending everything was okay.

One of the best papers I ever wrote with my mom was for a class in folklore with the late professor Alan Dundes, and it was about psychological implications of the Binding of Isaac, the story where God says to Isaac, "take your son, your only son, who you love" and offer him as a sacrifice.

This is according to the Jewish narrative and later the Christian narrative, which was informed by the Jewish story.

But the Muslims have their version, too. And according to their story, Ibrahim was ordered to sacrifice Ishmael, the son born from his barren wife's handmaiden, Hagar.

This is where the roots of Abraham/Ibrahim divide, where brother is pitted against brother, and we, the cousins a millennia later, fight it out.

It was one of her favorite biblical stories, and that's why she wanted me to write a paper on it.

"Sarah," she said. "The Binding of Isaac focuses on Abraham and the test of faith. But what about Sarah, Isaac's mother?"

The biblical Sarah was old and barren and had given up hope of ever having a child when three angels disguised as weary travelers came to her husband's tent in the heat of the day and promised that she would indeed bear a son.

And Sarah laughed.

Her laughter rose from that wellspring of desperation and of sorrow at not being able to conceive. Her laughter rose from the ludicrous notion that at such a withered age her womb would be opened. Her laughter rose from a place of disappointment, of bitterness, and yet, she laughed and didn't cry out in anger and frustration.

And the promise was true, and she did give birth to a baby, Isaac.

In the next chapter, Abraham takes Isaac to Mount Moriah to sacrifice him.

Now that I am a mother, it makes me literally sick to my stomach to think about the agony and dread the biblical Sarah must have endured, not knowing that God's command to her husband to sacrifice Isaac, and her baby boy, her only child, the light of her life, was only a test of faith, and that he would be returned safe and sound.

In the next section, the biblical Sarah is dead. Many Torah sages say she died of a broken heart, never knowing that Isaac lived.

I get it. Just like I now understand what Jono meant when he said he would kill his ex-wife for taking their children from him and disappearing if he ever got the chance. I get it. And I curl inward when I think about my kids and something happening to them, and I still have nightmares about that day when the sirens blared and we barely made it to the bomb shelter fast enough, and wouldn't have if it weren't for the help of some neighbor who scooped my son up at the last second before the rocket fell.

And I think about my mom. She was forty when I was born, and I was unexpected. She and my dad had tried to have a baby for years, and it didn't happen. In fact, she was already five months pregnant and convinced she was going through The Change when she went to the doctor for hormones.

"Well, you aren't going through menopause," Dr. Rubinstein told her.

"Then what's wrong with me?"

"Nothing is wrong with you. You're pregnant!"

And mom laughed. She laughed from that wellspring of desperate wanting, and then she hopped off the exam table in her little paper robe and danced down the hall.

No wonder she loved the story of the biblical Sarah and Isaac.

And I love it, too, although it hurts me to think about it.

According to Judaism, this very spot where Abraham's faith was tested, where his son Isaac was nearly slaughtered by his father's hand, and where the echo of Sarah's cry would have pierced the clouds and shaken the hills, is the Foundation Stone—the axis mundi, the center of the world—and it is inside the Dome of the Rock on the Temple Mount.

According to Judaism as well, beneath is also our Holy of Holies, and it's the sacred spot where we once had the Temple, before it was destroyed by the Romans—broken, burned, piece by piece, and all of Jerusalem smelled like roasted human flesh.

This was the beginning of the diaspora when the Jewish people were scattered to the winds, and again, it is the place we long for when we say, "Next year in Jerusalem."

My Muslim friends have a different story.

They say it is the very spot where Ibrahim's faith was tested, and where his son Ishmael—not Isaac—was nearly slaughtered by his father's hand. This is their third holiest site, and it is the place where they believe Muhammed ascended to heaven.

Anyway, today, the Dome of the Rock is beautiful, standing where the Temple once was. It is a masterpiece of blue and white and green mosaic tiles, and it reminds me of ripples in the ocean, of sea foam, of waves all the way out in the middle of the raging desert.

On top of it, the gold dome gleams in the sun and shines in the moon, and for folks all around the world—Muslim, Christian, and Jew—it is part of the Jerusalem skyline.

And it's a political and religious flashpoint, and I guess we should talk about it.

Temple Mount—*Har HaBayit*, *Al Aqsa*—is the bleeding heart of the Old City, and one of the causes for renewed conflict between Jews and Palestinians.

Temple Mount has different names because when a city is cleaved to by those who think they love her best, you choose your own names to identify and possess.

And right now, the place is fraught with tension. Muslims can enter the Temple Mount from one of several gates—down quiet roads, or a busy shuk, there are many veins and arteries flowing to the Temple Mount. Non-Muslims can only enter during specific visiting hours on specific days through a heavily guarded entrance. No laptops allowed. And the police who check our bags can decide that they don't want to let you in.

Many Palestinians believe that Jews are trying to take their holy site away from them, and while we say we aren't, there *are* Jewish activists who go up to the Temple Mount to pray, which they're forbidden to do under a status quo agreement between the Israeli government and the Waqf.

"We have the right to pray on our holiest site," they say.

But it's like throwing a match into a pile of dry leaves sprinkled with gasoline.

"*Allahu Akbar! Allahu Akbar!* God is great! God is great!" the Palestinians chant over and over and over, and some throw stones, and shove, and the police and army swarm the compound with tear gas.

Both Jews and Muslims yearn for this place, and every year it becomes even more polarized and rife with tension. And that's the part that hurts. It's beloved by both sides, and it reminds me so much of the story of King Solomon where two mothers claim the same baby.

"She's mine!" says one woman.

"No, she's mine!" says another.

"I know," says King Solomon. "Why don't we cut the baby in half! And each of you can take a piece!"

"Yes," says the first woman.

"No! Don't hurt her! She can have her!" says the second.

And from the second woman's answer, King Solomon knew that she was the true mother, and the other wasn't.

Jerusalem is like that baby, only neither mother will relent. And Jerusalem will be ripped to ragged pieces by those who say they love her best.

Today, the whole area is controlled by the Waqf, and yet it is the holiest site in Judaism. And again, it is literally the place where Jews all around the world face to pray—unless you're at my synagogue in Culver City, California in the middle of July for services on the beach and Rabbi Zach says while he strums his guitar, "You know what, gang? We're supposed to face east when we pray, but if we turn east, we're just facing a parking lot and a gas station. Let's face west instead and watch the sun set because that is, like, way more special."

I'm down with that because the world is round anyway.

As I've said, I'm not particularly drawn to shrines. I still feel nothing when I touch the Western Wall. But the hands that placed the stones in the first place were holy. And the hands that touch them today are holy, and that's what matters.

I guess it goes without saying that I don't want to rebuild the Temple that the Romans destroyed. Not even a little.

Because I like who we are: a rebellious group of arguing Jews who stay up all night discussing Big Ideas while candles melt wax into puddles.

And that's who we became while living in the diaspora when we moved from Temple Judaism to Rabbinic Judaism, when we had to because the Romans destroyed the center of our religion.

I *like* that we have no High Priest—because let's be real: we got enough trouble with the Rabbinate in Israel telling us what stores can be open, how to get married, and who is even a Jew. I'm pretty sure that if the Temple were rebuilt, the most sexist, homophobic, noxious dude of *all* would be in charge. Because that's how political power seems to work.

And that won't work for this rebellious Jewess, who will wear what she wants and eat what she wants and kiss who she wants and say what she wants so long as she does her best to be kind and fair and hurt no one.

And my skin and bare collarbone hurts *no one.*

I want to have faith that it would be different, but seriously? Look at the evidence: All I need to do is look down on the Western Wall plaza and see how women are hindered from praying the way they want, *detained* for carrying a Torah, spat on by angry young men. Ain't nobody got time for that.

Not me. Not my kids.

Besides. Have you seen how Israeli contractors build stuff?

The Temple would look like Dizengoff Center, where people literally need a map to get through it without getting lost! We would be trapped for days wandering around with our goat sacrifices. I guess we'd start to hallucinate, and start gibbering—not from the Spirit of God, but just from dehydration.

But let's be real: Shmulik or Pinchas running the project would bring the cheap dry wall, and the whole thing would crumble into ruin after the first rough winter.

Also, let's talk about goats. I like goats. Goats are adorable. Do we really want to go back to a time we sacrificed goats?

So no, I don't want to rebuild the Temple.

When the Second Temple crumbled we proved our strength. The Romans said we wouldn't make it without our holy heart intact, and suck it, Romans, we did.

We became this wonderful, contentious people, loving, striving to be a light.

We took the best of the Temple with us in our blood and bones, and instead of trying to rebuild something we no longer need, I want to take all that energy and effort and just keep on making the world a better place for everyone.

Goats included.

But still. Even though stones and shrines carry little meaning for me, there's something about the Foundation Stone that compels me, that moves me, that holds my imagination and my feelings in its grasp, and I really want to see it.

I want to touch it. It's an irrational feeling, but it makes sense, too.

Because this story we tell about it matters to me, and it reminds me of my mom, and it reminds me of me, too, or the me I want to be because the woman I was named for, my great grandmother, was named for Sarah, and as Gideon said to me outside Jaffa Gate the night after the terrible thing happened in Migdal HaEmek that I can't remember, and just hours before I stood there trembling by Damascus Gate, "Sarah Imenu is where it's at." The biblical Sarah took a leap of faith and left the community she knew for all her life. She ached, she suffered, but we remember that she laughed.

But actually getting to touch the Foundation Stone isn't so easy, because only Muslims are allowed inside the shrine, and burly Waqf officials guard the site, with their arms folded and their legs spread.

Last week at the restaurant, Mahmoud showed me photos of his wife inside the Dome of the Rock. She was all in black, but her face was shining as she touched the Foundation Stone. Her eyes were lipid pools even in the dim light.

"That's one of my dreams," I told him. "I really want to go in there and touch the stone."

Mahmoud looked at me for a long few seconds while I ate my shawarma. "You get to touch everything else around here. Maybe if you get rid of the wall between the West Bank and Israel, maybe if you get rid of the checkpoints, and the different roads, maybe if you give us back our homes and our dignity and our rights, we'll let you touch that stone. It's just a stone, after all. What does it matter anyway?"

I came back today to the roof where I first fell in love with you, Jerusalem. Where I stood with my friends, where we held each other. But I'm alone, and it's cold today, and the sky is shifting every second. Seething, weeping, my beloved, my Jerusalem City in Pieces. Your fault lines shaken, your people thrown to different sides as the chasm deepens. As the rift widens.

Everyone is quiet.

"*Mah shlomcha?*" I ask a soldier.

"Tired."

"*Kif halak?*" I ask a merchant.

"Tired."

I am tired, too.

But I am back on this roof again, the clouds so close just like those stars that summer I stood beneath your sky.

And I still look up, and know that there are those of us across that rift, our fingers barely brushing, still, as we whisper, "I'm so sad."

"I know. And so am I."

Leila and I are having hot chocolate at the Austrian Hospice, again. Okay, *she's* having hot chocolate, and I'm having a beer.

The sun is out, and the birds are singing in the garden, but Leila's eyes are swollen, and her cheeks are blotchy, and I can tell she's been crying.

She touches the mermaid on my arm. She knows why I have it on my right hand: "Jerusalem, if I forget thee, may I lose my right hand."

Her eyes are shining.

"I love Jerusalem as much as you do," she says, and I know that to be true.

She came here by choice, like I did. She could live anywhere else in the world. She could be sipping cappuccinos in a cafe somewhere in Copenhagen, or climbing the Eiffel Tower, or reading a book in Central Park, or anywhere, really, because, like me, she has two passports. Egyptian and Danish, but she's chosen to live here.

"I don't know if you realize this," she tells me. "But the man I'm engaged to is a West Bank Palestinian."

"Yeah, I know," I tell her. "He's from Ramallah, right?"

"Yeah, he lives there now, but no. He's actually from Jerusalem. He was born over near the Nun's Ascent in the Old City. His mom is from the Old City."

"So what's the problem?"

"His parents got divorced, and his dad went to Jericho, in Palestine. And he went with his dad because he was fourteen, and he wanted to be around his dad, so he didn't get Jerusalem residency, like the other Arabs in the Old City and East Jerusalem. He became Palestinian, and he hasn't had any luck getting East Jerusalem residency even though he wants to live here now."

"I'm so sorry," I say.

"He came here for a while secretly and ran a juice stand outside Damascus Gate. His Hebrew is perfect. It's even better than his Arabic because he grew up in Jerusalem. But he dated this chick who ratted him out to the police, and they came to arrest him, so he's on their list, and it isn't safe for him to come back here without a permit."

"Even though he was born here," I say quietly without a question mark, because I get it. I think about other friends of mine who planted olive trees that were uprooted, and I also think about my mom and my great grandmother who loved Jerusalem with such hunger, such ferocity that somehow they passed it down to me, and it's in my DNA.

It's my birthright to be here, and walk freely here, and I'm so grateful for that, but Leila's fiancée, who was *born* here, can't.

"So that means if I marry him, I have to move to the West Bank. And I'll lose the right to come to Jerusalem without special permission."

"I'm so, so sorry."

"And I love Jerusalem just like you do. But I love him, too. And the laws here mean I have to choose."

"My great grampa was in the SS," Franz says to me while we share a spliff at midnight in the garden of the Austrian Hospice, and I spit out the swig of wine I just took from the bottle.

A nice boy. Blond hair and Harry Potter glasses, and in deepening shadows, inside a building that's nearly two centuries old, looking out on a skyline that's far, far older, we could be at Hogwarts.

The whole place smells like apple strudel even though the kitchen's empty. That and nard oil . . . sweet and musky.

There are a few of us sitting there on this ledge in the garden—they're all eighteen. I did the math, and they're young enough to be my kids—but it's midnight in the Muslim Quarter and the only light is from the moon, a single Hanukkah candle, and the green mosque across Al-Wad.

I'm high and I can't stop laughing at the Hanukkah candle. It's the kind that Chabad gives out in the shuk—but it's spring already. But that's okay. In Jerusalem, nothing and everything makes sense, you take what you get, you look up, up, up at the sky, do a fist bump, and say thank you.

But back to the Nazi thing.

"Is that why you're here?" I ask him, because that would make sense. Some kind of *T'shuvah*, as we say in Hebrew—literally, a turning back and making amends.

"I'm here because in Austria we have to join the military—just like Israeli kids. And if you don't want to do the military, you can take part in national service, so that's what I'm doing."

"Right, but why *here*?"

"Maybe because of my great grandfather. But also because his son married a Jewish woman from Poland, which I guess makes me Jewish somehow, right? Even if I had a Christmas tree?"

"Do you think of yourself as Jewish?"

"No. But I don't think of myself as Christian either. Identity is a stupid construct. So is religion." He pauses. "That's why this whole mess in Jerusalem is so stupid."

"How do you mean?"

"It makes no sense. This place has no natural resources. No oil. No gold. It isn't really on a trade route. It's just desert. And yet, people are killing each other over it, over all this land no bigger than a fingernail in the grand scheme of things, over some kind of claim to dead land, over a stupid story about how God gave this land to someone and not someone else. It fascinates me. And I can't understand it. So that's why I'm here."

He takes another long drag on his spliff.

"What's your excuse?" he asks me.

"I guess I'm trying to figure it out, too."

I'm not the only one who's lonely sometimes, and looking for love.

Last week, I went out with a vegan guy I met on Tinder. He was eating hummus in the Christian Quarter when we both swiped right.

He's from Canada and he's a peace activist, one of these guys who meditates and went to India and lived in an Ashram for a year. But then he almost punched the waiter in the face because there was butter on his baked potato, so yeah.

The guy I dated before told me that he loves Jerusalem the most in the whole wide world—he loves everything! The stones! The fragrances! The people! Except for all the Arabs. "They're like insects," he told me. I asked for the check.

The guy *before* that picked me up by Jaffa Gate with this great song in Arabic bumping on the stereo. "Awesome song," I told him. "You like it? It's one of Hamas's songs—it's about liberating Aqsa from the filthy Zionists!"

Rivky sits across from me at a bagel place in the Jewish Quarter. She's got long blonde hair curled at the ends. It's a wig and it's made from real hair, and "it cost three thousand dollars," she tells me, twirling the ends. "It's real blonde hair from several women," she says when I ask.

Rivky has seven kids, all under nine. She's married to a rabbi. She wears heavy black stockings even in the summer, and blouses buttoned up to her dimpled chin. Her breasts are high and firm and full of silicon, and I know because she let me touch them. Rivky hasn't had sex with her husband in three years.

"He just doesn't want me anymore," she tells me, a tiny thread of mascara running in a slim black river from her eyelashes. "I don't think it's me. I just think he doesn't like sex. He was never that into it."

I dated someone like that once, and it's hard.

"The thing is, I love sex," she says. "I started masturbating in seminary. All the girls did it, and anyone who says different is a liar. The thing is, it would take me too long to, you know, and I was the only one brave enough to buy a vibrator online. I remember picking it up from the post office by Jaffa Gate—not the one that used to be in the Rova," she says, referring to the Jewish Quarter. "It was purple, and really cute, and it was in this plain brown package, and I just put it in my purse with my prayer book, and went back to my room and spent the next three days there, and it was bliss."

She takes a bite of her bagel, and wipes her eyes with a pink tissue. She opens a little mirror and reapplies her lip gloss. Her mouth is full and soft. I know, because I've kissed her.

She lowers her voice.

"I had an affair once," she tells me. "Just once. Last year. One of the Yeshiva kids who came for Shabbat. He was 19. I was 29. He shtupped me behind the Austrian Hospice at one in the morning. Right in the Muslim Quarter! We could have been murdered! I made him pull out, and he got angry at me for making him spill his seed, which he said was a sin. I can't believe I did something so terrible, so risky, so *wrong*, and yet so . . ." she pauses and her cheeks flush. "So *life* affirming!"

She lowers her voice.

"A lot of people are happy," she says to me in a whisper. "And some days, I am too. I have my beautiful children, and I go to pilates. But I'm lonely. And the community doesn't help because we're all supposed to be happy, and if you aren't, you can't tell anyone. Marriage isn't a guarantee you'll be happy. Look at me." She buries her face in her hands and weeps right there in the middle of the bagel place in the middle of the Jewish Quarter where everyone is looking but pretending not to.

It didn't occur to me when we moved here that I would be raising Israeli kids, but I am.

And I take that seriously. But it isn't easy, because Israel is not a normal country. Let me explain.

We cut each other off on the highway, but will help a total stranger carry her baby carriage onto the bus.

And we will steal your parking space at Mamilla Mall, but will pay for your coffee when you're five shekels short.

We scream at our neighbor because her dog peed on our geraniums, but we will be the first over with a basket of food when her mother dies.

We cheat on our taxes, but give to charity.

We are cynical. We are optimists.

We litter in the park, but plant trees.

We draw lines. But reach across them.

We can be tough. We can be brash. We can be rude, but we will bring down joy with tambourines and timbrels, and we will join hands and dance the Hora with total strangers.

We have all grieved over someone killed horrifically and violently—a parent, or a lover, or a friend, or neighbor, or God forbid, a child. And this place is so small, so close, so *fraught* that even if we haven't felt the violence touch our own families, we still feel it, and you can see it in our eyes when the news broadcaster announces, "a bus has blown up in Talpiot." "There has been a car ramming at Pisgat Ze'ev." "There has been a shooting in Tel Aviv." "A young girl was stabbed to death in her bedroom in Kiryat Arba."

And it's true, we are a strong and mighty nation, but we have never known a day of peace since we came into being. We are panic-stricken, guilt-ridden, and that fear does something to us, and you can see it on the roads and in our lines and in our homes and when we vote.

We are messed up and PTSD-riddled, angsty, angry, handwringing, nail-biting people.

But still, we stay out all night and swim in warm sea water, or argue with our friends on crowded corners, or drink whiskey until sunrise, or dance until our feet hurt and then stop for a minute and keep on dancing. We choose life with our arms and eyes wide open.

We are full to brimming.

We are not a normal country.

We are in pain at times, but joyful still. We make mistakes, and struggle, and defend. But we keep on moving on that spiral through history because this is where we are meant to be, and we are a miracle.

❖

"Is the Mayor of Jerusalem nice?" my son asks me.

"Some people think he is," I answer.

"Do you like him?"

"I don't think he treats all his constituents fairly."

"What does that mean?"

"It means he and the government treat Jewish Israelis better than Arabs."

"So he wouldn't be nice to me?"

"No baby, he would be nice to you. Why do you think he wouldn't?"

"But I'm also an Arab," my blonde, blue-eyed, Hebrew-speaking Jewish child says.

"No dude, we are American-Israeli Jews."

"I know. But I thought we are also Arab."

"Why do you think that, baby?"

"Because you are teaching me words in Arabic like '*salaam*' and '*kifek?*' and you listen to Arabic music all the time, and you read that Mahmoud Darwish guy's poetry to us."

"Okay, but learning another language and culture doesn't mean we belong to it. We are Jewish, baby, with an amazing and rich history."

"Well, I *know* that. But why can't I be both?"

I have no words.

It's afternoon, and it's been quiet for a few weeks and I take the kids to see the macaw that lives on Via Dolorosa, only he flies away, breaks out of his cage, and flies high, high above the Old City, a speck of color, before he disappears.

"He's probably dead," my son says.

"No, he's just free," my daughter says.

"Maybe he's both."

We see Abu Ibrahim and he shows us some old Roman coins that smell like dirt and gives my son a penny from 1932, and we see the Fabric Merchant and he lets my kids touch this fabric embroidered with Salahadin in battle that he smuggles from Palmyra, Syria. It's the softest thing I have ever touched, and it's spun from silk and gold.

I wonder what happened to the family with the loom and the skeins, if they're still in Palmyra, or if they got out, or if they're dead.

But it's afternoon now, and we're hungry, and my son walks into this kosher pizza place in the Jewish Quarter—really good pizza, and everyone eating and working there is dressed accordingly: the dudes are wearing yarmulkes or black hats, and the women are in long skirts and scarves.

Shabbos has just ended and they've got good pizza.

So my son bellies up and in his sweet clear voice asks, "May I have pepperoni, please?"

"No, this place is kosher."

"Oh. Okay. May I have pepperoni . . . *Be'ezrat Hashem*, with the help of God!"

"You mean, *Inshallah*," my daughter says.

"I mean both."

If there's one thing I've learned about counting the minutes and the hours and days and weeks in the Old City it's that time is measured in Shabbat sirens and church bells. And in the call of the muezzin that echoes off the stone. It's also measured in the different holidays and festivals—like in December, during Hanukkah, how the Jewish Quarter lights up with a million candles from the oil lamps placed in windows and outside. My eyes fill with tears when I think about all the long, bare years when we Jews had to hide our Hanukkah menorahs when we lived in the diaspora and it wasn't safe to be Jewish, and how now we light our Hanukkah menorahs and place them prominently outside, lighting the darkness for all to see.

Or how, in spring, the Christian pilgrims carry palm fronds through the Old City on Palm Sunday, singing and chanting and waving and dancing. I remember how one priest grabbed my hands and twirled me around the courtyard of the Church of the Holy Sepulchre, laughing and singing, until my scarf slipped and he saw the Jewish star necklace around my neck, and he asked, "Are you Christian?" and when I said "no," he dropped my hands and walked away, but how others took my hand anyway, and we waved the fronds and rejoiced.

Or, how now it's Ramadan, the Muslim holiday where the world is turned upside down, and evening is morning, and morning is night, where you feast from when the moon rises until dawn, and then fast during the day.

The nights are a time to celebrate, to eat with family and tell stories. The men smoke their cigarettes or their hookahs, and the night is soft. But during the day—especially when Ramadan falls during the dregs of summer, and everyone is hot and tired—the sun is pitiless, and time ekes by too slowly until the sun begins to set and the air fills with the smell of good things to eat.

I'll tell you the truth; it isn't simple to stand here on the last Iftar as Ramadan ends at Damascus Gate.

It's a beautiful night, and the gate is strewn with fairy lights, and it's so beautiful, but also so fraught, here on the seam where people of all faiths and faces cross each other without seeing, until violence erupts.

Right here in this spot, my friends get frisked for no reason other than the fact they're Palestinian walking home through Damascus Gate, and right here in this spot too many soldiers and police officers and everyday folk have been stabbed or shot and maimed and murdered, which is why the soldiers here stand with their guns pointed, especially just a week and a day after a Border Police Officer gave her life defending herself and her city.

Right here in this spot, I was hit with stones.

And yet, just inside the gate, in the Old City, families sit together as the fasting ends and a gentleness falls and softens everything, and still the soldiers stand with their guns out because they might have to shoot or die if they don't, and a young boy walks with his dad to the mosque with a gun barrel pointed at his back. And he grows up learning to ignore it or go mad, and he clasps his hands behind his back in defiance, and all these things are true and still the lights twinkle. I breathe in, and the air is sweet and smells like popcorn and Nutella crepes, and Orthodox Jews walk out after Havdalah and back to Mea Sharim, and Muslims walk out after evening prayers and up toward Salahadin. And from this spot, this broken spot, I see why the old ones call this the Gate of the Welcoming Embrace, even though it feels like we might suffocate. Except tonight is a night of one thousand stars, and Ramadan is over for some, and a new week begins for others, and it's peaceful, and maybe if we have another night like this and then another and another it all stacks up, and maybe we can have even another. But even if we can't, I'll keep coming here to try to see the beauty in all the everyday folk who just want to break their fast or break their bread quietly while the night unfolds and all the little stars threaded across the gate shine.

I still haven't touched the Foundation Stone, but I'm back on the Temple Mount with my friend Oriah.

Oriah means "light of God" in Hebrew.

Oriah had another name once, but we don't use it anymore. I've tried to forget it, because remembering it is bad luck they say, but it's hard because I knew her then when she had this other name, before the cancer riddled her lungs, again, after only a few too short years reprieve.

In Judaism we have a tradition—if you're sick, like really sick, you change your name. It's supposed to trick the angel of death into giving you more time. Actually, when my great grampa was a little boy he had diphtheria—he turned blue and cold in his mother's arms.

"He is very sick," the doctor told his mother.

"Change his name," the rabbi said. "It may give him a second chance."

So they erased his name and gave him a new one—Chaim. Hebrew for "life." He recovered.

He went on to marry my Great Gramma Sarah after she showed up in Chicago, after her love affair with the man on the roof.

So name changing in our world is a thing.

Oriah is still sick, but fighting hard. She's my age, which is really young for lung cancer. Obscenely young. But really, cancer is always obscene and always comes when you're too young, whether you're thirty-six like Oriah or sixty-three like my mom. You're always too young to sit there in the quiet room while poison fills your veins and nurses check your vitals, while the beep of machines measures time, counting down, tick tick tick tick tick. You're always too young to sit with your kids as my mom sat with me that brisk November day and say, "I have cancer."

And Oriah is way too young. She's got kids—eight of them. Her oldest is preparing for his Bar Mitzvah, and Oriah hopes she'll be there for it. Her youngest hasn't even started preschool. He's still in diapers.

And she *looks* young with the brightest blue eyes I've ever seen, lashless now. She has a smattering of freckles over her nose, and hair the color of cinnamon. At least she used to before it fell off.

She covers her hair, just as my mom did. She's been covering her hair since she got married—it's the custom for most Orthodox Jewish women. But now she has no hair, except little tufts that stick out sometimes beneath her turbans or her scarves or her pink baseball hat with the rhinestones around the brim.

But her favorite hair covering is a pink-and-silver wig that glitters in the sun. "Take *that*, cancer," she says. "I'll keep shining no matter what."

Oriah and I grew from the same earth in Southern California, we both like the color pink, and we both write, which is how we met. But we've chosen different worlds. She lives in a religious community in the craggy hills just outside of Jerusalem where the year is measured in Sabbath candles and fasting days. She sleeps in a sukkah in the fall and searches for bread crumbs with a candle during Passover cleaning. My year is measured differently. My kids and I spend Shabbat having dance parties to Red Hot Chili Peppers, Dr. Dre, and Edith Piaf. Sometimes we watch *Fiddler on the Roof* on Friday nights, not keeping Sabbath, but reveling in our history and our culture. We light Hanukkah candles and buy fresh flowers during Passover, because it's spring.

And at first she and I didn't get along. I thought she was too rigid. She thought I was too flakey. But cancer does things to people, and when she got sick again, she reached out—mostly because she had learned that my mom had died of cancer.

"I can't imagine what it must be like for my kids," she wrote to me. "Can you help me understand what you felt when your mom got sick?"

It's a question I couldn't answer—still can't, because even though she's been dead all these years, my feelings keep shifting. They ebb and flow—some days it's easier, and some days it sucks so hard I have to stay in bed. Even still, after all this time.

And I still haven't forgiven myself for what I did to her that afternoon when I pulled her scarf off and left her standing there in the fading light, her head stark beneath the soft tufts of silver hair while all I heard was that keening wail.

But now Oriah and I are connected, because cancer does that to people. It softens edges, humbles, and draws you closer if you're lucky.

It also can kill you.

And this morning Oriah texted me while I was drinking my jasmine green tea on the roof overlooking King David's Tower while the air was cool and sweet and the sun was crowning over the entrance to the shuk.

"Will you take me to the Temple Mount?" she wrote with the praying hands emoji.

And right now, with so much tension radiating from the very heart of the Old City, the Temple Mount is the last place in the whole entire world I want to go.

"Why make it worse?" I tell people when they ask if it's safe to go.

"But don't you think Jews should be allowed to pray up there?"

"Sure, but we aren't right now. There's a status quo agreement between Israel and the Islamic authority, and I respect that."

"But isn't it okay to go during certain hours if you don't pray?"

"Yes, but I don't want me being up there to seem like I'm trying to stir things up."

It depends on who I'm talking to—with secular Israelis, or people visiting from abroad with no connection to the ancient stone, they agree with this answer, and we go out for hummus at Abu Shukri or maybe a Taybeh beer at the Austrian Hospice instead.

But for many Jews like my friend Oriah, the Temple Mount should be back in Jewish hands.

Hell, I know some people who are even carrying hammers and nails and just *waiting* for the day that the Jewish people can build a Third Temple.

"You're so worried about Palestinian rights, but what about *Jewish* rights?" they'll ask. "This is our holiest space! How can you turn your back on the Temple Mount?"

For me, it's stone. Beautiful stone, gorgeous stone, but stone.

And then I'm sad again. Because I see the cleaving of this place over stone, and it hurts. I think about all the people I know who live in the city, like Abu Ibrahim and his buddies who play sheshbesh until one of their wives calls them in. Or Fadi and Mahmoud and all of them at the restaurant. Or Bracha who hands out red prayer string near the entrance to the Western Wall. I think about Gal and Idan—they're almost finished with their service and soon off to Thailand. And I think about Sharbel, the Druze Border Police Officer with the delicious smile who makes sure that only Muslims go in through the main entrances of the Temple Mount.

"Can we go?" Oriah texts again.

I take another sip of jasmine green tea.

"???" she texts, because I still haven't replied.

And I think about my mother standing in that grey light in her office years ago when I ripped the scarf from her head. And I think about Oriah staring at her phone, wanting this and waiting.

I don't have to go all the way up with her, I tell myself while I take a breath. I'll wait in line at the Robinson's Arch entrance with her, and maybe I'll go, or maybe I'll stay and meet her back at the Western Wall.

I'll see.

"Okay. Let's meet at Jaffa Gate at 10:30."

She texts back exactly eighteen hearts. The number eighteen according to Jewish tradition means "Chai," or "Life." Like my great grampa who changed his name to escape death, and did.

I see Oriah all the way from the stone steps leading up from Mamilla. Her pink-and-silver wig shines in the sun and she waves. I walk to meet her, and she's limping. She had fallen the week before, and chemo just does things to your body—it softens ligaments and weakens your bones, and when you fall, you fall hard, adding insult to injury. Her ankle bends to the side, and she wobbles and winces, but smiles with all her teeth showing.

"Hi!" she shouts, and I run to her and we hug.

She smells like Coppertone sunscreen—the kind my mom slathered all over me before we'd head down to the beach every Saturday. She looks good. Her cheeks are pink from the heat, and *damn* is it hot out, and we're both dressed modestly because one thing Muslim and Jewish religious leaders can agree on is women need to be covered.

I'm covered from collarbone to ankle, wearing the very same black dress I wore when I stood in the stuffy room in front of stern old men with long white beards next to the man I once loved during our Jewish divorce.

"You are banished, you are banished, you are banished," the rabbis had him say to me while I stood there in this very same black dress with my arms out to receive the folded piece of paper that would end our marriage.

And I'm sweating, and I can see Oriah is, too, in her festive pink-and-silver wig, and long pencil skirt, and TEVA-Naot sandals and long-sleeve purple t-shirt. Modest dress and Middle East really don't mix. No wonder even the smallest thing can erupt into a war. We're all sweating and hot and annoyed and ready to come to blows over parking spaces, let alone sacred spaces.

In fact, that last long hot summer my ex-husband and I spent together, we had no aircon, and I wonder sometimes if we would have stayed together if we could have just cooled off.

It's getting close to the time when they open the entrance to Temple Mount for non-Muslims, and they only give us an hour or two. So Oriah and I link arms like little girls and walk down David Street, through the shuk, toward the Western Wall, and she leans on me as we watch ourselves on the slippery stone.

"I brought you something," she says. "For taking me up to Temple Mount. This is so so special to me, and I am so grateful to share this day with you."

My heart heaves in my chest. I still haven't decided if I can make myself go up when I feel it's the wrong thing to do. I think about Fadi and Mahmoud who pray at the mosque every day, I think about Um Ibrahim who is teaching me Bedouin embroidery and Arabic words beyond "thank you" and "please" and "good morning." I think about all my Muslim friends, and what they'll think of me if I go up there with someone who wants to pray in Hebrew.

Oriah reaches into her small leather purse and pulls out a package wrapped in blue-and-silver paper.

"I hope you like it."

I unwrap the slender package and pull out a delicate friendship bracelet—strings in shades of blue knotted and twisted and braided together with a tiny peace sign charm. I slip it on and it fits perfectly.

"I love it!"

"I didn't make it. I asked my daughter to make it for you."

We walk through security at the Western Wall, putting our bags on the conveyer belt and stepping through the metal detector. There's an old woman sitting just beyond the entrance to the Western Wall plaza holding scarves for women to wrap around their shoulders or their legs if they aren't dressed modestly enough. You can walk through with your hair uncovered, but bare shoulders and bare thighs are forbidden at the holy site.

She gives us a nod of approval as we pass, and I think again about those bearded rabbis with the same piercing eyes in the room where I got my divorce.

There's a long line waiting at the entrance for non-Muslims, and we get behind a couple speaking German. Behind us, a group in long purple robes speaks quietly in a language I can't make out, but I like the sound of it, like water moving over stones on a river bank. From a distance we hear clarinets and singing, "*Am Yisrael Chai!* The people of Israel live!" and a joyful band of celebrants dance out on the Western Wall plaza near where we're standing. The men wear yarmulkes and some women are wearing scarves over their heads, despite the heat, and they're floating light over the stones while a red-faced boy on the brink of manhood stands in the center, looking mortified and pleased at the same time.

"Ooh, a Bar Mitzvah!" Oriah squeals, and we watch the processional join hands in a circle around the boy while they sing.

Her eyes light up, and she sways with the music and I do too.

I love faith when it's pure and joyful, and *this* is pure and joyful. Although the boy looks like he would love to crawl and hide under the ancient stone, you can see him smiling too. From generation to generation, at our most awkward we stand before the community and the Torah and become an adult in the eyes of the Jewish world. Before we reach Bar mitzvah age, all of our mistakes are our parents' responsibility, but once we reach that age when we stand before our community and read from the Torah, we take responsibility for our own actions.

I didn't get it then when I was a Bat Mitzvah, and I wonder if this boy just a few years older than my kids with the smattering of pimples on his chin, and braces, and a Spiderman yarmulke gets it. Probably not. Probably none of us do until we watch our own kids grow up and remember being pulled between childhood and adulthood.

A few of the celebrants beckon to the people in line and the man in the purple robe behind me joins in. The German couple takes pictures, while the circle widens and the music swells and everyone shuffle-dances to the side, hands clasped, left foot right foot left foot right foot then toward the boy in the middle . . . "*Am Yisrael am Yisrael am Yisrael chai.*"

One of the celebrants sees us dancing on the sidelines, beams at us, and reaches out and grabs Oriah's hand and pulls her in.

She doesn't hesitate even though dancing with strange men goes against her observance. She joins right in, shuffling from the limp. She reaches for me, and I take her hand, and join the circle.

Left, right, left, right, left, right and in toward the middle, toward the Bar mitzvah boy. She's singing, and her face is glowing, even though she's limping, and even though her cheekbones are hollowed out, and her green eyes have no lashes.

"*Am Yisrael Chai!* The people of Israel *live*!" she sings along as she dances between me and the other man.

And I see how lucky I am that I'm here to see this in the shadow of Temple Mount by the Western Wall plaza, the seat of yearning for our people. And the seat of yearning for another people, too. It's one of those tiny miracles that happen in Jerusalem every second, but we miss it too often because we come laden with our own stuff that makes us heavy, when instead we could feel so light if we just let go and joined hands.

The song ends and the processional heads toward the Western Wall where the red-faced kid with the Spiderman yarmulke will read from the Torah and become a man in the eyes of Jewish law. Oriah is smiling and glowing as she wipes sweat from her brow and reaches into her purse for a bottle of water. She drinks long and deep and hands it to me.

"That was amazing!" she says. "Wasn't that amazing? Didn't you feel HaShem right there?"

I did.

"You know, I'm not supposed to dance with another man," she confides in me.

"Yeah, I know—I was wondering about that."

"Well, he was celebrating a Bar Mitzvah, and celebrating with other people is one of the greatest things we can do, even when it means we're uncomfortable. Honoring his joy is a service to God and diminishing it would be the opposite."

I think about that line while the Temple Mount gates open.

I look at my friend, at her radiant smile, her glowing eyes, shining with love.

Am Yisrael Chai! The people of Israel live.

She reaches for my hand.

"I know this isn't easy for you, dear friend," she says to me. "I promise I just want to feel as close to God as possible today. Come with me."

And holding hands, we go through the gates.

The Map Seller is angry because there are no tourists in Jerusalem.

"It used to be that it would take me nearly an hour to walk from Jaffa Gate to my store," he tells me. "But now, it takes me five minutes. There are no more tourists in the Old City. Everyone is scared."

"I'm sorry."

"The latest tensions," he sighs and looks at the ceiling. "What is it doing to us? It is destroying us. Let me tell you something. All this talk of Aqsa, all this talk of the Temple Mount. I don't care. I really don't care. You can build your Third Temple for all I care. Go on! Build it!" The Map Seller pauses with a twinkle in his eye. "But for God's sake, just build it close to my shop. I could use the business." He winks.

The first time I met the Map Seller was my first time away from home, and I was wearing shorts—blue jean cut-offs, my legs tanned and all scratched up from rappelling down the face of a cliff the day before, and I had my hair lobbed to my chin and super blonde, and I had an IDF t-shirt and no sense of nuance. I was sixteen, and I was with that summer group, and we passed through Muristan Square, and I saw maps in the window.

That was one of the only rules I broke that summer—when I snuck off and went into the shop even though we were supposed to finish our falafel and follow Opher and Gali straight to the Western Wall.

Because maps!

OMG maps!

I'm a total map geek. It started when I was a little girl and my parents gave me one of those relief globes with the mountain ridges and valleys in 3D, and I would trace my fingers over her face. I would close my eyes and spin it, my fingertip poised just over the surface, skimming it like a new leaf over water, until the globe would stop and I would look down at wherever my finger rested.

That's how I learned about the moon face of Mongolia, and the green plains of Tanzania, about the sweet rivers of Ireland, and the cliffs of Patagonia.

That globe was the beginning of a big dream. That globe is why I want to sleep in a forest that smells like pepper and green, by a river always flowing, and float through a city hewn from ancient rock, with thin air blowing from the edge of the Sahara. And why I want to ride camels and swim in deep water even though I'm scared. Why I want to take a train across Siberia and pick jacaranda petals in Eritrea.

That globe is why I don't want deep roots in one place in this earth. I want to see *every* place on this earth and never know that I've reached my final destination until I close my eyes for the last time and see only stars.

And that globe is why I love maps, and why I found the Map Seller. He has the best maps—maps of the biblical lands of Judea, Crusader maps with knights galloping into battle, maps drawn by more recent cartographers who told the story of Jerusalem through each line and each name assigned. He has British maps and American maps. Ottoman maps, too. Maps that showed the Holy Land from the sea. Maps that weren't really maps at all, but drawings of walled-off fortresses with towers. My favorite map at the time had a dragon on the side.

But many years passed—enough that the Map Seller doesn't even remember the times I sat with him that first summer, looking through his stacks of maps, at the different ways that people saw the world back then. Each map is a folktale, really.

After I was stoned at Damascus Gate, I didn't go back for years. When I finally did, I discovered the Map Seller hadn't changed. He sits in the same chair, near the same window. But he doesn't know me, and I don't tell him that he should.

(Oh, the funny things that I want sometimes. Because really, why should he know me anyway? Jerusalem is set in stone, but people flow through like a river, always changing. And yet, I want to be remembered.)

"What *is* this?" I ask, looking at a map in the center of the room.

"This is the Clover Map of Jerusalem," he answers. "She was drawn in 1581."

The map is simple and perfect, a circle with three leaves surrounded by a big blue sea, with a little finger of land at the corner that says "New World." Look closer and you'll see that Jerusalem, of course, is in that shining circle center of this imagined universe, and the three leaves branching from it are labeled "Europe. Asia. Africa." And all around, in the ocean, there are serpents and mermaids, roiling waves, and a ship tossed between Europe and the New World. The world according to 1581. Asia doesn't get farther east than India. Rome shines almost as grandly as Jerusalem at the bottom of Europe. And America? Almost doesn't exist.

This was the way it was in 1581.

"Look how they saw the world," the Map Seller says. "This is my favorite map because Jerusalem is the center, and America hardly even matters!"

And that's why I love this map. Not just for the aesthetic, but for the history it tells, and I keep going back again and again to stare at it, and once, when the glass was removed (and if you promise not to tell anyone), to touch it.

But one day, the map is gone.

"Some Russian oligarch living in Paris bought it. He wants to hang it in his bathroom. That's how it is, sometimes," the Map Seller says.

"I wanted to buy it!" I tell him. "After my book on Jerusalem comes out, and I make a million dollars, obviously." I'm not being serious, and the Map Seller understands.

He laughs. "*Inshallah*, you will be successful."

"Well, doesn't matter anyway. Some oligarch has it in his bathroom."

He gives me sweet tea, and we drink.

But I'm back today to look at some lithographs, and the map is back, too. Well, not the exact same map I touched, but one just like it, and it's like seeing an old friend.

"I see you found another copy!" I say.

"Yes," the Map Seller answers. "It wasn't easy, but we are lucky. There are only a few prints left in the world."

And then I see the SOLD sticker on the left hand side of the glass frame.

"But you've sold it already!" I say, as my face falls.

"Not really," he smiles. "I put SOLD on it so no one would buy it. I'm saving it for you after your book is successful and you have your million dollars."

Today, Jerusalem is crowded, and she's angry and pushing and shoving, and people are shouting and bumping into one another accidentally on purpose. She makes my skin crawl today.

It's breakfast and I'm eating masabacha at my favorite table at Arafat Hummus, warm pita dipped and perfect, and the room fills with Ismat's cigarettes that he chews on hungrily, stopping only to grind one out and light another.

("Know why he does it?" his wife whispered to me once. "It's to drive out the Jews from this restaurant because they're so health conscious! I tell him it's stupid, but it's his way of resisting, and we know it could be worse.")

My eyes burn.

Keshet and I just took her dog for a walk around the Old City. Keshet is wearing a rainbow tie-dye dress, and her cheeks are pink.

"She's such a good dog," Keshet says, patting her head. "She's big and scary looking, but she just wants to be give love." The dog nuzzles her hand and looks at her with limpid eyes.

Keshet speaks to her in Yiddish. "*Gutte vulf, gutte vulf,*" she says.

Outside her front door, she has a little garden full of colored stones—they look like Lucky Charms cereal, except each stone is shaped like a stone, smooth and round. Just like the pills my mother had by her bedside after she died, the ones I swallowed one by one. Pink Hearts, Yellow Moons, Orange Stars, Green Clovers, Blue Diamonds, Purple Horseshoes.

But today, the garden is half empty, more hard dirt and gravel than rainbow rocks, and the missing ones are strewn all over the stones in a little trail toward the steps leading to the Western Wall.

One by one, Keshet picks them up, and places them in her garden and I join her.

"The kids do it," she says. "They take the stones and throw them around the street. I pick them up, and they do it again."

"So what's the point in putting them back?"

"Because slowly, slowly, these kids will see how important these colored stones are to me, and they'll begin to understand that they can't win, that I'll keep picking them up and putting them back, and then they'll stop. But even if they don't, I have to assume they will one day. Otherwise, what's the point?"

I reach down and pick up a purple one—my mom's favorite color—and place it in the garden. Each thing we do matters, even if it's destroyed. We can always pick up the pieces.

Outside the hummus place, the woman smoking a cigarette who looks like my mother offers me a hit when she sees me staring longingly.

"I quit," I say. It's mostly true, except I'm standing there, breathing hers in because it reminds me of those moments with my mom tucked around the corner from my grandparents' house when she would sneak off to smoke and I would come with her.

"When?" she asks.

"When I was pregnant, ten years ago."

"You have kids?"

"Two!"

"I have grandchildren already. Two."

She sucks in smoke, coughs, and laughs. Then coughs again, and laughs a second time.

"Enjoy your time, sweetheart," she says as she grinds the cigarette underneath her shoe. "Enjoy it. It goes fast. Maybe I'll quit, too. Living here is dangerous enough right now."

Rivky is pregnant again, and she rests her hands on her little belly—you'd only notice it because of the way she's holding it, like it's precious. Her diamond engagement ring catches the sunlight with a flash.

We're sitting in Hurva Square and her kids and my kids are chasing the pigeons, and one little dove.

She looks tired—there are blue shadows under her eyes, and even though her breasts are full and her stomach pooching out a little, she looks thinner somehow. Her cheekbones are raised and pointy, and her chin is a sharp triangle.

But she smiles, and her eyes are glowing, and she rubs her little belly, and she sighs.

I offer her a bottle of water.

"I bet you're wondering why I did this to myself again," she looks down and laughs.

I remember how sad she was the last time we met, how she told me that her life feels like a sham, how her husband didn't have sex with her, but, people are complicated, and she looks happy.

And I'm happy for her, but I ask anyway.

"Why?"

"Because this is my life," she says and takes a sip of water. "This is my life. All of it—the good and the bad. And I made a decision to accept it, and never leave it."

"You mean, like, leave your husband?"

"Well, yeah, and also the Old City."

She looks down at her hands and her cheeks flush pink. She's told me about masturbating, about cheating on her husband, about her quiet desperation. I've seen her cry. And yet I've never seen her blush.

"What makes you stay?"

She looks at me like I'm insane, her eyebrows crinkle, and she shakes her head.

"Really?" she asks. "Really? Look around you." She lifts her hands from her belly and gestures in all directions. "Look around you!" she says again.

"Look at this place! I am living inside the ancient walls of Jerusalem—the holiest place on earth, honoring our beautiful and holy history, and I am raising my children here, which is honoring our beautiful and holy future. And I am a link in this beautiful chain, praise God."

She pauses for a moment, and looks down.

"And besides," she says quietly, her voice like the fog, and her hands cradling her belly again. "If I leave, I would lose my children."

She looks up at me, and her eyes swim with tears.

Her littlest son stumbles over his own shoelaces, and he falls to the ground.

"Oy, Shlomo Yitzhak, come here, baby," she calls to him.

He runs over, and she kisses his little knee.

And I look around at the ancient stone around us, enveloping us, holding us, *cradling* us just as Rivky is cradling her belly, just like I did when my babies were growing inside me, just as all mothers do. And I think about all of us who came before and birthed our babies, and all the mothers who have yet to even be born, and how we are linked perfectly and sacredly in our devotion and our love of our children, a beautiful chain of frustration and of hope.

Shlomo Yitzhak scampers off, and her hands return to her rounded stomach.

And then she beams. "Oh!" she says. "The baby kicked!"

It's morning, and I'm looking for some sweet ginger for Rivky who is still feeling nauseous from the growing baby, and for a change, Jerusalem is dancing with a red balloon. Fadi and I meet at Damascus Gate, and we're going to get coffee (okay, and cigarettes) on his way to work and on my way to where I'm staying. There are kids break dancing over the steps—Taylor Swift, then Justin Bieber, then something in Arabic. They're flipping in the air.

Just a few days ago, an old mother ran at a group of Border Police at the gate with a knife—or maybe a pair of scissors—and they shot her dead before she could stab them.

Shortly after she died, the story hit the news: Her son had been killed accidentally by soldiers at a checkpoint the year before. "It was a mistake," they said. But he was dead, shot, wrong place at the wrong time, driving while Palestinian, no excuse.

And his mother, broken, cleaved down the middle with grief, wanted to join him, so she came to Damascus Gate and ran at the soldiers, and they shot her.

I'm a mother, and I'd be lying if I said I didn't understand.

I can't tell if that's blood on the ground, or just a shadow.

"My friend saw the whole thing," Fadi says to me. "You know, the guy who sells oranges? Hatem? He said that she didn't even have a weapon, but she ran at the soldiers and shouted, "*Allahu Akbar*, and they just shot her."

"That's not what the police say, but the whole thing is just awful."

"I wasn't there," he tells me. "Hatem was and I trust him. But even if it's true, and all she did was shout *Allahu Akbar*, I understand why they shot her."

"What do you mean?"

"Maybe they thought she had a suicide vest. Maybe they thought she had a gun. They didn't know, and they're young boys, just a few years older than my son, and I understand it. I would have done the same."

"You would have shot her?"

"If it's your life or her life, wouldn't you?"

I can't answer that. I think about my friend's brother on that bus from Gilo to Jerusalem, newly married, his body blown up in a million little pieces, and his yarmulke the only thing they could find 100 meters from where he sat.

And I think about my kid who will one day wear combat boots and carry guns because that's what it means to be Israeli, and I think about Fadi's kids, too.

Two Border Police walk over with their guns on their backs to the guys selling crepes. They're bigger than the kids behind the stand. The kids look up.

My body goes rigid, and so does Fadi's. I can feel him next to me, poised, tense, just as I am. We're watching but we don't move.

I wonder if the kids are in trouble. I wonder if the Border Police could be, too.

I look at Fadi and the pulse beats in his jaw. His fists are clenched. I realize mine are, too.

Are the kids going to be arrested?

Could one of them pull a knife?

We don't move.

One of the Border Police steps forward, and I want to grab Fadi's hand, but I don't.

"Hey, can we get five crepes?" he asks, handing the kid fifty shekels.

"Sure, brother," one of the kids answers. "No problem."

Fadi and I laugh and laugh until tears fill our eyes.

"Want a crepe?"

"No, but yes."

Today, at the grocery store by Jaffa Gate, after my daughter hissed at me on the walk over, and I snapped back at her for being a little brat, my daughter says, "We sure fight a lot, don't we, Mama?"

"Yeah, we do," I say, and I kiss the top of her head.

"But we also know how to love each other."

"Yes, we do, too." I kiss her again.

She turns around to face me full on, her face so unlike mine with her hazel eyes and those lashes I would fkn kill for, and the freckles on her nose all cute and small, her smile so much her own, but her character a bright mirror in front of me, match-match.

"Mama, did you know that you make me the most angry I've ever been, but you also make my heart feel the warmest it ever feels?"

I smile and say nothing while I remember the mad swing back and forth between loving and hating my own mom, and the way my daughter can also bring me to the brink of batshit crazy and full throttle joy.

"I guess this is how mothers and daughters do," she added while she reached for my hand, and I felt my heart explode. "Can we get ice cream?"

We pick the same flavor, and laugh.

And I swear I can hear my own mother laughing, too.

The picture of my mom and Benny Sharon is still in my wallet, and I've shown it to the old guys who play backgammon, Abu Ibrahim and all of them. I've shown it to Musa, and Fadi, my friend Keshet from the Jewish Quarter, Kivork the grandson of the Armenian photographer in the Christian Quarter, and Bracha who hands out red string by the Western Wall. But no one knows Benny or my mom.

And I am looking for her everywhere.

Today, I'm looking for her in Omar's shop.

Omar's shop is one of my favorite places in the Old City. It looks like the inside of a pirate ship, and it smells like ginger and old paper and hashish. The walls are lined with books and newspapers, and little porcelain statues. There are little tables listing against the bookshelves—some are silver, some are wood. My favorite one is a mosaic with a peacock in the middle, his tail feathers splayed like thousands of tiny jewels, and on each table are baskets with old coins from far flung lands, and photos.

Behind the counter is a giant poster that says, "Visit Palestine."

"I'll tell you the truth," Omar says. "This poster has nothing to do with my Palestine. This was a poster the Jewish Agency made before 1948, and it's actually Zionist propaganda."

I had heard this story before.

"So why do you have it hanging up if you know the truth?"

"Because it makes me laugh that people can be so stupid. Especially my Arab brothers when it comes to Palestine. They are a little too hallelujah about everything"

There's a giant NO SMOKING sign in Hebrew, English, and Arabic, but I've never seen Omar without a cigarette, and sometimes, we smoke together. Sometimes, tobacco. Usually hashish. Except on Ramadan. And then it's only hashish because, "a holy month needs a holy spice."

The first time I went into Omar's store, I combed through the photos in the old shoe boxes to look for ones of my mother.

There weren't any. But I did find a picture of a little kid on a bike that reminds me of my Uncle Charlie, and next to the pictures, there's a little silver bowl that kids in Syria would use for comfort—the bells inside make a pretty sound and the bowl is inscribed with prayers, and when a little one has a nightmare his or her parents fill it with water and he drinks.

"She was a beautiful lady," Omar told me when I showed him her picture that I keep with me. "Good bone structure. But you don't look like her."

"Well, thanks a lot."

"We all need to know our limitations. That isn't to say you aren't a beautiful woman in your own way. But you need more jewelry."

He handed me a moonstone ring he made out of silver.

"Not that I'm one to talk," he said. "I have funny ears, and my eyes look a little E.T.—you know, the alien from the movie—they're too wide apart, and my hair is like this," he boinged one of his curls. "A little grey hair. Possessed! Like a man drunk on love! But I am charming," he winked and kissed my hand, and twirled me around while the Buena Vista Social Club soundtrack played merrily in the background.

Today, Omar is heating up coffee with a blowtorch. "This is authentic Palestinian silversmith coffee," he says, and the truth is, he burns it every time, but I love it anyway.

Omar passes me a joint, and I take a hit.

He's on one of those streets that you won't find unless you're lost. It's off the main road, several streets over, a twist and a turn, and three flights of steps. I found it because I was lost, and I was standing in the middle of his street watching an Arab brother and sister play the exact same game as a Jewish brother and sister on the exact same street in the exact same way, but turned from another, and not seeing.

This happens all the time in Jerusalem, and I was standing there and looking at them, left and right, when Omar came out and asked if I could tell that the buildings on either side of the street were built at different times.

"What do you mean?"

"Look at the stones here," he said, and he ran his hand over the chiseled rectangles, rough but flat across each face. "These are Ottoman stones. They had the technology to cut them straight and even. But over here," he said, pointing to the building with the bright blue door where he was standing, "the stones are oddly shaped, big and small and bumpy. Different, like me! These are from the Mamulk period—almost one thousand years old!"

"Is this your shop?"

"Not only is it my shop," he said proudly, tipping his little gray cap. "It is my house. I was born in it. My father was born in it. *His* father was born in it. And *his* father was born in it."

I wonder if they knew my great grandmother, if she wafted by with her long black hair streaming down her back at sunset. I wonder if his great grandfather or someone in his family saw her kiss that man on the roof, or if maybe Omar's great grandfather was the man she kissed and loved enough to never forget.

Today, outside in the heat of high noon, the Jerusalem municipality is working on the road.

"See?" Omar tells me. "The stabbing intifada was a good thing."

"Dude, no!"

"Relax, I don't mean the killing—that's not good. Killing is not good, no way! Not good for the soul to kill. Not good for the Palestinian soul, not good for you, either. But look!"

I look outside at a cloud of dust as a guy with an orange vest drills into the pavement. "He's fixing things! Finally! I'll give him coffee," Omar says. "Even though he's a Jew he appreciates Arabic coffee," Omar winks.

"Okay, but what does this have to do with the intifada?"

"Ah, yes. Well, when the stabbing intifada started, the Israelis realized that they have to pay more attention to the Old City and what's going on here. This street has been a mess for an entire generation—the steps broken, the ramparts unable to accommodate a wheelchair. Like my aunt couldn't even visit unless we carried her," he says. "But look around the Old City. You'll see the Jerusalem municipality is working, really working on making it nicer. They're fixing the streets, they're painting the doors—like mine, it's festive blue! And they've even given me a garbage can in front of my shop! You would not believe me if I told you how long I have been asking for a garbage can. Such dignity for me and my people in that stupid garbage can!"

He gets up with the coffee, and heads outside to the man in the orange vest. "You, sir! You should be the mayor of this town!" Omar shouts over the drill. "For you are a gentleman and a scholar!"

There's this story in our family that was passed down from generation to generation to my mother from her mother who got it from *her* mother (the same woman with the long black hair who lived fearlessly in the Old City and kissed a stranger on the roof), and it goes like this:

"There was a family—a father and a mother and two children—and when the father was learning with the rabbi, the two children died. This was before Sabbath, the Jewish holy day, when time slows, and the world all around rests. The mother put her two children's bodies in one of the back rooms, and when her husband came home, and asked where the kids were, she said, 'I'll tell you when Sabbath ends.' They lit the candles and ate the festive meal. They prayed and sang and talked and laughed, and the following evening when three stars shone in the new week's sky, only then did she tell him the truth about their children."

"Why didn't she tell him sooner?" I had asked my mother.

"She wanted to give her husband one last joyful Sabbath before he found out the terrible truth. There would be time enough to grieve."

I'm thinking about this story now while I crouch in the bathroom of a magnificent home in the Jewish Quarter checking my phone.

It's Friday night—Shabbat—and outside the bathroom, the room is lit with nearly one hundred candles, and shadows dance along the walls and in between the dozens of people out there from all over the world who have come to this special home in Jerusalem to celebrate the holy day.

Dinner is delicious—roast beef and chicken and salmon, rice and potatoes and salad, fresh challah, sweet red wine.

The table is laden with the best silver and the china, a white tablecloth hand stitched, and the hostess wears all white with what appear to be real diamonds sewn onto her dress and turban. She looks like a queen.

Outside from the rooftop garden that smells like honeysuckle and jasmine, you can see the Old City stretch in a sea of twinkling lights . . . but beyond, East Jerusalem is seething. There have been protests and riots all day over the Temple Mount.

Some of the protestors out there are people I know, I'm sure. I wonder if Fadi is there, or Mahmoud. Or Leila, for that matter. And some of the soldiers out there are people I know, too.

During dinner, our host gave a special blessing to the brave sons and daughters of Israel who are out there defending us.

It's all we can think about.

Earlier that day I stood surrounded by angry men yelling, "Death to the Jews" and "With blood and fire we will liberate Aqsa."

And I saw the anger on their faces—real anger—and I felt angry too.

I saw one guy I know from Fadi and Mahmoud's restaurant, waving his fist and chanting with the rest, and he looked at me and I looked at him, and I wanted to say to him, "But you *know* me. How can you say these things?"

But I didn't. It wasn't about me. It wasn't him about him, either. I looked away.

And later on that day, there was the boom of a stun grenade and hundreds of people were running toward me, the same ones who were chanting "Death to the Jews" only moments before, the same people who were so angry, but now their faces were all stricken—identical masks of sheer terror, eyes bulging, mouths pulled back into a rictus, shouting, screaming. I had never seen such a thing before, and I was afraid, too, because there was that loud noise, and there was smoke, and so many people, and I ran with them, and in that moment, I was just as Palestinian as they were. Except I'm not, because I'm Jewish, and whoever fired that stun grenade did it to protect people like me, except I was in this terrified crowd of people, and if someone shot at us with rubber bullets, I would be just as hit as they were, and we were all there, sweat dripping, fingers splayed, and I could smell my fear like a wild animal—like I smelled in that room the night with the Grey Man, like I smelled by Damascus Gate.

Oh God, we are so human. So, so *human* with our blood and our sweat and our stink from fear and yearning, and our bones, too. We are so easily torn apart, and broken, so emptied, and left like corn husks to dry in the wind.

After the smoke cleared and I walked for a long time around the walls, I called Keshet because I needed a hug.

She took me to this little store around the corner from her house, and I bought a ring that reads, "May God bless you and protect you." I've been twirling it around my fingers all evening, and I think about all the Shabbat dinners my parents and I shared, the thousands of candles we lit, the prayers we said.

"May the Lord bless you and protect you. May the Lord make you like Sarah, Rebecca, Rachel, and Leah, may the Lord, the Merciful

One, holy be God, give you peace in your heart, joy in your soul, and may He make you one with the universe."

And I'm in the bathroom now checking my phone in secret because on Shabbat you don't use electricity, but there are protests and riots, and Jerusalem is tearing itself apart, and I have a news alert that a Palestinian terrorist burst into a family home during their Sabbath meal just an hour ago and butchered several people. We don't know yet how many, but at least one is dead, and that's all I know—that not far from this very house where people are celebrating and praying for children of Israel, out there is a family ripped apart and torn to shreds and their blood is all over the kitchen floor.

And I think about that, and my mom and my family, and my children with their father, and I think about that mother from the story my great grandmother passed to her daughter and to her daughter and to me.

So I turn off the phone and say nothing to diminish the joy in the room on Shabbat.

It's late afternoon, and Fadi needs to catch the bus back to Ramallah to see his father who is sick, so we are walking up Al-Wad Street toward Damascus Gate.

"I'll never forget this corner," he tells me as we pass a little slip over to the right, just past the Austrian Hospice, right by the corner where the old women from Battir sit and sell bitter greens.

"What happened?"

"It's the corner where the soldiers asked for my ID. It was my first year in the Old City, 1997."

1997 was the first time I was in the Old City, when I fell in love with Jerusalem that summer that led me to this moment.

I don't tell him this though.

"I didn't have my ID yet," Fadi continues, "so I told them I didn't have one. I was so stupid, and I didn't think."

He pauses.

"So what did they do?"

"Okay, so then this soldier—he looked younger than me, I swear. He even had those things on his teeth . . . braces. He grabbed one arm, and this other soldier grabbed the other, and they took me all the way up this street, to Damascus Gate, and there were maybe twenty soldiers standing there. And then they started beating me."

I cringe as we walk together along the path that he was dragged—up the shuk steps where the roads come together, and out the gate toward East Jerusalem.

"They kicked my head, and my back, and they broke my nose, and then one of them starts crying, and I just didn't think, and I asked him, 'Why are you crying?' and he said to me, 'Why did you have to come here? Look at what we did to you!'"

By the time he finishes the story, we are outside Damascus Gate, between the guys who sell chocolate crepes and the soldiers who stand behind metal barricades. Fadi looks down at his feet.

"It was right here," he says.

The same spot where I stood staring at my blood on my hands.

Autumn

It's still summer technically, but the days are getting shorter, and there's gold spilling in little pockets of the Old City alleyways even as early as three in the afternoon.

I'm in bed because I took a nap at noon, which we do sometimes in Jerusalem when it's still hot out (or when it's cold and the rains splatter across the window).

But now I'm awake and dry-mouthed, haggard, groggy. I'm tired, and I feel heavy, and I want coffee, and I'm hungry, except I'm not, and I'm restless, but I don't want to move, and I'm all the things, so I figure I should take a walk.

I spend twenty minutes putting on makeup this afternoon high above the Old City in the room with the purple windows overlooking the Christian Quarter. Salmon-peach concealer under my eyes, a little powder and some blush. I lined the tops of my eyelids with black eye pencil, and filled in the eyebrow my ex used to call Alec. As in Alec Baldwin. As in bald.

I wear skinny jeans and a tank top, silver flip flops, my nose ring and a toe ring, and my hair is long and loose. I take a selfie.

(I edit out the lines around my eyes.)

I head downstairs past the French guys cooking in the kitchen, and everything smells like garlic, butter, and ennui.

I fist bump the guy in the front ("Want anything?" "Nah.") and head down the little street toward the Jewish Quarter.

It's still warm out, but the shadows are deepening, and the sky is burnished. Autumn is close and you can see it in the change in light, and in the fruit that's filling the market stalls.

Because now it's Elul. The Hebrew month before the New Year, when people take stock, and kids blow rams horns jubilantly through the alleys of the Jewish Quarter all the way to the Western Wall. I'm following that sound now, because it's woken me up.

Even with my headphones on, Taylor Swift (yeah, yeah, give me a break) bopping away, the shofar pierces through, and I take one ear bud out, and I want to feel it—the air around me, the fragrances of spices and sweet fruit, the smell of sweat and baking bread.

I take the other ear bud out so I can really hear it.

The sound of the shofar—just like we did back in the old days, just like we've always done.

The sound, too, of many languages, and I'm flowing with it, wherever it takes me, the kids laughing, the shofar blasting, all the different sounds in a warble and ripple, and I'm part of it, too.

And now I'm smiling.

I go down the steps on the south side of the Jewish Quarter—I can see the Mount of Olives, and beyond that, Jordan, smoky and pink in the distance.

And the sun is soft on my skin while I pass others who are covered, the men in black hats, women in their wigs. They must be roasting. The mothers with their scarves tied into turbans, bright colors, blue and green, jewel tones, like peacocks. The Beis Yakov girls in long skirts, the tourists wrapped in shawls.

I know that by the security entrance toward the Western Wall, where they'll check my bag and my body through the metal detector, that a woman with a wig and covered everything will hand me a scarf to drape over my body, and I don't want to go there. I don't feel like going through a metal detector, or having my body covered, or really being anywhere except right here where I can watch the light fade off the stones and see Jordan shimmering in the distance.

So, I stop walking, and sit on the steps before the entrance and look over the plaza. I look toward the Temple Mount and I see the golden dome gleaming in the fading light.

There's a woman near me. She looks old, but maybe she isn't. She's wearing all black, her hair covered, her eyes deep-socketed, her face woven with wrinkles. I can see a tuft of hair peeking through where her scarf meets her forehead, and it's grey and sparse. Her eyes are green like peridot, like sea glass. She smiles, and she's missing four teeth that I can see, and the rest are brown and grey.

In her hands is a spool of red thread, five shekels a string, plus a blessing! Such a bargain! I've probably seen her a hundred times sitting there, the same spot, holding her thread with her right hand and rattling the tin cup in her left.

A kid with black hair and black eyes blows a shofar next to me, and it echoes off the steps, off the stones, and farther in the distance, off the hills. But more than that, the blast shakes me. It wakes me up, and makes me look around, and then inside at all I have. The moments spent drinking coffee with friends. My rooftops. My friends and my family and my friends who are like family. The guy I kissed on my favorite rooftop, who just texted me. My kids. And this place, this moment in the gloaming as the light fades from pink to plum, as the birds fly home, while I sit and watch the entire world all around me soften.

And I look at this woman who could be my mother if my mother had lived without dental care, without sunscreen, if she had hidden her hair, and had had to beg for money—this woman, old enough to be a grandmother to my children, sitting on her folding chair with her string and her cup.

And I go up and sit by her feet, and hand her five shekels, and she tears a piece of red string with what's left of her teeth, and I remember how when I was seven years old, my mother tied a piece of red string around my left front top tooth and tied the other end to the door, and then slammed the door and the tooth popped out like a little pearl while my mouth filled with blood.

I miss my mom. That's no secret. And every day I'm looking for her here because I know she was here, and it mattered to her being here enough to make me come, too.

"Thanks," I tell the woman beside me while she ties the string around my wrist and says a prayer.

"May you be healthy, and happy, and may you have many children," she says, and I smile. And then she gives me the once over, from the top of my bleach blonde head to my toenails, painted black. "And may you realize one day—God willing—that a true Jewish woman dresses like a queen!

"A true Jewish woman," she continues, "takes pride in her appearance. She covers her hair and her arms and her legs, she protects what is the most sacred."

It's funny how similar this is to the religious Muslim women, and even the Christians—how we women put on our scarves and shawls and robes and head coverings to enter sacred spaces, how we hide our skin.

I think of something Um Ibrahim said to me just last week: "Hijab actually enables women—it empowers them. Because when you wear hijab, you can see, but are unseen. Think of what power that is."

"You could be so beautiful," the woman with her string and cup says to me again. "You could be so beautiful if only you dressed like a queen."

And I'm torn between wanting to stalk away, and wanting to laugh, between white hot anger that this woman—a stranger!—is lecturing me on how to dress, and why I should cover myself, and at the sheer absurdity of it all.

But then she beams, and she *does* look regal, her eyes bright, even though her smile caves in.

And I think about how I got dressed earlier— my tank top, my flip flops, my makeup, and my nose ring and toe ring, how I put coconut serum on my hair, and how I line my eyes. All these things that I do to cover myself, just as she does—to be beautiful, to be noticed.

And then I think about my great grandmother who left her little village in Poland, who traveled to Jerusalem, who kissed a stranger on the roof, who refused to cover her hair, and whose stories shaped my mother, who named me for her and sent me here.

"I'm good, thanks," I tell her.

She smiles sadly, and shakes her head the way I imagine most people do when they walk past her sitting there.

The last time I saw my mother was in her bedroom in Los Angeles.

But lately, she's everywhere in Jerusalem—she's so close, and it's what I wanted to happen when I started living here, but now that it's happening it sometimes hurts so much I can barely breathe.

Like right now.

The radio's on in our little room, and I'm listening to this song in Hebrew, and it's called "Apples and Dates," and it's a song about a woman whose husband no longer loves her, and it's sad.

I haven't heard it on the radio in years.

I first heard it that summer when I was sixteen—the first summer in Israel, the summer I fell in love with Jerusalem—and it's the song that was playing on the tape deck when my mother kicked me out of the car on Sepulveda Boulevard a few months after I got back to LA.

God, I wanted to be in Israel so badly, to feel my hair whipping across my face on a hot night, chasing the dawn back in Jerusalem on that roof again, teetering on the seam between coastal plane and desert.

Instead: SAT class every Thursday from 6:00 to 8:00 p.m. The girl who had flown through the night on that song, high with every breath of life reduced to sharpening No. 2 pencils and bubbling the letters on practice tests and getting rides to and from everywhere with her parents.

I knew every synonym for "frustration."

Vexation.

Anger.

And on that night, as the leavings of that long summer in Israel drained into LA autumn, we listened to this song on the car tape deck, my mother and I.

And she could do nothing right.

Nothing. From tapping her fingers in time with the music, to trying to sing along to words she didn't know. To trying to understand her wild, willful girl who wore shirts that were way too tight, and eyeliner that was way too dark, who was madly in love with a country ten time zones away.

Nothing.

"Mom, you don't know Hebrew, so stop trying to sing along."

She stopped singing, stared at me in a way that shrunk me in half, jerked the steering wheel to the right, and screeched across three lanes of traffic on Sepulveda Boulevard.

She leaned over me and shoved the passenger door open.

"Get out."

I got out, and walked the rest of the way home.

We had dinner that night as usual—spaghetti and meatballs, salad with pieces of avocado on top. Like nothing had happened.

The next time we rode together, she played Bach. Or maybe Beethoven. Like nothing had happened.

And now, ten time zones away from the place where I was stuck and seething, I listen to this song again. I sing along while my kids cut shapes out of paper with matching pink scissors.

"Mama, you shouldn't try to sing in Hebrew."

And for those few moments, I remember how it felt that summer with the night wrapped around me, how it felt to feel at home so far from home.

And how I would give ten years of my life just to be back in that car with my mother listening together, just so I could tell her that I didn't understand the words, either.

My son has a homework assignment, and he wants my help, not that I can understand many of the words, since they're in Hebrew.

But, my little boy who still sleeps with his stuffed camel doll we got in the shuk is patient, and explains when I get frustrated by the Hebrew printouts he hands me.

"Mama, can you go to the Google thing and look up Teddy Kollek?" he asks.

Teddy Kollek, first mayor of "United Jerusalem," of the Four Quarters of the Old City, the West and the East, the mayor who hours after Jerusalem came under Israeli control, ordered that milk be sent to Arab children. The mayor who said, "I got into this by accident . . . I was bored. When the city was united, I saw this as an historic occasion. To take care of it and show better care than anyone else ever has is a full life purpose. I think Jerusalem is the one essential element in Jewish history. A body can live without an arm or a leg, not without the heart. This is the heart and soul of it."[1]

We read all this online, but it's not enough.

"I have an idea," I tell my son. "Forget Google, I want to talk to someone who actually *knew* the mayor."

We head through the winding streets, the light gold and peach through the spaces in between the stone walls, until we reach Sami's place.

Sami has a plate of cookies out and is bent over his sewing machine. He looks up and waves.

"Baby, this is the Mukhtar of the Syrian Orthodox Community, and a good friend of Teddy Kollek. He *knew* him," I tell my son, pointing to the picture of Teddy and Sami on the wall behind the sewing machine.

"What was he like?" my son asks, his face covered in cookie crumbs.

---

1 Erlanger, Steven; Marilyn Berger (January 2, 2007). "Teddy Kollek, Ex-Mayor of Jerusalem, Dies at 95." *The New York Times.* Retrieved January 3, 2007.

"Teddy Kollek was honest," Sami answered. "He was humble. He was kind. He understood that in Jerusalem there are three different people who love her—the Christian, the Muslim, and the Jew—and he understood that it was his job to serve all three equally, and with respect and dignity!"

My son writes all this down.

"Was that helpful?" I ask him.

"Yeah, the cookies are really good."

I'm walking with a tall man with golden skin and the warmest brown eyes I've ever seen.

I would know his face anywhere because I've been looking at it ever since my father asked, "Who is Benny Sharon?"

Now I know.

He's a man who lives in Jerusalem and has three children, and a wife, and he still walks around the Old City and I'm sure we've crossed paths a million times before without knowing that we share a person together: my mother.

He met my mom on Kibbutz Gesher Haziv, and he traveled down with her and with a German girl with white blonde hair and cobalt eyes to the Old City where the three hung out and walked around and talked to strangers.

"Your mom was a very special woman," he says. He doesn't elaborate, even though I push.

I met him because that photo was burning a hole in my wallet.

It's not that my dad asked again or anything happened, it's just there's only one person that I know in this whole entire country who knew my mom, and that person is me.

My kids never met her, although my son has her wrists, and my daughter has her chin. We don't have family here besides each other—except when my dad and his wife visit—so there's no aunt or cousin who can meet me for a drink and talk about the old days in LA, who knew my mom when she climbed trees and swam across big dark lakes and planted begonias in the garden.

And the hardest part is that each day takes me further and further from her last breath, when the entirety of her existence was sucked down and spat out into that last golden thread.

And I'll tell you the truth: I am lonely, and I miss her, and sometimes, I am tired of being a mermaid who can go anywhere, because the one place I want to be most of all is with her again.

So? I shared the photo online with a few words about my mother and how she shone when she stood next to him, and within a few hours I had a message from a woman with the same exact eyes as the man in the picture.

"That's my dad. Want to meet him?"

Benny doesn't talk much now, except he's showing me around the Old City, and we stop at Muristan Square for coffee, and the guys there know him—the same ones who know me.

Fadi and Mahmoud say hi. The Map Seller waves.

"What was she like?" I ask him.

"She liked to sing. She loved Jerusalem, but she wrote many letters back home. She was homesick."

Like me, sometimes.

He really doesn't say much, and I wish he would, but I know what he's doing. He's taking me on the same roads she would have walked when she was with him. He's showing me the same places that she loved, that shaped the stories that she shared with me, that shape the way I see it now.

And together, we walk through the shuk, and he buys some spices—200 grams of zatar—and we both say hi to the guys at Jaffar where the kenafe is perfect, and in the end, I walk him out Damascus Gate, past the very place where I was stoned that night, past that place that helped me here to find him and my mom, with no clear answers, but I look into the eyes of an Israeli man who knew her, an Israeli man who helped her fall in love with this place so she could raise me to love it, too, and even though he hasn't told me much, it is enough.

The Juice Man squeezes the best pomegranate juice in the world. Really, you should taste it. It's so good. And you should listen when he talks, even though he mumbles, like the time I was sitting there and Salafis came in all in white and began railing against the Zionist Entity, in their South African accents thick as the mud at the bottom of black coffee.

"It is more important to be Muslim than Palestinian," the Juice Man tells them while he wags his crooked finger in their young faces.

"I'm not even Palestinian," he says a little louder while he presses juice from the ruby red fruit. "My family is from Spain. We came here when they kicked us out, with the Jews. But I am Muslim. It is not good to worship an idea. Only God. Now drink. The juice is sweet. Now listen to your elders and learn something," he says to the Salafis.

He walks over and hands me a cup.

The Salafis drink. I drink. The Juice Man drinks. The juice is sweet and bitter.

The Mukhtar of the Syrian Orthodox Church and I are having coffee on Saturday morning while he finishes hemming a dress with his sewing machine. A man in a black suit and a black yarmulke comes in.

The Mukhtar stops the machine.

The man sells halva, a sweet sesame treat, and he's from the Jewish Quarter—I know him, though not well. I've sat with him over coffee while our kids played at the park in the middle of the Jewish Quarter. He's a handsome sweet talker who sells sweet things, too—with a discount for the ladies. Wink.

Keshet warned me about him, and he did, too.

"I'm a slave to God and women, in that order," he told me. I appreciated his honesty.

He greets the Mukhtar in Arabic, and the Mukhtar greets him in Hebrew, which I guess makes them friends. He says hi to me.

"I'm so sorry to hear about your dad, may his memory be a blessing," the Mukhtar says.

The Halva Guy's eyes cloud over. "It's been less than two weeks."

"I'm so sorry," I echo.

"I'm an old man," the Mukhtar tells the Halva Guy. "And I miss my parents every day."

"You're never old enough to lose your mom or dad," I say.

We all sit quietly.

It's funny how grief works.

People assume grief has a time table. Because unless you've lost someone, you expect there to be a timeline: From that last breath to burial to uncovering the mirrors again through a year marked in mourning, to "getting on with it already," to "moving on."

In Judaism, when your mom or dad dies, we mark the year in mourning—seven days with family and friends in the house and holding the bereaved close, then thirty days, and then a year. A beginning, a middle, and an end.

And while we tell ourselves to focus on the living, missing someone never goes away.

It changes, and we live with it, but it is never okay.

In the beginning, right after my mom died, I couldn't breathe. It was like drowning. Big angry wave after big angry wave crashed over me, knocked me over, spun me around. I would wake up and have to say the words aloud: "Your mother is dead. Your mother is dead."

You're smashed against a rock, drenched, maybe drowning, you choke and sputter, but then you realize the breathing spaces in between each wave are getting bigger.

You're shivering, still, but you feel sunlight on your skin.

So you open your eyes.

And the waters are mermaid blue, instead of ink—it changed somehow when your eyes were squinting shut . . .

So you lean back, the sunlight full on your face, and you float, float, float . . .

And it's almost okay again.

"Maybe I'm okay," you say, and you start to believe it . . . until the water swells around you, and another wave bares down, and you're back against the rock, smashed, bleeding, shaking in its icy blast.

Only this time you remember while you're clinging to the rock, "it does get easier. This too shall pass."

(And you hear this in your mother's voice, the way she whispered to you when your first love broke your heart when you were fifteen.)

"It does get easier. This too shall pass."

And it does.

And you take that chance and slip back into the waters where you float again, only just as you remembered while you were being smashed that it will get better, you remember, too, this time, "it does get worse."

And it does.

But the spaces between those brutal waves stretches wider, and in that time, you are (sort of, maybe, kind of) okay.

And you are.

And you remember in your mother's voice again, "This too shall pass."

But still, you know that it isn't gone, not forever, not the missing. It's always there, that wisp on the horizon, reminding you, "Enjoy this now, because the storm will come again."

And even though it *is* okay now, it still *isn't.* Not really. Not ever.

I say some of this out loud and the Halva Guy wipes his eyes. "I'm so blessed that I was there with my aba when he died. With his last breath, he asked me to wrap his Tallis around him, and help him lay tefiillin so he could pray. He closed his eyes, I swear to God, he closed his eyes, and he whispered the Shma, and I saw it happen. I am not a spiritual man even though I dress like this, but I saw it happen, I saw that breath turn golden in the light while the sun poured in through the window, and I saw my aba's essence condense into that one last moment, and fly."

The Mukhtar murmurs something in Aramaic. A prayer? Probably.

Tears pour down my face, because the Halva Guy describes exactly what I had seen happen when my father and I held my mother when she took her last breath, when every bit that made her who she was came down to that last second, and then poof. She was gone.

When we are born, we take our first breath, and when we die, it leaves us.

What matters is what we do in the space in between for however long we're given.

I'm still living in this place on the seam between the quarters, and it's my favorite place—it's the one with the bombass view, with the room with the giant bed with the wrought iron posts, and the purple glass windows and a view looking onto the Church of the Holy Sepulchre.

The building grew out of an old cistern seven hundred years ago.

And there's Wi-Fi and hot water, so basically it's my happy place.

The people who run it are Palestinians from Beit Hanina. We speak English when I come in, or maybe *shwei Arabi,* a little Arabic. I don't hide that I'm Jewish or Israeli. (I stayed here on Purim and paraded through in my mask and beads and shit, and wished everyone *Chag Samayach* and explained to the baffled backpackers from Belgium WTF was going on.) But once when I asked something in Hebrew, the guy running the desk said, "I'm sorry, I don't understand." When an East Jerusalemite says that, sometimes it's because he literally doesn't understand, and sometimes it's because he does understand but prefers not to speak Hebrew.

Whatever.

Meanwhile, I've heard the Israeli singer Ofra Haza blasting from one of the rooms, and I've seen a guy in a yarmulke stay here, and whatever. This is Jerusalem in all its layers. It's complicated and it's messy and it's gorgeous, too.

Anyway, I'm staying in my room there tonight, the room with the purple windows and the double bed overlooking the Church of the Holy Sepulchre. And while I walked down the street past one of the little alleys leading toward the Jewish Quarter, a man with a yarmulke started following me:

"You're a tourist?"

"*Lo*." I answer in Hebrew.

"Oh, I thought you were a tourist because you're so blonde, and your arms are so tan. I thought you were Swedish, you look Swedish. You look like someone I used to know."

"Okay, have a good day."

I walk a little faster; the tiny hairs on the back of my neck are standing up.

I get into the main room at the bottom of my building, and I shut the door, and two minutes later he walks in, and starts talking to me about some woman he used to know—a blonde woman just like me. Maybe I'm her daughter? Or her ghost? Where *is* she? "*It's you! I know it's you! Why did you leave me???*"

The woman working reception has always been courteous but businesslike with me. She's polite, but she's never been friendly. Each time I pay for my room, she takes my ID and copies it, and counts out exact change, and that's it. "Have a nice day."

The man says to her in Hebrew, "I want to stay here with her." He points to me.

"I don't speak Hebrew," she says.

"I want a room," he says in English.

"We don't have anything available," she tells him. "Do you know this man?" she turns to me.

"No. He followed me," I told her.

"I just want one room, I can stay any night that *she's* here," he shouts.

Now, you don't know this about me, but when I feel threatened, I turn into a she-beast that is part raptor, part lion, and part libertarian. And suddenly I speak fluent Hebrew.

"No," I say to him. "You need to leave. There is no room here, and you cannot stay here."

"Why not?"

"Because there is no room here. You need to leave right now." My voice is leaden and cold and every muscle in my face and neck and arms and stomach and legs and toes are flexed and ready to lunge if I have to. I do not want this man staying here. He followed me, and he frightened me, and I do not want him staying here. He is the man in that room in Migdal HaEmek. He is the men who threw stones at me. He is the man who beat me and drowned my cats. He is the Grey Man who squeezed milk from my breasts.

"But I have a right to stay here!"

No. No. No. Such a powerful word that I haven't used enough and I use it now.

"No. If you do not leave this minute, I am calling the police." I reach for my phone. "No, you do not get to stay here. Get out."

He backs through the front door, and he disappears down the street.

"Wow," the woman at reception says to me. "Your Hebrew is great. Where did you learn it?"

"I'm Israeli," I answer.

"But you're American. I've seen your passport."

"Yeah, but I moved here. And my kids taught me Hebrew."

"Did they also teach you to be so brave?" she asks.

I never thought of that, but I guess they did.

"Thanks for getting rid of that guy," she says as she goes back to the reception desk to answer the ringing phone.

And it was only then that I realize she and I had been speaking Hebrew the whole time.

And you ask me why I love this place—this complicated, messy, ancient city of broken pieces held together by chance and opportunity, by fear and love, and maybe a few lucky breaks.

"I went to high school in the Old City," Basem tells me in Hebrew when we pull out of the taxi stand by Damascus Gate. I'm sitting next to him because my phone is plugged into the charger in the front. He smells like cigarettes and Hugo Boss. Enrique Iglesias is on the radio.

"It was the school just inside the gate, on Al-Wad by the mosque."

"What was that like?" I ask.

"Just a school. It was closed half the week though," he says.

"Why?"

"The army would come in and shut it down."

"Why?" I ask again.

"Do the years 2000 to 2004 mean anything to you?"

"Oh." The bloody terrible years of the Second Intifada, the years when every siren was followed by another and another, when Jerusalem smelled like smoke and burning flesh.

"Yeah it was the intifada, and the army would come in and just shut us down, and so instead of sitting in the classroom and learning math and history, we would all go up on the roof and chuck stones off the sides."

I remember how the Journalist told me about the kids who would throw big old rocks off the roofs near Lions' Gate, the *fwish* of heavy matter hurdling down, the smash, then the splatter. These weren't little pebbles, they were bricks, sometimes they were boulders. They could pulverize your skull and turn you into pink and grey and red, sinew, bone, and blood if you were underneath. And they were children and they were the heaviest weapons they could find.

I sit in silence, saying nothing, and keep listening.

"It was messed up," he says. "Stupid kids all of us, and we did stupid stuff."

"That must have been a really hard time," I say, and I remember how my friend Fadi was pummeled to strawberry pulp because he didn't have the right papers.

And then I think of my eight- and nine-year-olds tucked in their bunk bed just a thirty-minute drive away, of their childhood spent with no real uncertainty, no barbed wire, no forced closures, no anger, no reason to climb a roof and throw things. And then I think of how we also spent a summer sleeping in bomb shelters and running over parched earth, and how like every Israeli, we all know someone killed or injured in a terror attack or war.

"It was hard," he says. "The soldiers would also come into the classroom and just look at all our faces, and if they didn't like one face they'd pull the kid out, even if he didn't throw stones. Even if all he did was just sit there without blinking. That made them mad: when we would stare back at them with no fear. But I don't blame the soldiers. They had their job and we had our job and I really just blame the school for letting them in and letting them shut us down and letting us have all that free time to do stupid and terrible things. Someone should have been the grownup."

We sit in silence for a while and he offers me a sip of his coffee. It smells like earth. I drink, hand it back to him, and he drinks, too.

There's banging and clanging by the Juice Man's shop on the very street where they say Jesus carried the cross on his way to crucifixion, and there between the sixth and seventh stations of the cross, a group of Palestinian men, sweating and smoking, huddle around a drain pipe. One has a hammer.

There's a nun, too—one of the Little Sisters of Jesus—and she's praying. A Muslim cleric who I recognize from Temple Mount stands to the side, and his face is stricken.

Z. is waving his arms, directing traffic and yelling at the guy with the hammer—"A little harder, no not there, hit the part that's lower. Yes, that's right, give the man some space!"

He's sucking on a cigarette, and the whole street is full of smoke, not just from him, but from five other guys who are standing there, too.

"What's going on?" I ask him.

"There's a kitten trapped in the pipe," he tells me. "Just a baby, we can hear him meowing." He puts his hand on the guy hammering the pipe. "Stop, let's see if it's still alive."

Three big men with their shirt collars unbuttoned and hair poking through and gold chains around their necks put their ears against the pipe.

I know one of these men. Just last month I stood in the middle of a crowd of people under a pitiless white sun by Lion's Gate while hundreds of Palestinians chanted, "We will liberate Aqsa with blood and fire!" including this man.

"He's alive, praise God!" he says.

A group of Russian pilgrims stop and begin to sing. The nun crosses herself again. The screw on the pipe comes loose, and Munir unfastens it.

It's cooler now, a blue sky autumn, and the man who I had seen shouting by Lions Gate about blood and fire cups his hands gently underneath the space in the pipe and takes out a little kitten no bigger than a chicken egg. The kitten is grey like soot, and he sneezes. His eyes are closed, not because of dust or dirt or out of fear, but because he's only a few days old.

"We can't just leave him!" someone says. "He'll die!"

"I can take him for a little while," says Z. "But I have to go to Jordan next week, so someone will need to be with him then."

He's tiny, and he's trembling. "May I hold him?" I ask.

The man who I saw yelling at the riots places him softly, almost reverently, in my arms. This big man who just last week shouted of fire and blood and armed struggle against Israel is holding this little kitten with as much love as I held my sweet babies when they were born.

"Be careful," he tells me in Hebrew. "Watch his neck."

The kitten reminds me so much of Crumbum, one of the two kittens the man I loved made "disappear" on that cold night many years ago in November. I nuzzle him. He mews.

"I have an idea," I say. And while I stroke the little kitten, I call a friend of mine who has about a million cats in Jerusalem. "Hey, what do I do with a newborn kitten with no mom?"

"Are you in the Old City?"

"Yeah, Muslim Quarter." I was in an area where most of my Jewish friends have never walked.

"Call the Cat Lady in the Jewish Quarter. She rescues cats."

I know about the Cat Lady. She's a hero. When the British first brought cats to Jerusalem during the Mandate years, the cats took the whole "be fruitful and multiply" thing very seriously, and Jerusalem is overrun with cats. Many are hungry, and most have no home. The Cat Lady wants to change that, so sets traps for cats all over the Old City and takes them to be fixed. Then she releases them where she found them. The sick ones she keeps until they're well.

My friend gives me the Cat Lady's number, and I call her.

"Hello?"

"Hi, are you the woman who rescues cats?" I ask while this tiny ball of fur snuggles against my chest.

"Who wants to know?" she sounds wary. I don't blame her. She's encountered problems with people in the Old City, and even the police.

"I have this kitten that we found in the Muslim Quarter. He's tiny. Eyes are still closed. I don't know what to do with him."

"Well you can feed him." She says, like *duh*.

"I can't. He's too young."

"It isn't rocket science," she scoffs. "Get an eye dropper."

"I can't keep a kitten this young," I tell her. "My life is too unpredictable. Some days I'm on a moshav, other days I'm in the Old City, I'm kind of all over the place . . ."

She sighs. "Fine, fine, I'll take him. Bring him to the main square in the Jewish Quarter and I'll meet you there."

She hangs up before I can thank her.

"Well?" Z. asks.

"I know a woman who can take him," I tell him. "She's in the Jewish Quarter."

"Oh, the Cat Lady? We know about her. She is a Kiddush Hashem, yo," he says in Hebrew. "A sanctification of God's name."

The sweating, smoking men line up one by one to pet the kitten. The pilgrims, too. The nun says a prayer. A few kids from the Muslim Quarter have come too, and everyone wants to touch him. I hold him to me tight, remembering the weight of those two cats that the man I loved got rid of, remembering the weight of my own babies, too, and remembering also the way my mom's hands felt in mine seconds before she died.

This kitten is that little, that fragile, and weighs so much against my skin while I hurry down Via Dolorosa, and turn right onto Al-Wad/Ha-Guy Street, the street with two names.

The street I love the most. By now, maybe you can see it.

The Old City is densely packed, and people live right on top of each other and often buy their milk and eggs and bread from the same places, but the worlds of the Old City are divided, too. It's as though people pass each other through plate glass windows, except when violence erupts, or when there's tension, and then we see each other but through a veil of suspicion and fear. There are exceptions, and these exceptions are the bridges that we need.

And that tiny kitten on that complicated street is that bridge between the quarters, from the blonde tourists from Sweden, to the kids from the Muslim Quarter, to three Yeshiva students, to the Border Police, and a Waqf guard, to a priest, an imam, and a rabbi. No, this isn't the beginning of a joke, it's the beginning of something better: People see the kitten, and see one another.

It hits me in a flash, and I feel warm all over, and the kitten purrs and nuzzles me, and I stop hurrying, and I walk more slowly down the street while people from all faiths and walks of life come to touch this little kitten, this mangy little creature that was only minutes ago trapped in a drain pipe.

"Where did you find the kitten?" a guy in the border police asks me.

"He was rescued by some guys in the Muslim Quarter," I tell him.

"Where are you taking him?" a Palestinian kid asks me.

"I'm taking him to the Jewish Quarter."

By the time I reach the Jewish Quarter, I'm crying.

Because in the epicenter of everything, where tension thrums, and Jerusalem is drawn and quartered, sometimes we need a miracle to keep us going. And sometimes we get one.

Winter Again

MY DAUGHTER LOVES to draw.

Through snack time and dinner we go through her sketchbook together, where she draws pictures and writes little stories.

She loves drawing people, and dolphins, and flamingos, and houses.

Sometimes, she sketches with pencil—a grayscale world on a white page. Other times, bright colors, like a picture of Santa Claus.

My daughter loves Santa. Even though we're Jewish and we light the menorah and we don't have a Christmas tree, she *loves* Santa.

We know a family in Ramle, just fifteen minutes away, that celebrates Christmas, and serves hummus instead of figgy pudding—a family that sings Christmas carols in Arabic, and serves maklouba instead of ham.

And every year they have an amazing Christmas party with a real, live Santa Claus that hands out cotton candy and speaks Hebrew and Arabic.

I also took my kids to the Christian Quarter during Christmas so they could meet my friend who dresses up as Santa year after year and strolls around in red and white, ringing a big old bell, chortling, granting wishes, and handing out candy canes.

She loves him, too.

So my daughter has experienced Santa, and she can't wait to go back.

And while dinner simmers on the stove and she drinks her hot chocolate, we are looking through her sketchbook until the end.

And there, on the last page, after pictures of smiling babies, and flamingos and peacocks and a goldfish named Pinchas, is one line of Hebrew in dark pencil.

She reads it out loud for me.

"All the Arabs hate the Jews and want to kill us and take our land."

I turn to face her and I put my hands on her soft cheeks.

"Baby, who told you that?"

"Yael at school."

"Baby, listen to me. It isn't true."

"But Yael says it is. She says there are people with knives who are trying to kill us and take our land."

We've talked about this before. In fact, I kept them home during the first days of the last terror wave so we could talk about it in safe, broad strokes before their friends or their teachers said something.

And now someone *did* say something, and my daughter has written in her special art book that "all the Arabs hate the Jews and want to kill us and take our land."

"Look baby," I say to her with my hands still on her cheeks while dinner simmers and her cocoa gets cold. "There are Arabs who want to kill Jews. They're called terrorists. And there are also Jews who want to kill Arabs. They're also called terrorists. There are bad people in the world. And there are also good people."

She looks at me skeptically.

"Remember when you met Santa Claus in Jerusalem during Christmas?" I ask her.

"Yes, Mama."

I know she remembers how Santa rode a camel, and how all the kids from all the quarters came up to him one by one.

"Do you remember Santa Claus was speaking a language you didn't understand some of the time?"

"Yes."

"That was Arabic. Santa Claus is an Arab," I say. "And most of the people there are, too. The kids you played with, their parents, the woman who gave you a present. They were all Arab."

"They don't want to kill us," she says. "They were nice."

"Exactly. And remember when Abdullah asked how old you are? How old you are really? He made you laugh. He's an Arab, too."

"He bought us ice cream."

"Remember the little kitten I told you about? How a bunch of guys rescued him from a pipe in the Old City?"

"Yes. Otherwise he would have died."

"They were Arabs, too."

Her eyes shone.

"And the little Star of David you wear around your neck?" I ask, pointing to the little necklace my daughter is wearing.

"Yes. It's my favorite."

"Yes, my friend Musa gave it to me, and he's an Arab."

"Oh! And then we picked up trash with Yusef and Luba—they spoke Arabic!" she said, remembering the day we cleaned up garbage in Jerusalem, before I even had to remind her.

"Yes, exactly!" I said. "Sweet Girl, it's true, there are people who are Arabs who hate us. And there are also Jews who hate Arabs. But it's more important that we also remember that there are people who are Arabs who are just like us—there are teachers and doctors and lawyers and gardeners and nurses and carpenters. And fire fighters and ambulance drivers and moms and dads and little kids and . . ."

"And Santa Claus!"

"Yes, and Santa Claus."

"Mama, why would Yael lie to me?"

"She isn't lying," I say. "She really believes its true, and . . ."

"Well, I have to talk to her tomorrow and tell her why she's wrong. Maybe she can come with us and meet Santa and Musa and the kitten, and we can see Yusef and Luba!"

And then my daughter picks up her pencil and turned back to the words, "All the Arabs hate the Jews and want to kill us and take our land."

And she turned her pencil over until the eraser touched the first letter. She pressed hard over it until it was gone. And then the next one. And the next . . . until all the words had disappeared.

There's something you should know about this place, and you'll see it when you're here. Jerusalem writhes on that ragged seam between the hearth and the desert.

Toward the West, and toward the sea, the land rolls across the sweet green fields and little towns. If you walk out Jaffa Gate and head straight for a few days, you'll hit the port city. There are rules, and there is order, and each step follows the other until you get to where you want to go. But toward the east, the land is austere and pitiless. The desert rages, and the wind howls. And Jerusalem is in between, both regal queen and a wild-eyed prophet, righteous, and despairing. She's there, and that's all.

She'll tease you into thinking maybe you can have her and have her completely, but don't be fooled: she can't be tamed, not really. Not ever. She's seen empires crumble to their knees, and grown men with swords and armor weep at her feet. She's carried the weight of millions of footsteps from all over the world; she's watched those who love her bleed to death.

Still, she endures, restless under a shifting sky.

One writer called her a black widow. But that isn't fair. Jerusalem isn't predatory. Jerusalem never asked for this. Jerusalem didn't make this happen. Jerusalem just is. Blaming her for the violence, for the bloodshed, for the terrible things carried out in her name is like blaming a woman for getting raped or beaten. Our behavior is not her responsibility, it is ours, and ours alone, and I think about this as I walk down an ascent, facing the golden dome that shines in the morning light.

This is the same set of stairs I ran down when I was scared so many nights ago, when the shadow of a little child frightened me, and when Um Ibrahim invited me in.

I hear a hiss and a screech, and I look down and there's a blur of grey and black and white and blue, and I see this kid no older than my son kick a cat down the ascent.

No reason. And something unfastens in me.

I'm standing in that little bathroom again while the man I loved held my cats under the water. It's cold and I'm wet, and I'm shivering and screaming and soaking with bath water and tears, and I remember how those cats used to sleep with me and lick my tears when I would curl up and cry myself to sleep. I remember those cats, and I remember the man I loved and what he did, and I remember other things, too, where I was frightened, and weak, and shunted off to the side, or kicked into a wall, and I yell at him, "Why are you doing this?"

The boy freezes. So does the cat.

"Why are you doing this?" I shout again.

The cat runs away, and the kid, too, and I just stand there trembling in the morning light. And in a wave it hits me:

Watching this cat get kicked down the stairs makes me angry.

Watching people get hurt makes me angry.

If someone hurt my kids, I would want to kill them. I would want to kill them dead. I would want to tear their skin off their faces and feed it to them. If you have kids, too, you get it. It's a primal instinct, and it comes from a wellspring of wanting to protect your young.

And inside me is this creature that is strong and brave and knows how to fight when it's important. I saw her rise out of me that morning years ago on the train, and again just a few days ago when that man followed me back to the place I'm staying.

She is strong, and imperfect, and hewn from fire. She has my mother's voice. And I turn around, and walk back toward the place where the Grey Man lives, and I know it's time to confront him.

I walk up the steps, through the Old City. By now, I could do it with my eyes closed.

I turn left and right, then left again, past the house with the red geraniums in the front where Leila lives, past the bakery where it smells like fresh bread. Up the steps toward my favorite church where there's a giant cistern underneath, and I swear I've heard mermaids singing from inside. Then right around the corner to the roof of the Church of the Holy Sepulchre where old men wearing long robes and crosses dip bread into thick lamb stew on top of the holy site. I walk down through the Ethiopian chapel, and out into the plaza, and then I turn toward Muristan, and I see the Map Seller who told me that his favorite map in the world is the one where Jerusalem is in the center, and the world falls accordingly. I see the Fabric Merchant who makes garments for all of Abraham's grandchildren.

I thread through one of the side streets and I can see the Cardo where Keshet and I drink coffee, and where Rivky wept.

And I think about all the things that make Jerusalem, Jerusalem—all these truths that we have to hold in our hands at the same time.

Like how if you fall down the flight of steps from the overlook to the Western Wall, someone will pick you up and ask if you're okay. I know this is true because I slip a lot. And every time I fall, someone is there to lift me.

And how on my favorite roof where the Four Quarters come together, ultra-Orthodox kids play, and Palestinian kids play, but they never play together, except this one time that I saw the Haredi kids' ball land over by the Palestinian kids, and one of the boys picked it up as though it might explode, just by the fingertips, as though touching it were dangerous, and he held it for three long seconds before he threw it back. That was the closest I have ever seen to the Muslim kids and the Jewish kids playing.

And how that's the same roof where I swiped right on "someone wonderful," and where I kissed him just a few days later, and where we fell in love unexpectedly at sunset, and where I imagine my great grandmother stood also at sunset with her hair long and black blowing in the wind while a stranger lifted her face to his in a moment that would change her life and bring her to the front stoop where she met my great grandfather.

And how Benny Sharon took me down that very street, so I know my mother was there, too, which means we saw the same thing through our different eyes, but still share it.

And how there's a door in an alley behind this very street, and the door is green and always locked, and Z. told me that when he was a kid, they used to say there is a three-headed basilisk that lives behind it, and spools through the tunnels of the Old City. I haven't seen it, but I believe it. And sometimes, late at night when I am walking through the darkened alleys and the world smells like a river of old coins, I think I hear him down there, moving underneath, hungry and waiting.

And how the Fabric Merchant has silk from Palmyra, woven by expert hands threaded with 14-karat gold. He sells fabric to priests and rabbis and imams. "Politicians deal in blood," he says. "I deal in silk and gold." And how I've touched his fabrics against my cheek, and it's the softest thing I've felt since I held my own two babies.

And how the Map Seller has never left Jerusalem.

And how Islamic charities give out food stamps to poor families, and they buy bread that way, because living in Jerusalem is expensive, and it's hard to make a living, and sometimes, the shopkeepers go an entire day without making a single sale. And how grandparents in the Jewish Quarter are so poor that they have to sell red string for a few shekels, how they pick up old bottles and cans, slowly, and recycle them just so they can buy dinner, and how the pilgrims and the tourists come to visit the holy sites, but they don't see the people and their need to survive is just as holy as any stone or cistern.

And how little boys in yarmulkes, and little girls in hijab line up to meet Santa Claus, and how the red and green and purple lights twinkle on crisp December nights.

And how in Jerusalem, the Jewish kids are afraid to walk in the Muslim Quarter, and the Muslim kids are afraid of the soldiers, and how the soldiers are probably afraid, too, sometimes. And how there are people in the Armenian Quarter who have never walked five minutes from their own from door because *they're* afraid of the Jewish Quarter and the Muslim Quarter, and how almost everyone stays behind their invisible walls, except for the mermaids who can go everywhere because they don't quite fit anywhere.

But how really, all of us in Jerusalem can be mermaids if we just swim.

And how all the terrible things that have happened are not my fault, just like all the terrible things that happen in Jerusalem's name are not her fault either.

The man with the missing teeth and the rainbow scarves isn't there when I walk to the building where the Grey Man works, and the front door is shut and locked, and when I ring the buzzer no one answers, and even though I'm ready to confront him, to fight him with the strength of my mother inside me and the mother that I am to *my* kids, he isn't there. Sometimes the pieces don't fall together, and sometimes, things don't make sense, and sometimes, it's uneven and untidy, just like the things I can't remember and the things that won't make sense even if I do remember them, and just like each one of us, and just like life. I think about how all these things are true and hard to hold together.

I'm heading back to the moshav to see my kids, and I'm waiting by Damascus Gate for a taxi.

In Jerusalem, there are Arab taxi drivers, and there are Jewish taxi drivers, and they both drive the same kind of taxi—white, with a yellow sign—and they both say "*Baruch Hashem,*" which is Hebrew for "Praise be to God," and "*Kus emekkkkk,*" which is Arabic for "your mother's vagina."

The only way to know for sure if the taxi driver is an Arab or a Jew is by his name, or by what language he uses when he talks to his wife.

And that's the funny thing—for how much we hate each other sometimes, we look alike. We use similar syntax. We shrug our shoulders and roll our eyes the same way, and praise God's glorious name, and curse each other's mother's vaginas.

And yet, there's this sense of the *Other.* Of wanting to know—is he a Jew? Is he an Arab?

I guess it boils down to tribalism. And trust.

"You know," my Jewish friend told me once, "I can't trust Arabs. I just can't. They'll be nice to your face, and then stab you in the back."

"You know," my Arab friend told me, "all those Jews are the same. Liars. Sneaky. You just can't trust them."

I tell both that I think people are people are people, and there are righteous people, and there are scorpions. And if we look for the righteous, we'll find them. They're everywhere.

(The scorpions will find us, too . . . no need to look for them.)

On my way back to my kids, the driver's name is Sami. It's a mermaid name—he can be either Jewish or Arab, and we're speaking Hebrew.

I'm tired. It's been a long day. *Hell*, it's been a long life, and I'm carrying the weight of it with me in my bags and in my skin.

My phone rings, and I look down: FADI.

"*Marhaba*," I say in Arabic. "Wssup," and then we switch to English, until we say goodbye: "*Masalaame*. Bye, yo."

"Do you speak Arabic?" the driver asks me in Hebrew.

"A few words."

"Why were you speaking it?"

"I was talking to a friend who speaks it."

"You have Arab friends?"

"Sure," I answer, wondering where he's going with this. Because in Jerusalem, things get tribal fast. Streets narrow, walls close in. I still didn't know if he was an Arab or Jew, but I knew he was drawing lines.

"Why?"

"Why not?"

"No, really, how do you know Arabs?"

"I live in the Muslim Quarter a few days a week."

We were stopped at a red light, and he turns to face me.

"Why?"

"Because I want to. And I'm writing this book about what it's like to live in the Old City."

"Aren't you afraid?" he asks.

"Nah," I say. "I'm not afraid." And then I decided to tell him the whole truth, about how I was once eighteen and standing in front of Damascus Gate, and about how they threw stones at me, and about how there was blood all over my hands and about how I was scared. So I tell him, but I also tell him about how one day I got tired of being afraid so I got over it, and I realized that the people in the Old City were just people as vulnerable and hurting and hopeful as anyone else. Just like me.

And that's why I stopped being afraid.

"I have to tell you something," he says in Hebrew. He clears his throat, and then he says something to me that I didn't understand because it was in Arabic.

"What does that mean?" I ask.

"It means, 'On behalf of my people, I am sorry for what was done to you.'"

He turns around and looks at me again. "Really," he says. "I take responsibility for this."

"You don't have to," I say. "You didn't do it."

"My people did it, and I love my people, and I am responsible to them, as they are to me."

In Hebrew, we have an expression: "*Kol Yisrael Arevim Ze le Ze.*" It means, "All of the People Israel is responsible for one another." It means we have to show up at each other's weddings to celebrate and funerals to mourn. It means we have to feed one another, and protect one another, too. But it also means that we are responsible for the mistakes that are made by our people and in our name.

"I get it," I say, and I think about Damascus Gate and being afraid, and I think about the Border Police who stand there behind metal barricades, frisking random people because they're scared, as well. "And I'll take responsibility for all the stuff we've put you through, too."

"Thanks," he says.

"And thank *you*," I reply.

There are scorpions, and there are the righteous.

And there are way more of the righteous than there are scorpions.

And a weight lifts—for me, and maybe for him as well. Not everything can be solved or understood, but this feels better, and I feel lighter, and he was quiet and so was I as we drove through the streets of the city we love together.

It was the necklace she was wearing that makes me stop breathing on the train to Jerusalem. Three sapphire blue charms on a silver chain, hanging still, in the web of sunspots just below her collarbone.

And I know that necklace.

Three blue charms for her three sons. The oldest, surely married (and divorced?) by now to the sweet-faced girl he would talk about all the time when he visited us that summer nearly thirteen years ago. The youngest, long out of the army, probably done with school, too, and back from India or Thailand or South America, the dreadlocks he would surely grow shorn long ago, and the Om tattoo he'd surely get forever stuck in the dip between his shoulder blades.

And then the middle one. A quick Google search could reveal that he's working as a chef in New York like he was the last time I saw him. Or maybe he's driving a taxi in Tel Aviv. Or maybe he's dead.

The middle one, who would make schnitzel from scratch on Sunday nights, who would tear up when Five for Fighting's "Superman" would come on the radio, who would give me his glasses to take to Anthro lecture, because we shared the exact same Rx, and I had lost mine.

The middle one, the one I still dream about when I pulverize my night with Jameson and three chasers of absinthe, or when I'm feverish and tossing and turning against burning sheets. The middle one, who shows up in dreams where I'm rooted to the ground and I know something terrible is about to happen—because it *did* happen.

The middle one, who grabbed my chai necklace carved from Eilat stone, pulled hard until the chain bit into my neck, tugged until the charm fell off in his hand, glinting in the center of his palm between the lifeline and heartline. "You will never wear anything that I didn't give you. Do you understand?"

The middle one, who made my two cats "disappear" in the middle of a stormy November night, who would squeeze the soft skin on my upper arm, covering it in little amoeba tattoos that changed color from blue to purple to green to brown, just like the leaves change, a bruise for all seasons. The middle one, who said he would kill himself if I ever left him.

The middle one who was fine until that morning when the memory of that necklace was seared into me, like the funny scar on my arm from where my mom bit me, like the stretch marks on my hips from the babies I carried.

The middle one, who I hardly think about, except with a gasp and a prickle of sweat under my arms. Or when I see that necklace on a train after so much life has passed between us.

I would know that necklace anywhere. The morning she burst into the bedroom, when I was naked except for a pair of underwear, one sock, and my chai necklace, stark and white in a pool of sunlight. I remember when she came in screaming and hit her middle son across the face, shoved him back on the pillow. I couldn't look at her eyes. I didn't want to see myself reflected back, trembling. So I looked at her necklace.

I would know it anywhere. Three charms, one for each son.

The first, her favorite, the last, her baby. And the middle, her "failure," her "mistake," her "worst disappointment ever." The middle one, the son she spat and cursed. "You're just like your father, damn him to hell," she railed that morning in the light, while we cowered against each other, and I stared at her necklace, glowing like three gas flames.

The middle one, the man I loved.

She was visiting for his graduation, all those years ago. She was supposed to stay for ten days. She and her favorite and the baby.

We wrote an itinerary: Chinatown for dim sum. Pier 39 for clam chowder in sourdough bowls. A boat ride to Alcatraz. A hike in Muir Woods. Dinner at Thai House after her middle son walked across the stage, accepted his diploma, and threw his hat in the air.

We had vacuumed and dusted and bought a futon from Ikea. We went to Whole Foods for cucumbers and tomatoes and salmon filets and green lentils. We hung a silver mezuzah on the door. This was when I worked in a flower shop on Durant Avenue, a little place that paid me in petals when we didn't make enough in sales, so I brought home Gerber daisies (white), Peruvian lilies (pink), and three purple irises.

Their father was supposed to come, too. I never met him, but he would "break his teeth in English" on the phone when we would talk long distance, and he had a big laugh with soft edges. He spoke with the same inflections as his middle son, a pause, a lilt, and then a race to the finish. He drove a taxi, and wore a mustache (for when he would drive through East Jerusalem, or Kfar Kassam, or the Galilee) and a yarmulke (for when he would drive through West Jerusalem or Tel Aviv, or Modiin).

He used to be in the special forces.

Each week, he would take his middle son, *his* favorite son, who he loved, to the army, dropping him off with a hug and a kiss and a blessing on his head. And on Shabbat, despite birth order, his middle son would receive the first blessing: "May the Lord make you like Ephraim and Menashe."

But when we picked them up at the airport, he wasn't there.

"Where's Aba?" his middle son asked.

"He can't come."

We arrived back at the apartment in a van we rented from Hertz. We each kissed the mezuzah as we walked in.

"Nice apartment," his mother said. "Pretty flowers."

We chopped salad from the cucumbers and tomatoes. We grilled the salmon and cooked the green lentils.

Two days after they arrived—Tuesday—the four of them drove to the marina to talk about his father. I stayed home, and waited. My stomach felt like a washing machine with only a stone inside.

I waited.

I watched the *Maury Show*.

I waited.

Then *Jerry Springer*.

I waited.

I went outside and walked around the block.

I waited.

The fog leaked in from the bay.

By the time I was pacing in front of our apartment, the sky had turned the color of spoiled clams.

They drove up, the four of them in the van. The mother and the favorite and the baby wouldn't look at me when they walked up the steps to the apartment. And the middle one, the man I loved, staggered out of the driver's seat, his face the color of the fog, and his eyes just as opaque.

The truth seeped out like sewage: his father was in jail for raping a neighbor. Or so the neighbor said. But really, they were having an affair, and she was angry that he wouldn't leave his wife, so she made up this lie, or so his father said.

His father who taught him how to fly a kite and then an airplane. His father, with the exact same profile. They'd line up side by side like those funny vintage cutout portraits, match-match. His father who bought him his first pack of gum when he turned six, and his first pack of condoms when he turned sixteen.

He went into the bathroom and threw up.

He graduated the next day. He walked across the stage. He accepted his diploma. But he didn't bother to throw his hat.

We went to dinner at Thai House. We used chopsticks, the plastic clinking against our plates the only sound as we picked up pieces of chicken, tofu, and steamed cabbage. No one spoke until . . .

. . . midway through, his mother shoved the plate away, and said "I hate this place," and lurched from the table. Her favorite chased her down the street, while the middle and the baby stared at their plates.

The days passed sullenly. We did what we were supposed to. We slept and woke and brushed our teeth and showered and dressed and ate and got in the car and did the things we had planned—the trip to Pier 39, the boat ride to Alcatraz, the hike in Muir Woods. His mother didn't speak to him, and the more he tried to speak to her, the angrier she got.

"You look like your father," she hissed while we drove back over the Bay Bridge. "You have his nose."

He clung to me that night, when all was quiet.

"He loved me best," he spoke in low tones. "So she can't anymore."

He touched his nose. "She's right. I hate my nose."

We fell asleep curled toward each other.

That was the last night he was still okay.

And I loved him, I loved him hard, and it was good for nearly twenty-three months. We had our apartment and late night chicken sausage with sauerkraut at Top Dog, and we'd watch *The Simpsons*, and listen to Natasha Atlas and Eviatar Banai and The Shins, and he'd pound Jack and I would sip Smirnoff Ice—but never again. If there's anything I've learned from that time, along with "never let a man tell you he will kill you," is never drink Smirnoff Ice. That shit is nasty.

I don't remember much about that time except the apartment and the windows and the flowers on the table and the mezuzah we hung on the door, and the poster of Gustav Klimt's *The Kiss*, and the way the chain bit into my neck when he tore my necklace off me.

I don't remember much about that time except for the sound of blood through my face, and collapsing in a heap inside the closet because the world seemed too big, too vast, too empty.

But I *do* remember that if I stood on the arm of the couch, I could see the twinkling lights of the city. I *do* remember that I thought about jumping. I *do* remember that I put my feet on the ground instead.

I will never blame myself for staying and loving him even after that morning and all the other terrible mornings that followed. Those terrible, horrible mornings that began terrible, horrible days, when my world shrunk so little that it could be measured in coffees and minimum wage and waiting for the train.

I will never blame myself for wanting to jump in front of the train every night at 9:50 p.m., when I would hear the howl of the train through the tunnel, cutting a hole in the night.

I will never blame myself for staying until that very last second when I took my own life in my hands and ran.

Because I was there that morning when his own mother lurched at him and clawed his face. I was there with him, half-naked in the white light of the sun, when her eyes went blank and her face twisted and she lunged. I was there and screaming, "Don't hurt him, don't hurt him, don't hurt him," while she clawed and bit and scratched and chanted, "I hate you, I hate you, I hate you," over and over and over again to her middle son, the man I loved, the man who would nearly destroy me with him.

But he didn't destroy me. Because I'm still here, and on the way to Jerusalem to climb a roof and see Fadi for lunch and Keshet for coffee. He didn't destroy me; he couldn't. And you know what else? I may be broken in places, but I put the pieces together again and soldered them with gold, and he did not destroy me. Nor did the man in Migdal HaEmek on that night I can't remember, or the guys who threw stones at me by Damascus Gate on the night I remember all too well, nor the Grey Man who I will one day confront.

And all of this comes together while I'm staring at that woman with her necklace with the three charms, the necklace I would know anywhere, even if I didn't remember her face.

She looks up, and I want to say something. I want to tell her how she broke him, and how he tried to break me. I want to tell her about the cats that "disappeared," and the time I couldn't breathe, and the morning I clawed a sewer grate because I had dropped the only twenty-dollar bill I had in the world down it.

I want to tell her about all these things that make me who I am, the beautiful and ugly, all of it.

But her face looks tired, her eyes woven in a web of wrinkles and sun spots.

And I'm a mother now.

And I can't imagine a world where I would be able to hate my son or my daughter, and not hate myself, too.

She looks at me, her head tilted to the side.

Even if she remembers that girl, it isn't the woman in front of her—although she's in there, still half-naked with that sock, still lying on that bed with her dress pulled up, and her thighs sticky, still standing by Damascus Gate sniffing her own blood, still standing in that room overlooking the Old City with milk dripping down her breasts . . . still broken, still grieving for her mother, still aching. But she isn't the only me anymore.

The world is full of broken pieces, and the world is full of people who want to put them back together. There are scorpions and there are the righteous and I am a mermaid in between all of these things.

And I've changed enough in all these years, and especially this last one—to smile at her—but I've also changed enough to know I don't need to smile if I don't want to.

The train doors open.

"Pretty necklace," I say, as I get up and walk straight ahead, toward Jerusalem and the love of my life, where the broken pieces come together, imperfect and beautiful.

Acknowledgments

THERE IS NO way I could have written this book without being challenged and supported by so many wonderful people:

Thank you to my agent Fern Reiss for telling me that this idea about living in the Old City would make a good book, for her patience and advice, for sushi lunches and Thanksgiving dinners, and making me believe I could do this. Thank you to Jonathan for his tireless work, and to Daniel, Benjamin, and Ariel for being such great people and so welcoming. And thank you to the Jewish Speakers Bureau for giving me the professional platform to talk about living in Israel and my time in Jerusalem.

Thank you to editor Abigail Gehring and the incredible team at Skyhorse Publishing for taking on this project, and their diligence and faith in it. Special thanks to proofreader Alison Swety and production editor Chris Schultz.

Thank you also to my babies, M. and E., for being (mostly) great kids, and the best thing I've ever done in my life.

Thank you to:

Ruth for being the best Savta my kids could ask for, for ice cream sundaes, and for being there for me when my mother couldn't.

Hillel for being the best Saba my kids could ask for, and for being such a great support and friend.

Boaz for being the best Aba my kids could ask for, and a terrific ex-husband.

Hagar for being the best "Ima Horeget" my kids could ask for, and her family for the way they treat my kids like part of their own.

Gil Nachmani, on whose couch I basically wrote most of this book, for his kindness and support and for challenging me to think beyond the present and far into the vast and distant future, and for explaining to me why it's wrong to say "like, light years into the future."

David Leichman and Miri Gold and their children and grandchildren for being my family here in Israel, and for Leich Cream for being the best ice cream in the whole wide world.

Bradley Burston and Varda Spiegel for being great mentors.

James Oppenheim #otjo fire and furry, and for a world where it's always Wednesday. And for taking a chance on me when I wanted to work for *Times of Israel,* and for reminding me that love is better than fear, and for the amazing, inspiring Rachel Oppenheim who radiates real beauty and warmth and charisma.

Tzvi Maller and Leigh Maller, Yoni and Ricka Razel Van Leeuwen, and Nachum Aranov for reminding me to be less angry. #Heart2Heart #Primal

Rabbi Levi Margolin and Aidel Gestetner for the Chumash, which helped me connect to my time in the Jewish Quarter in a real and meaningful way.

Rob Eshman for finding all the goats, and for helping me find the threads of all these stories to tie together into this book.

Daniel Sokatch for introducing me to my favorite roof and my favorite cistern. I couldn't have written this book without these highs and lows.

David Rose for a day in Ramallah that pushed me well beyond my comfort zone.

David Horovitz for giving me the perfect title for this book, for his integrity, and for holding all of us at TOI to such high standards.

Linda Amar for her wisdom, comfort, and keeping all of us sane at *Times of Israel* when David is holding us to those high standards.

Jessica Steinberg for reminding me to be authentic and vulnerable.

Gavi Nelson for taking over my job at *Times of Israel* for a month so I could do *this* job.

Raphael Ahren, Amanda Borschel-Dan, and Jessica Steinberg for helping me come up with pseudonyms.

Miriam Herschlag and Anne Gordon for their tireless work on *Times of Israel*'s ops and blogs, and Elie Leshem for publishing my first blog on *Times of Israel*.

Luke Tress for taking a video of the day I got my mermaid tattoo.

Ira and Boris Ginzburg and the creative team behind Jerusalem City Stories for their unique vision of Jerusalem, which helped inspire many of the stories in here.

David Abitbol for his tireless work and for showing me Jerusalem through a different lens (and getting my good side on camera).

Oren Rosenfeld for introducing me to the best hummus in the Old City.

Avi Issacharoff for helping me through Damascus Gate after so many years.

Tova Hametz for being a rainbow and a bridge in Jerusalem, and a woman I admire.

Nancy Lamb for being a great writing mentor, and for being such a dear friend to our family for many wonderful years.

Mohammed Manasra for being a friend I can trust. #99

Ryan Lifchitz for showing up at exactly the right time one morning in Jerusalem and framing the idea for this book into words.

Boaz Fletcher for the pepper spray (because you never know) and the Talmudic references.

David Brundige, Micah Baskir, Stephane Dudley, Preston Peterson, and Jeff Rigler for reading so many of my false starts over the years.

Jonathan Kessler, for his ideas, insight, and for bravely trying new scotch.

Ahava Emunah Lange for being a stunning example of love and faith.

Karen Byer Silberman for being a source of inspiration through writing and art.

Kfir Pravda and Benny Akler and the team at Pravda Media for giving me my first job in Israel and teaching me so many tools of the writing and new media trade.

Bill Goldman for speaking truth to power. May his memory be a blessing and inspiration to us all.

Jonah Light, Asher Ragen, Andi Nussbaum Frenkel, Yael Ben-David, Jon Mitzmacher, Opher Rom, Kim Bardy, and Ronen Kleinman and the staff at Young Judea who helped me fall in love with Israel in 1997 and 1998, and to various roommates and bus buddies, Shoshanna Slutske, Esther Pasternak, Rebecca Werre Kessler, Rachel Bethke, Rebecca Braun, Claire Golden, Lisa Swid, Nathan Glatt-Holtz, Joshua Saidoff, Sasha Gersten Paal, and Allison Fisher, Zachary Abraham, and Yves Sztjnkryczer. And to the Israelis who made me want to come back to Israel again and again and again: Matan Goldberg, Daniel Eisenberg, Noam Zwilling, Kesem Daliyot, Ben Engel, Elad Ben-David, Micha Carsenti, Sofi Zvili Sinai, Limor Margolin, Vered Lamhot, and to the beautiful Tova Streets—may her memory be a blessing always.

The people of Kibbutz Gezer and Kibbutz Mishmar HaSharon for putting up with my shenanigans when I was a teenager. I am sorry for all I put you through. :P

Leanne Ravid, Bernice Keren, Mona Guterman, and Claire Shilo, for strong coffee and stronger friendship.

Woolf Marmot for his wisdom.

Sara Bader (Sazi) of Talma Travel Israel for her diligence and patience and helping me get safe and sound to America to see my family.

Lynn Schusterman and the Charles and Lynn Schusterman Family Foundation for their vision, and for the ROI Community—especially

Elissa Krycer, Justin Korda, No'a Gorlin, Adam Margolis, Orli Rashba, Ariel Hirsch, Arielle Cizma, Emily Bernstein, Eric Kessler, Galit Romanelli, Marcus Frieze, Renana Levine, and Talya Levin, and Yael Schuster for nominating me to be part of this wonderful community.

Rabbi Yoni Gordis, Rabbi Michael Adam Latz, Rabbi Chuck Davidson, Rabbi Sharon Brous, Rabbi Lisa Gruschcow, Rabbi Miri Gold, Rabbi Levi Weiman-Kelman, Rabbi Susan Silverman, Rabbi Yossie Bloch, Rabbi David Wolpe, Rabbi Zach Shapiro, Rabbi David-Seth Kirshner, Rabbi Naomi Levy, Adam Weisberg, Rabbi Levi Margolin, Rabbi Menachem Creditor, Neshama Carlebach, Rabbi Jerry Goldstein, Rabbi Zach Shapiro, and Rabbi Allen Maller for their spiritual leadership.

Mike Smouha for the ramen. Always be ramen.

Naava Shafner and Ima Kadima for the incredible work they do to empower women.

Uri Blau for being one of the first to say, "Wow, that's a great idea—you should write a book!" when I said I wanted to live in the Old City.

Aimee Dawson for nearly thirty years of Saskia and Lieneche.

Laura Ben-David for sisterhood and for selfies and a wild night at the Waldorf, and Rachel "Rose" Landis Rosen for over thirty years of Broadway musicals, for sleepovers, and for reminding me to never read the comments.

Elana Messner for reminding me that even though I was overwhelmed and heartbroken, I had a glass elevator.

Benji Lovitt for being hilarious and making me LOL.

Jessica Apple, Liza Rosenberg, Shari Eshet, Zimra Vigoda, Aviv Benedix, Rebecca Gindin, Cornelia Reich, Timna Seligman, Samantha "Sam" Fisher, Nicola Davis, Leanne Ravid, Bernice Keren, Mona Guterman, Claire Shilo, Laura Ben-David, Rahel Jaskow, Karen Brunwasser, Yael Schuster, Therese (Tini) Neuman Vardi, Karen Brunwasser, Anne Gordon, Deborah Gilboa, Linda Amar, Steve Leibowitz, Sara Lapping, SB, and Sarah Kass, and all other mermaids who understand the exquisite beauty and the agonizing pain of living between worlds and being many things at the same time.

Founder and Criminal Mastermind of the *Daily Freier*, Aaron Scheer, for reminding me about good times with the Palestinian Jewish fortune teller at Tiv Tam. Thanks also to the creative team including Lee Saunders Chava Ewa Kovacs and Tali ZelikovIch ("the writer known as Mia Deych").

Rebecca Gindin, Adi Shifris, Noa Harel, and Cornelia Reich for the warm scarves for those cold Jerusalem nights.

Hugo Schwyzer for reminding me to be honest when I write—and to find the crucial line between telling the truth and hurting someone.

Dani Tal for showing me Jerusalem through my mother's eyes.

Meredith Lewis for my first writing gig at *Kveller*, which led to Jordana Horn recommending I write for *Times of Israel*, which led to everything else.

Deborah Kolben and Molly Tolsky for being such patient and wonderful editors at *Kveller*, and our OG team of contributing editors: Mayim Bialik, Carla Naumberg, Tamara Hansen Reese, Jordan Horn, and Adina Kay-Gross.

Rabbi Alan Maller for shaping a synagogue community that is inclusive and nurturing, and for officiating over my daughter's Simchat Bat.

Rabbi Zach Shapiro for telling me it's okay to face the sea when I pray instead of the parking lot.

Matthew Kalman for introducing me to so many wonderful people in the Old City, including the Fabric Merchant, and for being an inspiration, and a kick ass journalist and friend.

Various assorted taxi drivers for their heartwarming stories, and the challenging ones, too.

Special teachers and educators in my life: Principal Hal Hyman, Billy Jean Gerren, Muriel Ifekwunigwe, Richard Cohen, Karen Lee, Jan Cohn, Randy Rutschman, Robert Cole, Andy Piligian, Raney Draper, Susan Miller, Alfee Enciso, Stu Bubar (I'm sorry!), Dr. and

Rabbi Miriam Hamrell, Eileen Ettinger, Dr. Ron Hendel, Dr. Ibrahim Muhawi, Dr. Robert Alter, and Dr. Alan Dundes.

Robert F. Kennedy for bringing my parents together on March 18, 1967 "across a crowded room."

My amazing, loving, and wonderful family: Beatrice DeRusha Century and Kris Yang, Joey DeRusha, David, Merav, Rachel, Sheyna, and Sarah DeRusha, L'nor Wolin, Marc Wolin and Goldie Shnitzer Wolin, Michael David Wolin and Ashley Suzanne Fogerty, Adam Arthur Wolin and Sarah Rose Hattem, Genna, Jason, Eva Lillian, and Noah Murray Fessinger, Lisa and Steve Singer, Erin and Pat and Brett, Devi Singer, Ralph Buck and Chris Freeman, Pat Allen, David, Adrienne, Elana, Jonathan, and Corie Messner, Allen and Maria Tuttle, Sarah Tuttle Thorn, John Thorn and Paige Imaculata Thorn, Marikathryn, Mike, Hannah and Lauren Debnam, James and Martha Tuttle, Carrie Tuttle, Margaret Tuttle and Michael Greenblatt, Bobbie and Rem Remedios, David Tuttle, Howard and Peg Tuttle, Howie, Susan, Rose and Elijah Tuttle, Kate, Bill, Walker and Kendall Tuttle, Sam, Erin, Claire and Chase Tuttle, Allison Hawley Crawford, Fred Crawford, Anna and Misha Labovsky, Eliza Crawford, Mike Hawley and Helen Fox, Caren Singer and Robert Wolin, Rick Tuttle and Rebecca Rona Tuttle, Dan Rona and Remy Ruiz and Haydn Rona-Ruiz.

And to those who are no longer with us on earth but in our hearts: Goldryn and Bernie Singer, Fred and Mary Emily Tuttle, Mimi and Murray Wolin, Evan and Monica Remedies, Judy Singer, Gene Allen, Eva and Ray Messner, Tim Harris, Sherman Tuttle, Howard and Eleanor Tuttle, Alta Carter and Burton L. Tuttle, Dick DeRusha, Max and Esther Singer, Bob Rona, Barbara Rona, Mimi and James Babcock, and Tsiryl and Chaim Blonder.

Dear family friends—those with us here on earth, and those who are always in our hearts—friends who have been sources of inspiration and strength to my family: Bruce and Toni Corwin, Lenore and Jack Wax, Eva Wax, Francine Hamberg, Julian Hamberg, Jon Friedman, Alex White, Craig Cunningham, Pearl Ricci, Phyllis and Leon Ruderman,

Sandy and Karen Weiner, David Weiner, Irwin and Rachel Levin, Gerri and Joe Cochrane, Sarah and Lindsay Conner, Sally Weber and Malcolm Katz, Jerry Weber, Aaron and Esther Buchsbaum, Dr. William Wexler, Gavriella Roisman, Adina Weber and Reuven Barkan, Risa and Mark Gordon, Marna Tucker and Larry Baskir, Beverly and Mark Schwartzman, Ben and Tracy Austin, Noah and Julie Austin, Nancy Lamb, Congressman Howard Berman and Janis Berman, Congressman Henry Waxman and Janet Waxman, Supervisor Zev Yaroslavsky and Barbara Yaroslavsky, and Mayor Tom Bradley.

Tsiryl (Sarah) Blonder for kissing a stranger on a rooftop in Jerusalem and falling in love with the Old City, and for Chaim Blonder for falling in love with the headstrong woman wearing a slip on a stoop in Chicago.

Bernie Singer for my vocabulary and my sense of humor, and for his unconditional warmth and love.

Goldryn Malka Singer for the legacy of chicken soup, her unconditional warmth and love.

Judy Singer for her bravery, her grit, her fierce loyalty to family, and her unconditional warmth and love.

Cousin Devi Singer for her independence and her creativity, and her unconditional warmth and love.

Uncle Allen Tuttle and Aunt Maria Tuttle for welcoming me with open arms, for taking me to church, and for their dedication to family, and their unconditional warmth and love.

Sarah Tuttle Thorn for doing my hair and for sharing Gramma Mary Emily's looks and personality and for being with me when my mom died and for her unconditional warmth and love.

Uncle James Tuttle and Aunt Marty Tuttle and Cousin Carrie for their love and acceptance and good humor and their unconditional warmth and love.

Aunt Margaret Tuttle for all those trips to LA and Israel, for all she does to inspire and encourage, and for her unconditional warmth and love.

Aunt Caren Singer and Uncle Robert Wolin for family, for coconut water and kombucha, for sea urchin with sriracha, for gin martinis at Musso and Frank's, for inspiration, for love, for support, for FAMILY, for the angels, for cozy nights on my gramma's couch while a fire crackles merrily in the fireplace, and for showing me, truly: "no day but today."

Rebecca Rona Tuttle for being a wonderful stepmother, for loving my dad, and me, and my kids with such fierce loyalty.

My dad Rick Tuttle for being my role model on how to be in the world, for his love, for his dedication, for his bravery, for swagger, and for being my moral compass. Whenever I need advice, I know that if I ask him for the right answer, I may not like it, but it'll be the right answer.

Maida "Muff" Singer, my mom, my muse, and for being the reason I write.

The incredible team at *Times of Israel*, for all their work and dedication to getting the story right.

And Chef Todd Aarons and the wonderful folks at Crave Gourmet Street Food for nourishing me, and for being a true *maayan*—a watering spring—for Jerusalem, a watering spring we desperately need.

Special thanks to Jerusalem friends and folks I've hung out with and climbed roofs with in the Old City:

Noah Austin
Aviv Benedix
Jennifer Spitzer
Stephane Acel-Green
Steve Rothman
Daniel Sokatch
Malynnda Littky
Inga Kastrone
Nuha Musleh
Karen Brunwasser
Omar Zaro
Maryn Demirjian
Adam Weisberg
Oren Rosenfeld
Dani Tal
Tova Hametz
Eric Stark
Rahel Jaskow

Scott Brockman
Jon Marco Church
Dan Goldman
Rabbi Lisa Grushcow
Iris Finkelstein
Issanis Kassissieh
Tawfeeq Badrieh
Mohammad Manasra
Noura El Zokm
Sami Barsoum
Rame Nabolse
Wassim Razouk
Anton Razzouk
Maral Amin
Crystal Henle
Daniel J. Levy
Matthew Kalman
Roel Geeraedts
Adar Weinreb
David Seidenberg
Bilal Abu Khalaf
Yassir Barakat
Laura Ben-David
Apo Sahagian
Roi Frey
Michelle Chabin
Hannah Spiegel
Aia Khalaily
Ahmed Maswadeh
Oren Feld
Liza Rosenberg
Matt Wulkan
Kefa Kader
Naava Shafner
Harvey Stein
Omer Amir
Harry Flaster
Guy Tidhar
Riad Anwar
Mordechai Ben Avraham
The special family that hosted me on Shabbat
Miri Shimony
Kaspar C. Goethals
Johannes De Bruycker
Daniel Gottesman
Hadrian Gosset-Bernheim
Rahel Jaskow
Tova Saul
Moran Tal
Sister Bernadette and the staff at the Austrian Hospice
Jeff Seidel
Leanne Ravid
Bernice Keren
Claire Shilo
Kobi Shilo
Woolf Marmot
Gil Nachmani
Mona Guterman
Kirsten Mcintosh
Maureen Marcus Thal
Jonathan Kessler
Sam Fisher
Chaim Motzen
Jeffrey K. Said

Mike Smouha
Avigail Kormes
Opher Rom
Jesse Lerner
Shira Mazor
Michal Bruck

Richard Behar
The staff at the Citadel Hostel
The folks at *Caravan's Journal*
That one girl with the green eyes, and the kid with the broken arm

A special thank you to the first people who read this manuscript—with all the spelling and grammar mistakes and tpyos:

Daniel Sokatch, James Oppenheim, Jonathan Kessler, Rob Eshman, Uri Blau, Anne Gordon, Leanne Ravid, Bernice Keren, Ady Stern, Mona Guterman, Claire Shilo, Woolf Marmot, Padraic Hussey, Diogo Monte-Mor, Josh Kellogg, Jedediah Jack, Gil Nachmani, Tova Dvorin, Sam Tsirah, Rebecca Ehrenpreis, Eric Stark, Eli Leshem, Naomi "Simenoff" Goldman, Yaniv Golan, Laura Ben-David, Bradley Burston, David Leichman, Barak Raz, Rob Eshman, Lisa Alcalay Klug, Dan Getman, Ohad Shabtai Raoul Wootliff, Rebecca Fontes, Uncle Neil Ginsberg, Shay Rabineau, Mike Smouha, Sarah Kass, Ami Kaufman, Uri Blau, Rick Tuttle.

And another special thank you to the folks who helped me choose which photos to include: Deborah Blank, Vivian Nathan, Nour Radouai, Rebecca Fontes, Lorit Kaplan, Sam Mercado, Josh Aronson, Emily Aronson, Ari Marc Wachsman, Sandra Yosef-Hassidim, Daniel Newbrun, Grant Crankshaw, Mary Theresa Martin, Patrice Hollman, Claude Pierrot, Yaakov Campbell Lui-Hyden, Jesse Buckner Alper, Mark Matchen, Anami J. Naths, Eivind Skildheim, Andy Green, Rinat, Rond, Katrine Jutrem Cohen, Rachel Risby-Raz, David Rose, Gail Doering, Lorit Kaplan, Simon Rainsborough, Caren Shapiro, Samantha (Sam) Fisher, Michael Hilkowitz, Colin Shapir, Joanna Saidel, Keith Brooks, Anna Hecht, Krystle Herbert, Shoshana Rachel Slutske, Jack Bershtel, Simon Stout, Tova Hametz, Leanne Ravid, Judy Stein, Bernice Keren, Shira Pasternak Be'eri, Avi Nires, Polina Labovskaya, Janice Wheeler, Paul Mirbach, Mary

Keary Stojanovic, Chip Blumberg, Liza Rosenberg, Sue Liberman, Jacob D. Lustig, Ciaran Blumenfeld, Bernice Keren, Seth Menachem, Chaya Gruber, Miri Shimony, Neshama Carelebach, Lauri Donahue, Sharon Marks Altshul, Elaine S. Black, Maureen Marcus Thal, Yaniv Golan, Holly Rosen Fink, Shari Eshet, Adrie Ro-McLean, Anna Moyer Budovitch, Gil Nachmani, Menachem Creditor, Eric Strimling, Jane Smelt, Khaled Latif, Sebastian Naitsabes, Andrea Licht Simon, Lois Germain, Lucia Lior, Russell Wolff, Alene Wright, Keren Ann Burgman, Genevieve Fenster, Simona Weinglass, Sarah Vanunu, Shira Koeningsberg, Apo Sahagian, Michael Adam Latz, Jessica Burnsweig, Deborah Kallick, Elana Hassan, Rebecca Ehrenpreis, Drorit Bick Raiter, Rahel Jaskow, Gary Rudoren, Gavi Nelson, Aviv Benedix, Sally Abrams, Marie Kemp, Paul Hemphill, Yvette Marie, Laura Ellen, Mark Sirota, Elliot Evans, Inga Kastrone, Steve Aagard, Ezra HaLevi, Shai Reef, Vera Grodzinski, Rachel Bell, Kay Picquet, Adele Raemer, Jeffrey K. Said, Sharon Bershtel, Zachary Abraham, Melanie Levin, Joshua C. Karlin, Asad Jafari, Jonathan Morgenstein, Seth Menachem, Hugh Schwyzer, Yael Swerdlow, Ricky Katz, Riana Goren, Laura Ben-David, Judy Zinkin, Elena Katz Fries, Melissa Beth Milgram, Debbie Grossman, Nancy Metviner, Brennan Kurfees, Hedy Rubin, Josh Gerstein, Emmanuel Pribys, Jonathan S. Kessler, Rivka Cohen, Arielle Hanien, Lexi Rae, Bee Schneider, Sara Lapping, David Tuttle Cohen, Julie Paris, Maya Lan, Chana Shenderovich, Enno Raschke, Rafi Gassel, Stuart Drucker, Harold Goldmeier, David Youngs, Sruli Broocker, Zsuzsi Schindler, Abdalla Abdalla, Benji Lovitt, Brian Burch, Yitzhak Ben-Moshe, Stuart Soffer, Nicola Davis, Ralph Buck, Hanna Anton Salman, Nikah Fialkoff, Janel Amador, Annabel Timan, Marc Shabsis, Riad Anwar, Eyal Nevo, Noam Simon, Gavin Shrell, Ilansky Naftali, Ido Avrahami, Tal Cherni, Ynon Lerner, Ofir Dahan, Oren Oppenheim, Daniela Daniela, Ruthie Mashal, Bobby Rootveld, Dorit Sasson, and Cable Neuhaus.

And finally: Thank *you* for being part of this story, too—for inspiring me to write it—and for being willing to look through new windows and open new doors into different worlds.

Next time you're in Jerusalem, look me up and we can get kenafe or some coffee together. You know where to find me.